OpenGL Programming for
Windows 95 and Windows NT

OpenGL Programming for Windows 95 and Windows NT

RON FOSNER

ADDISON-WESLEY DEVELOPERS PRESS
An imprint of Addison Wesley Longman, Inc.

Reading, Massachusetts • Harlow, England • Menlo Park, California

Berkeley, California • Don Mills, Ontario • Sydney

Bonn • Amsterdam • Tokyo • Mexico City

Library of Congress Cataloging-in-Publication Data

Fosner, Ron.
    OpenGL programming for Windows 95 and Windows NT / Ron Fosner.
       p. cm.
    Includes bibliographical references and index.
    ISBN 0–201–40709–4
    1. Computer graphics. 2. OpenGL. 3. Three-dimensional display
systems. 4. Microsoft Windows (Computer file) 5. Microsoft Windows
NT.   I. Title.
    T385.F663   1996
    006.6—dc20   96–20193
                                                       CIP

Sponsoring Editor: Mary Treseler
Project Manager: John Fuller
Production Assistant: Melissa Lima
Cover design: Jean Seal
Set in 10-point Palatino by A&B Typesetters, Inc.

4 5 6 7 8 9   MA 00 99 98 97

4th Printing January, 1998

To
Sue and Rachael—
I couldn't have done it without your help, patience, and love.

Contents

Preface

I originally was a user of graphics systems. My formal education was as a chemical enginee, specializing in the simulation of chemical plants. However, when I graduated—in the early 1980s—there was no real interface other than a dump of numbers. As a user of such systems I always found that I could learn a lot more about a system if I could plot the results. If there was no plotting system, I wrote a routine to plot out data, using a line printer. The first company I worked for hired me to write the visual front end for its chemical plant simulation system. I was going to write a line-graphic interface using the built-in line characters found on the video adapter of most IBM-compatible PCs. This was practically state-of-the-art back then! Luckily for me that was just before oil prices dropped, which meant that oil companies (our major customers) soon halted new construction of chemical plants. The ripple effect soon had me out of work, since no one was buying my company's expensive software.

This was actually a godsend (after I got over the shock of being laid off). I made a career choice to pursue computer graphics rather than get a job in a chemical plant somewhere. I was soon working as a computer consultant, happily helping clients solve their data analysis problems. After a while I ended up working for what was then the hottest company in PCs, Lotus Development Corporation. Remember, this was in the mid-1980s, and Lotus was *much* larger than Microsoft! Working at Lotus was an epiphany. People working there *tested* the code that the programmers wrote! Such an environment! When I was later asked whether I wanted a full-time job as a programmer, I jumped at the chance. I happily spent the next nine years working on various projects, usually on the graphics side of things. When I worked on Lotus 1-2-3, I decided that I had to try to force the product to have a better charting system. I was familiar with UNIX workstations and the software that ran on them. Even though there wasn't yet a PC that could run in 24-bit color in 1024 × 768 resolution, I could clearly see that this was the direction things were heading. It wouldn't be long before PCs would be able to perform 95 percent of the work of a then current $40,000 workstation. I set my sites on better color support, higher-resolution display support, and 3D graphics. None of the other competing products at the time had support for these items.

About this time Lotus was getting beaten up for lack of a Windows spreadsheet. Windows was getting pretty widely accepted. It had an API that supported graphics at any resolution (so long as it wasn't too high), and it had better color support, but it didn't have 3D graphics. Almost, but not quite there yet. I played around with writing my own dynamic 3D graphics routines, but when you tacked on the Windows overhead, they ran unacceptably slowly. I soon read that Microsoft had contracted with Silicon Graphics, Inc., to write a portable 3D graphics interface that would work on a Windows platform. SGI had pretty much the entire UNIX 3D graphics market and was an engineering company. This meant that it built the solution, then went looking for problems to solve. The problems solved were all manner of visualization problems. All I had to do was wait a few years to see what developed. What happened was Windows NT, a 32-bit operating system. This was the first requirement for a portable graphics language. Next came the 3D graphics API itself. SGI had migrated its native API into something called OpenGL, a portable, open-architectured, extensible 3D graphics API. I had experienced OpenGL on workstations, but now that power was going to the PC! This was the moment I had been waiting for. With Windows NT 3.51 with its native OpenGL support, I quickly wrote a collection of 3D demos that far outsurpassed anything that was running on a PC. Armed with the demos and with projections about how 3D was going to be important to everybody in the next few years, I went before the VP of Desktop Products and stated my case. It was probably the terrain map connected to a SpaceBall that lost my case. Somehow using this weird ball-like thing on my desk to control the flyover of a landscape made me seem more like a computer graphics zealot than a spreadsheet programmer. I made my pitch to a few product managers who actually could see that in a few years, interactive 3D graphics would be important. I contented myself with writing a few magazine articles about virtual reality and 3D graphics, while wasting my time implementing more 2D business graphs using an inherited architecture from a long-defunct product, and waiting for a chance.

My chance came when Microsoft announced Windows 95. Buried in the product specs were OpenGL support and the reworkings of Windows to be a successful games platform. OpenGL was good. Being a gaming platform was better! This meant that there would be not only support for animated graphics but also better sound support and a new input system for things other than a mouse. I tried one last time at Lotus to get buy-in, but at that time it was fighting a losing battle for market share, and there was little enthusiasm to make a radical leap and architect a new stellar graphics system. So I decided that I needed to devote more time to working on visualization tools and 3D graphics systems. It was time to quit and form my own consulting company.

About this time Addison-Wesley contacted me about writing a book about OpenGL programming for Windows. The results of that conversation are in your hands. It's been a rocky path getting here. I'm very glad that some of my clients were patient when I disappeared for a few weeks before a writing deadline, even though I did mention beforehand that it probably would happen.

Microsoft has been twiddling with the OpenGL/Windows interface, so I continually had to make changes in chapters to keep the information current. The final thing to happen was the imminent release of OpenGL 1.1, which is an order of magnitude better in terms of rendering speed and support for writing faster applications. But since I wanted to write a book about *fast* 3D graphics, it was important to take a look at version 1.1 to see what it offered. And it does offer a lot! I've included most of the features that were added to version 1.1, so you should be all set when you're ready to try it out.

Not all of the features of OpenGL are covered in this book. I didn't want to rewrite the *OpenGL Programming Guide,* which already covers OpenGL's features. This is a book about how to program OpenGL in a Windows environment, how to program it to be fast, and how you can make it easy to use OpenGL in your programs. I cover all the aspects of creating, viewing, and animating a scene. Specific tips along the way give you specific information about how to make your code as fast as possible. All the source code is included on the CD, so you can experiment with the examples on your own. The examples build on one another; by the end of the book you have most of the important features of OpenGL in one place and with a convenient wrapper about them that makes them easy to use. Feel free to pull 'em apart and reuse whatever you like. I've tried to avoid letting any mistakes into the code, but that's impossible, so watch out. If you find a problem with the code or the text or just want me to expand on some topic, drop me a line. Check out the README.TXT file on the CD for all the latest information.

I wrote this book because I believe that 3D graphics will be one of the most important features in computers in the next decade. It's indescribable what you can demonstrate to people when you have a fast, interactive 3D environment. I'm doing my best to promote this conviction, and the book you hold in your hands is the best way that I know of to prove it to you as well. Now go and do something with it!

Acknowledgments

I would like to thank the following people for assisting me in the writing of this book: Hock San Lee of Microsoft, Neil Trevett of 3D Labs, Igor Sinyak of Intel, Jeff Morris of Lotus Development Corporation, Bruce Campbell of AOD Software, and Mary Treseler of Addison-Wesley, who gave me lots of support, which I dearly appreciated.

List of Figures

List of Listings

1

Why 3D? Why OpenGL?

I mean, if we're promising to make graphics on the PC better than on a Silicon Graphics workstation, we sure as heck are going to make them better than on a $200 game device.

—Bill Gates

OpenGL is rapidly becoming the industry standard for high-quality 3D graphics applications. It's available on a variety of hardware platforms and operating systems, including Microsoft's Windows 95 and Windows NT, IBM's OS/2, DEC's AXP and OpenVMS, and X Windows. OpenGL was written with the express intention of becoming a thin software interface to underlying graphics hardware—an arrangement of proven success in the graphics workstation market and now being popularized by its introduction into the personal computer market. With the introduction of OpenGL for Windows 95 and Windows NT the most popular operating systems in the world now have the same high-quality 3D graphics capabilities that were used to produce such excellent 3D renderings as found in the movies *Jurassic Park, Toy Story,* and *Twister,* and many of the models regularly seen in the TV series *Babylon 5* and *Space: Above and Beyond.* Not only a fun technology, high-performance 3D graphics are regarded as an important one as well. *PC Magazine* recognized this when it awarded its 1994 Technical Excellence Award for operating systems to Windows NT Workstation version 3.5. As part of the award citation, *PC Magazine* asserted: "By implementing OpenGL on NT, Microsoft brought workstation-class graphics to the PC, and—finally—genuine 3D graphics to Windows."

Good 3D capabilities are becoming an increasingly important part of many fields, including CAD/CAM (computer-aided design/computer-aided modeling), architectural design, product design, financial analysis, computer animation and simulation, multimedia applications, World Wide Web applications using VRML (Virtual Reality Modeling Language), statistical and scientific visualization, medical imaging, publishing, and game design and implementation. With OpenGL on Windows this capability has moved from the realm of the workstation into the much larger domain of the PC.

What's So Important about 3D?

We are already seeing the effect of this transition on the hardware companies as they all scramble to take advantage of the standardization of a well-defined API (application program interface). By mid-1996 a wave of new products will be taking advantage of this 3D capability, producing an explosion of products in fierce competition. Silicon Graphics Incorporated (SGI) in particular is heading off in a new direction, away from simply dominating the graphics workstation market and instead targeting the consumer personal computer market. If that sounds strange, take a moment to think about it. Would you rather be selling $30,000 machines to an audience of around 250,000 customers or adding an additional business of selling software targeted at 200 million customers, especially if they might be repeat customers?

SGI is not alone in targeting game customers. Microsoft is not above entering the "lowly" game market as evidenced by its huge introduction of Windows 95. After all, it was really just an upgrade to an operating system, not anything startlingly new. Yet the huge furor when it was introduced was caused in no small part by the enormous advertising effort expended by Microsoft in an effort to get people to upgrade—to a new operating system with new capabilities. One of these capabilities is an excellent redesign and enhancement of the video interface, in addition to new input, sound, and networking libraries in the form of the Game Software Development Kit (SDK). Microsoft is betting that it can make a PC the ultimate, generic game platform (which just might steal most of those new customers that SGI is looking at, plus a sizeable chunk of the home game-console market!). What could be better than selling them all new $50 copies of your new operating system? Will Microsoft pull it off? I think so. They have the resources and the talent, and they don't get scared by a high entry fee. When asked if Microsoft will be in this market for the long run, Bill Gates stated: "Well, we've never been capital-constrained."

But don't get the idea that everyone is interested strictly in games. In fact, people are just looking at prior history. CD-ROMs were not that commonplace until a few killer games requiring CD-ROMs came on the market. Within three years just about every PC sold from that point on came with a CD player. Since CDs are much cheaper to sell software on than if the software were on multiple floppies, most large programs come on CD, and it's been a much better deal all around.

Customers suddenly get a few hundred megabytes of stuff instead of 15 or 20, and a whole new industry has grown up around the creation and use of CD-ROMs. A few of the more astute players in the computer business, mostly SGI and Microsoft, noticed this cause and effect and set out to build the next incremental wave of improvement: better graphics. But how could they get it started?

Well, just as games launched CD-ROMs into respectability, games can also launch better 2D and 3D graphics. Microsoft in particular is spending huge amounts of cash and hiring some of the best talent in the industry to bolster its standing in the video and graphics arena. The real need is to get the equipment capable of handling 3D graphics into the hands of consumers, and what better proven method than that provided by the CD-ROM model, especially when the industry has agreed to steer it in that direction!

With the release of DirectX, Microsoft's game interface, and the release of OpenGL, the high-quality 3D API, the PC platform is being transitioned into the equivalent of a personal workstation for less than $5000. In fact, since Windows 95 and NT are 32-bit platforms and not entirely different from X Windows, most workstation software vendors will probably come out with PC versions in the near future, driven simply by market size. When I was at a C++ conference in 1989 and talking to another engineer, who happened to develop workstation software, he looked down his nose with obvious disdain when I told him I wrote PC software. With a wave of his hand he dismissed its importance and said, "Oh, how much of that stuff can you sell?" When I mentioned that in the last year we'd sold almost $500 million, his jaw dropped and he was literally speechless, since a workstation software company with sales of $10 million was considered to be doing rather well. Herein lies the effect of having a large customer base!

In change lies opportunity. The September 4, 1995, issue of *Business Week* had a cover story on 3D graphics. That such a staid business publication should devote its cover story to a particular type of computer application is amazing, but perhaps it's a good indication that more than a few people are aware of what the next couple of years will bring. In fact, a quote from the article brings home the point: "In these early days of the 3D boom, demand is growing at such a rapid pace that plenty of suppliers should be able to make a buck off the third dimension."

Although that quote is directed mostly at the video manufacturers, it's just as true for anyone writing the software to take advantage of this new capability. If you've watched the industry for any length of time, you know that when a technology gets hot, developers who already are established are worth their weight in gold. Of course, we're at a junction. There might be OpenGL programmers, and there might be Windows programmers, but very very few are both. Opportunity beckons.

Learning OpenGL on Windows

The introduction of OpenGL onto a Windows platform entails its own edification of a new legion of graphics programmers, since the blending of a workstation-based graphics API with a common PC operating system ushers in an entirely new realm of programming on the PC. That's where this book comes in. If you're interested in fast rendering of high-quality 3D images on Windows 95 and Windows NT, you've come to the right place. This book makes heavy use of Microsoft's Visual C++ programming platform, the C++ programming language, and the Microsoft Foundation Classes (MFC) as wrappers to the generic Windows API, but it starts off with a generic C application that can be compiled from any 32-bit C compiler that provides access to the OpenGL headers. With some minor work you can run OpenGL programs with compilers from Borland, Symantec, or Watcom. This book will cover the basics of creating an OpenGL program, from the selection of the appropriate pixel format to the arrangement of the device context and rendering contexts. We'll touch on everything that you'll need to know about OpenGL on Windows in detail so that you have a good basis to further expand your 3D graphics programming expertise. In the later chapters we'll cover how to go about enhancing OpenGL programs to get the maximum speed out of them.

From using display lists and texture maps to finding out about OpenGL enhancements that may be residing, hidden, in your video driver: We'll start programming a real application and take it step by step through enhancements, applying what we've learned about increasing OpenGL rendering. We'll cover how to program OpenGL's Modelview matrix and explain how to use it to get the effects you want. We'll start off by programming a simple OpenGL program to demonstrate setting up Windows to run OpenGL. We'll go into detail about the pixel format specifier and why you should understand what it is and how it's important for a Windows programmer to know how to program it. We'll write a few tools so that you can examine the OpenGL implementation on your computer and how that implementation can be different on the same PC.

Along the way we'll get introduced to some tools that Microsoft provides—but doesn't really document—for measuring a program's speed; and no, I'm not talking about the profiler! We'll learn how to provide rapid animation under Windows without bogging down the user interface. And as we go through each step, we'll be building up an application that you can experiment with and use. The MFC OpenGL View Class will give you some hands-on experience at designing, creating, programming, and optimizing an OpenGL 3D animation program. You'll learn how to measure OpenGL calls to see what arrangements perform faster, how to select one video mode over another, and how to precompile primitives into display lists for rapid rendering execution. We'll also collect some programming tricks that you can use to further enhance the rendering speed.

Summary

OpenGL is an operating system– and hardware platform–independent graphics library designed to be easily portable yet rapidly executable. It brings a standard 3D graphics library with the hardware-enhanced ability to perform lighting, shading, texture mapping, hidden-surface removal, and animation onto the Windows platform for the first time. Some of the main features of OpenGL include the following:

- *Texture mapping:* the ability to apply an image to a graphics surface. This technique is used to rapidly generate realistic images without having to specify an excessive amount of detail. For example, you could create a wooden floor by painting the floor's rectangular surface with a woodgrain texture.
- *z-buffering:* the ability to calculate the distance from the viewer's location. This makes it easy for the program to automatically remove surfaces or parts of surfaces that are hidden from view.
- *Double buffering:* support for smooth animation using double buffering. A smooth animation sequence is achieved by drawing into the back buffer while displaying the front buffer and then swapping the buffers when you're ready to display the next animation sequence.
- *Lighting effects:* the ability to calculate the effects on the lightness of a surface's color when different lighting models are applied to the surface from one or more light sources.
- *Smooth shading:* the ability to calculate the shading effects that occur when light hits a surface at an angle and results in subtle color differences across the surface. This effect is important for making a model look "realistic."
- *Material properties:* the ability to specify the material properties of a surface. These properties modify the lighting effects on the surface by specifying such things as the dullness or shininess of the surface.
- *Alpha blending:* the ability to specify an alpha, or "opacity," value in addition to the regular RGB (red/green/blue) values. The alpha component is used to specify opacity, allowing the full range, from completely transparent

to totally opaque. When used in combination with the z-buffer, alpha blending gives the effect of being able to see "through" objects.

- *Transformation matrices:* the ability to change the location, size, and perspective of an object in 3D coordinate space. This gives you the freedom to change an object's size and location just by modifying the elements of the matrix.

OpenGL is an interface that's designed, maintained, and enhanced by the OpenGL Architecture Review Board (ARB)—a collection of interested software and hardware companies, including Digital Equipment Corporation, Evans and Sutherland, IBM, Intel, Intergraph, Microsoft, and Silicon Graphics. These companies have a vested interest in seeing that OpenGL becomes *the* standard for high-quality 3D graphics. The introduction of OpenGL as a native part of the operating system on the Windows NT 3.5 platform in mid-1994 and its ability to run directly on the initial release of Windows 95 marks the onset of high-performance 3D graphics capabilities on a PC. The pressure to provide a 3D library with texture mapping and lighting capabilities has been building for a long time, and now it's here! Already hardware companies are starting to provide video boards that have built-in OpenGL routines—hardware that can easily speed up the average OpenGL program twenty to fifty times. This pushes the rendering speeds for simple models, say, less than 100,000 polygons, to video frame rates, the rate needed to provide the true illusion of motion. Due to the marriage of a slim API linked with underlying accelerated graphics hardware, we are now seeing PC-based 3D applications that were unthinkable just a few years ago.

2

OpenGL for
Windows Programmers

We're rich as son-of-a-bitch stew but look how homely we are, just
as plain-folksy as Grandpappy back in 1836. We know about cham-
pagne and caviar but we talk hog and hominy.

—Edna Ferber

This chapter is intended for programmers who are either new to OpenGL and learning it on a Windows platform or experienced with OpenGL on other platforms and learning the Windows-specific requirements for getting an OpenGL program up and running under Windows. This chapter covers the basics of getting a window ready to accept OpenGL calls. This involves getting a device context for the rendering window, selecting a pixel format, creating a rendering context for OpenGL to operate on, and, finally, cleaning up after all this preparation and creation. In this chapter we will cover just the interface layer between Windows and OpenGL—what you need to know about it and how you go about manipulating it.

Although it's great that Windows finally has a real 3D API, the irritants that are part of GDI (graphics device interface) programming have to be endured. If you're new to Windows programming, GDI refers to the Windows native 2D graphics API. For those of us who've been making a living at Windows programming, GDI is a necessary evil. Much like any other graphics API, GDI has its own quirks and eccentricities, and for most Windows programmers GDI's quirks soon become part of the background noise of programming under Windows.

Fortunately *most* of the GDI quirkiness is gone from Windows OpenGL programming. In fact, getting GDI to work in an OpenGL window isn't that easy! However, for most OpenGL implementations, there's a platform-specific interface that requires twiddling before you can fire up OpenGL, and Windows is no exception.

Six basic steps are required to use OpenGL calls in a Windows program:

1. Getting a device context for the rendering location
2. Selecting and setting a pixel format for the device context
3. Creating a rendering context associated with the device context
4. Drawing using OpenGL commands
5. Releasing the rendering context
6. Releasing the device context

Those are the steps. However, even a Windows programmer won't be able to make much sense of them, since OpenGL programming requires functions that are entirely new to Windows, starting with Windows NT 3.5 and as an additional subsystem on Windows 95. Let's examine a bit of the terminology involved with setting up Windows to use OpenGL calls.

Overview of Device Contexts, Rendering Contexts, and Pixel Formats

We've already mentioned GDI, Windows' original 2D graphics interface. GDI is capable of drawing to the screen, to memory, to printers, or to any other device that provides a GDI interface layer and that can process GDI calls. This makes it simple to give your program the ability to print out a diagram that's on the screen, since the drawing command essentially remains unchanged. GDI accomplishes this by a rendering "handle" to the currently selected device. This handle is called the *device context*, or DC. All GDI calls pass through a DC, and the DC does the correct thing. You can create a DC for the screen, do your rendering, switch to a printer DC, and render using the same commands again; what you saw on the screen will show up on the printer.

A *rendering context*, or RC, is the OpenGL equivalent of the GDI DC. An RC is the portal through which OpenGL calls are rendered to the device. The device context is, in part, GDI's repository of state variables (the current color of the current pen, for example); the rendering context plays a similar function for OpenGL's state variables. You can think of both of them simply as a data structure that keeps the state of the current settings and routes calls to the appropriate device. That's pretty much how they are going to be treated in this book. Creating a DC and an RC before you start making your OpenGL calls is simply part of the ritual that you have to execute before you can use OpenGL functions. In this chapter we'll examine what you need to know about DCs, RCs, and pixel formats and then describe the library function I've created that takes care of all this stuff for you.

Pixel formats are perhaps the only interesting part of the Windows OpenGL interface, and that's because you can modify the pixel format to suit your needs. Modifying the pixel format is one of the areas that you can preselect in your program to optimize your OpenGL program, with no other changes to your OpenGL code. It's also one of the least-discussed areas of Windows OpenGL programming, since it's an entirely new part of the Windows API, created just for OpenGL. If you're just interested in getting OpenGL up and running without getting into minute details of how the rendering device can be set up, you can skip the next section. The OpenGL initialization functions of the library will take care of setting all this up for you. However, if you're interested in optimizing your program to get the maximum rendering speed out of it, you should spend some time studying the next section.

Pixel Formats

Pixel formats are the translation layer between OpenGL calls (such as an OpenGL call to draw a pixel with an RGB triad value of [128,120,135]) and the rendering operation that Windows performs (the pixel might be drawn with a translated RGB value of [128,128,128]). The pixel format that you've selected describes such things as how colors are displayed, the depth of field resolution, and what additional capabilities are supported by the rendering context you've created. The Windows OpenGL API has four functions that handle the pixel format. These are shown in Table 2.1. We'll describe each of the functions and how it's used.

Pixel Format Function	Description
ChoosePixelFormat( )	Obtains a device context's pixel format that's the closest match to a pixel format template you've provided.
SetPixelFormat( )	Sets a device context's current pixel format to the pixel format index specified.
GetPixelFormat( )	Returns the pixel format index of a device context's current pixel format.
DescribePixelFormat( )	Given a device context and a pixel format index, fills a PIXELFORMATDESCRIPTOR data structure with the pixel format's properties.

Table 2.1   Functions for Manipulating the OpenGL Pixel Format

Pixel Format Structure

The capabilities of an OpenGL window depend on the pixel format selected for the OpenGL rendering window. The properties of this format include

- Single or double buffering
- RGBA or color indexing
- Drawing to a window or bitmap
- Support of GDI or OpenGL calls
- Color depth (depth = number of bits)
- z-axis depth
- Stencil buffer
- Visibility masks

In Windows these values are set for each OpenGL window, using a data structure called the **PIXELFORMATDESCRIPTOR**. The pixel format has to be selected before the OpenGL rendering context is created. Once the pixel format is set for a rendering context, it cannot be changed.

The exact values of the **PIXELFORMATDESCRIPTOR** that are supported depend on the implementation of OpenGL that is running, the current video mode Windows is running in, and the video hardware you currently have installed. Generally you can be sure that you have at least the "generic" Windows implementation of OpenGL. This is a software-only version of OpenGL that's provided by Microsoft, and it's an important consideration if you intend your OpenGL programs to be distributed widely. You can be fairly sure that the generic implementation will be the slowest. If your computer has a video board that supports OpenGL, you're getting *some* assurance that your OpenGL programs will run faster. However, even if a board has OpenGL hardware, there is no rule that the manufacturer has to provide a device driver to completely reroute calls to the hardware. Some manufacturers may implement only a limited set of OpenGL calls, leaving the generic driver to perform the rest. Such an implementation is called a *Mini Client Driver*. So the only way to be sure of the capabilities of your target system is to run tests and see what is present.

The following structure can be found in the Windows include file WINGDI.H

```
typedef struct tagPIXELFORMATDESCRIPTOR
{
    WORD  nSize;
```

```
    WORD   nVersion;
    DWORD  dwFlags;
    BYTE   iPixelType;
    BYTE   cColorBits;
    BYTE   cRedBits;
    BYTE   cRedShift;
    BYTE   cGreenBits;
    BYTE   cGreenShift;
    BYTE   cBlueBits;
    BYTE   cBlueShift;
    BYTE   cAlphaBits;
    BYTE   cAlphaShift;
    BYTE   cAccumBits;
    BYTE   cAccumRedBits;
    BYTE   cAccumGreenBits;
    BYTE   cAccumBlueBits;
    BYTE   cAccumAlphaBits;
    BYTE   cDepthBits;
    BYTE   cStencilBits;
    BYTE   cAuxBuffers;
    BYTE   iLayerType;
    BYTE   bReserved;
    DWORD  dwLayerMask;
    DWORD  dwVisibleMask;
    DWORD  dwDamageMask;
} PIXELFORMATDESCRIPTOR,
*PPIXELFORMATDESCRIPTOR,
FAR *LPPIXELFORMATDESCRIPTOR;
```

Table 2.2 is a breakdown of each element found in the **PIXELFORMATDESCRIPTOR** structure. You can consider this breakdown as a way of setting up the properties of the canvas that you are going to paint on with your OpenGL program, so you should have a good grasp of what those capabilities are.

Structure Element	Description
nSize	Specifies the size in bytes of the data structure and should be set to sizeof(PIXELFORMATDESCRIPTOR).
nVersion	Specifies the version of the structure (*not* the OpenGL version!).
dwFlags	A set of bit flags that specify properties of the pixel buffer. The properties are generally not mutually exclusive; however, there are exceptions. The following constants are defined:

- `PFD_DOUBLEBUFFER`: We want or have double buffering. This flag is important if you want fast rendering, since you usually draw to the hidden, or "back," buffer, then swap it to the front. This flag and `PFD_SUPPORT_GDI` are mutually exclusive in the release 1.0 generic implementation.

- `PFD_STEREO`: We want or have a stereoscopic buffer. This flag is not supported in the release 1.0 generic implementation.

- `PFD_DRAW_TO_WINDOW`: We want to draw to a window or device, or for the device driver to support it.

- `PFD_DRAW_TO_BITMAP`: We want to draw to a memory bitmap or for the device driver to support it.

- `PFD_SUPPORT_GDI`: We want or have a buffer that supports GDI drawing. This flag and `PFD_DOUBLEBUFFER` are mutually exclusive in the release 1.0 generic implementation.

- `PFD_SUPPORT_OPENGL`: We want to use OpenGL, or the device supports it.

- `PFD_GENERIC_FORMAT`: The pixel format is supported by the generic implementation. If this bit is clear, this pixel format is supported by a device driver or by hardware. See the next entry.

- `PFD_GENERIC_ACCELERATED`: New with OpenGL 1.1, this flag is used with `PFD_GENERIC_FORMAT` to differentiate between the various driver types.

- `PFD_NEED_PALETTE`: The buffer uses RGBA pixels on a palette-managed device. This means that a logical palette is required to achieve the best results. The colors in the palette are specified according to the values of the `cRedBits`, `cRedShift`, `cGreenBits`, `cGreenShift`, `cBluebits`, and `cBlueShift` members. The palette should be created and realized in the device context (DC) before calling `wglMakeCurrent()`. Also see the next entry.

- `PFD_NEED_SYSTEM_PALETTE`: Flag used by OpenGL hardware that supports only one palette. To use hardware accelerations in such hardware, the hardware palette has to be in a fixed order (for example, 3-3-2) in RGBA mode or match the logical palette in color-index mode. In the release 1.0 generic implementation the `PFD_NEED_PALETTE` flag doesn't have such a requirement. That is, if only `PFD_NEED_PALETTE` is set, the logical-to-system palette mapping is performed by the system. However, if `PFD_NEED_SYS-TEM_PALETTE` is set, you should take over the system palette in your program by calling `SetSystemPaletteUse()` to force a one-to-one logical-to-system palette mapping. If your OpenGL hardware supports multiple hardware palettes and the device driver can allocate spare hardware palettes for OpenGL, then this flag may not be set. If a format requires `PFD_NEED_SYSTEM_PALETTE` but your program ignores it because it doesn't want to mess up the desktop colors, it won't get maximum performance but should still work. The `PFD_NEED_SYSTEM_PALETTE` flag isn't needed if the OpenGL hardware supports multiple hardware palettes and the driver can allocate spare hardware palettes for OpenGL. The generic pixel formats don't have this flag set.

- `PFD_SWAP_COPY`: Not found in the original Windows NT 3.5 implementation. This is an advanced flag that depends on your OpenGL implementation and its extensions. If this flag is specified, it's a hint that you want the back buffer *copied* to the front buffer when the buffers are swapped. This is different from the default behavior, whereby the back buffer becomes undefined when the buffers are swapped. The contents of the back buffer are not effected. Also see the next flag.

- `PFD_SWAP_EXCHANGE`: Not found in the original Windows NT 3.5 implementation. This is an advanced flag that depends on your OpenGL implementation and its extensions. If this flag is specified, it is a hint that you want the back buffer *exchanged* with the front buffer when the buffers are swapped. This is different from the default behavior, whereby the back buffer becomes undefined when the buffers are swapped. The contents of the back buffer are swapped with the front buffer. Also see the previous flag.

- `PFD_DOUBLEBUFFER_DONTCARE`: Used only when calling the `ChoosePixelFormat()` function. This means to ignore single or double buffering when selecting a match for a format you've set up.

- `PFD_STEREO_DONTCARE`: Used only when calling the `ChoosePixelFormat()` function. This means to ignore the stereo flag when selecting a match for a format you've set up.

`iPixelType`   Specifies the color type of the pixel data. The following types are defined:

- `PFD_TYPE_RGBA`: The pixel color is specified as RGBA values. Each pixel has four separate color components: red, green, blue, and alpha. This is the setting you want in most cases; however, your hardware will determine what you get.

- `PFD_TYPE_COLORINDEX`: The pixel color is specified in a lookup table. Each pixel uses a color-index value to look up a palette value instead of an RGBA value. You'll need to use this setting (and set up a palette) if the RGBA setting fails to render colors satisfactorily or if you need to perform palette animation. Note that some featuers (lighting and texture-mapping, for example) don't work or require more work when using color-index mode. You might need this if the system has 256 colors or fewer.

`cColorBits` Specifies the number of color bit planes in each color buffer. For RGBA mode it's the size in bits of the color buffer. This value doesn't include the alpha bit planes. If you're currently in "true color" mode (16 million colors, or 24-bit color), your hardware supports 8 bits per RGB color. So the value of `cColorBits` would be 24 bits ($3 \times 8 = 24$). If you're currently in 256 color mode, the values for `cColorBits` will never be greater than 8 bits. Values will generally range from 4 to 32. For color-index pixels it's the size of the color palette. Note that you generally prefer to use RGBA mode over color-index mode. If you select color-index mode, you should set up the palette.

`cRedBits` Specifies the number of red bit planes in each RGBA color buffer. For example, a value of 3 indicates that eight (2^3) different intensities of red are available.

`cRedShift` Specifies the shift count for red bit planes in each RGBA color buffer. That is, it's where the red bits can be found in the color buffer. The shifts for red, green, and blue will all be different. For example, in an 8-bit, 256 color mode, the last two bits in an 8-bit color value are usually the two blue bits. The blue shift value would then be six.

`cGreenBits` Specifies the number of green bit planes in each RGBA color buffer.

`cGreenShift` Specifies the shift count for green bit planes in each RGBA color buffer.

`cBlueBits` Specifies the number of blue bit planes in each RGBA color buffer.

`cBlueShift` Specifies the shift count for blue bit planes in each RGBA color buffer.

`cAlphaBits` Specifies the number of alpha bit planes in each RGBA color buffer. The alpha bit plane is used to specify the opacity of a color. Alpha bit planes are not supported in the release 1.0 generic implementation.

`cAlphaShift` Specifies the shift count for alpha bit planes in each RGBA color buffer.

`cAccumBits` Specifies the total number of bit planes in the accumulation buffer, which is used for accumulating images.

`cAccumRedBits` Specifies the number of red bit planes in the accumulation buffer.

`cAccumGreenBits` Specifies the number of green bit planes in the accumulation buffer.

`cAccumBlueBits` Specifies the number of blue bit planes in the accumulation buffer.

`cAccumAlphaBits` Specifies the number of alpha bit planes in the accumulation buffer.

`cDepthBits` Specifies the number of bits of the depth (*z*-axis) buffer. Generally this value is 0, 16, 24, or 32.

`cStencilBits` Specifies the number of bits of the stencil buffer, which is used to restrict drawing to certain areas.

`cAuxBuffers`	Specifies the number of auxiliary buffers, which are not supported in the release 1.0 generic implementation.
`iLayerType`	Specifies the type of layer. The generic implementation supports only the main plane, although the following values are defined: • `PFD_MAIN_PLANE`: The layer is the main plane. • `PFD_OVERLAY_PLANE`: The layer is the overlay plane. • `PFD_UNDERLAY_PLANE`: The layer is the underlay plane.
`bReserved`	Not used. Must be zero.
`dwLayerMask`	Obsolete in OpenGL 1.1 or later. Designated the layer mask, which is used in combination with the visible mask to see whether one layer overlays another.
`dwVisibleMask`	Designates the visible mask, which is used in conjunction with the layer mask to determine whether one layer overlays another. If the result of the bitwise-AND of the visible mask of a layer and the layer mask of a second layer is nonzero, the first layer overlays the second layer, and a transparent pixel value exists between the two layers. If the visible mask is 0, the layer is opaque.
`dwDamageMask`	Obsolete in OpenGL 1.1 or later. Specified whether more than one pixel format shares the same frame buffer. If the result of the bitwise-AND of the damage masks between two pixel formats is nonzero, they share the same buffers.

Table 2.2   Elements in the PIXELFORMATDESCRIPTOR Structure

The generic implementation (up to OpenGL 1.1 on Windows NT and Windows 95) supports 24 pixel formats. Installed hardware may change or add additional capabilities. Each format is referred to by number (from 1 to n), but the ordering can change, depending on various factors, so don't rely on the numbers to remain the same.

The pixel formats are grouped according to their properties. The primary property is the color depth, which ranges from 4 bits per pixel, through 8, 16, 24, and 32 bits per pixel. Eight formats are defined for the color depth specified by the display driver. These are referred to as the *native formats*. The remaining non-native formats are divided among the other color depth values. These formats are grouped according to pixel type (RGBA or color index), single versus double buffered, and the depth of the depth buffer. Note that you can have a double buffer only if the format specified is a window, not a bitmap. Any additional formats that might be provided by OpenGL hardware are called *device formats*.

Selecting and Examining a Pixel Format

Now that we've examined what goes into the pixel format structure, let's use it to examine pixel formats. The Windows function that fills a pixel format structure is `DescribePixelFormat()`. The following code fragment illustrates how it's used:

```
// create a device context from the current window
CClientDC mydc(this);

// get a pixel format descriptor variable
PIXELFORMATDESCRIPTOR pfd;
int MaxNumberPixelFormats;

// if it succeeds, it returns the total number of formats
MaxNumberPixelFormats =
 DescribePixelFormat(
        dc.m_hDC,           // pass in a DC
        1,                  // select the first pixel format
        sizeof(pdf),        // size of struct to fill
        &pfd);              // ptr to struct

if ( 0 == MaxNumberPixelFormats )
        {
        // Something went wrong....
        // print out a message to the debug window
        TRACE("DescribePixelFormat Failed with "
                "%d\r\n",GetLastError()) ;
        }
```

The class `CClientDC` creates a device context. This is Windows' way of describing the selected window's identity and properties. The function `DescribePixelFormat()` is called with the argument of 1 to describe the first pixel format. If this routine succeeds, it returns the total number of pixel formats on the system. If it fails, it returns a value of 0. A successful call fills in the `PIXELFORMATDESCRIPTOR` structure, which can then be examined.

Figure 2.1 shows the tool I've provided for displaying the pixel formats available on your PC. The source code can be found on the CD under Chapter 2/Pixel Format Enumeration Program. To use the program, you can either type in the name of the executable image, PIXELFMT.EXE, from a command prompt, or you can launch the program from the file manager. Once the program comes up (assuming that you don't get a message stating that OpenGL is not on your system!),

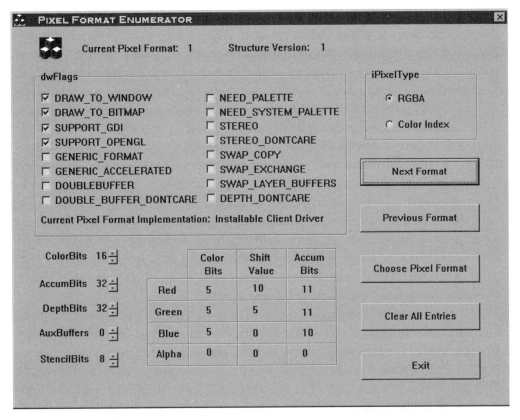

Figure 2.1   Pixel-Format Enumerator

you'll see a dialog box that is the main display of the pixel-format enumeration program.

You can press the Next Format or the Previous Format button and watch as the program runs up and down the listing of the pixel formats found on your system. You can use this program to explore the formats available on your system. Take a note of the formats, and then change your video settings and run the program again. You'll see the formats change in accordance with what's currently running on your system. For example, if you're running in video graphics array (VGA) mode, you'll never see a color depth greater than 256 colors, even if your video hardware is capable of it. And, as I'll get into in the next section, the program can also be used to try various pixel-format template values that can then be passed to the OpenGL interface layer to see what it then returns to you as its "best match."

Generally when you start out, you'll have a pretty good idea of what properties you'll want in an OpenGL program. You'll know right away whether you want to render to a window or a bitmap and whether you want OpenGL support. If you're going to be displaying some animation or some other rapidly changing scene, you'll want a double-buffered window. If you're going to be using a lot of colors or OpenGL's lighting effects or you need nondefault colors, you'll want an RGBA window and probably a color depth of at least 16 bits.

Once you've selected the main attributes for your window, you need to ask the system for such a window. This is where the next function comes in. **ChoosePixelFormat()** takes a **const** pointer to a partially filled-out pixel format structure—one that you've filled out with your desired pixel format attributes—and the function matches it against the available pixel formats, selecting one for you. The pixel format structure you passed in is filled out with the selected format attributes, and the function returns the index value of the selected format. It's up to you to check to make sure that the selected format is acceptable and to retry with different values if the selection is not acceptable.

In the PIXELFMT program you may have noticed that you're able to edit the values in the dialog box. This feature allows you to use the ChoosePixelFmt button to take the entered-in values and call **ChoosePixelFormat()** and then see what the returned values are. Note that not all of the entries have an effect on the chosen pixel format. The further you get away from the primary properties, the less effect the values will have on the chosen pixel format. Basically, color depth, z-buffer depth, and the flags have the major impact on the returned pixel format.

Finally, when you've found an acceptable pixel format, you call the next of the pixel format functions, **SetPixelFormat()**. This function takes a DC and a pixel format index and selects that format for the window associated with the DC. The entire process of filling out a desired pixel format descriptor, calling **ChoosePixelFormat()** to get a match, and then calling **SetPixelFormat()** to select the format for the device context can be illustrated as follows:

```
CClientDC mydc(this);
int SelectedPixelFormat;
BOOL retVal;

// Now create a pfd and fill it with what we'd like
PIXELFORMATDESCRIPTOR pfd =
    {
    sizeof(PIXELFORMATDESCRIPTOR),// size of this pfd
    1,                            // version number
    PFD_DRAW_TO_WINDOW  |     // support window
```

```
        PFD_SUPPORT_OPENGL |   // & OpenGL
        PFD_DOUBLEBUFFER,      // & double buffering
    PFD_TYPE_RGBA,             // RGBA type
    24,                  // 24-bit color depth
    0, 0, 0, 0, 0, 0,  // color bits ignored
    0,                  // no alpha buffer
    0,                  // shift bit ignored
    0,                  // no accumulation buffer
    0, 0, 0, 0,        // accum bits ignored
    16,                 // 16-bit z-buffer
    0,                  // no stencil buffer
    0,                  // no auxiliary buffer
    PFD_MAIN_PLANE,     // main layer
    0,                  // reserved
    0, 0, 0            // no layer, visible, or damage masks
    };

// get the device context's best-available-match
// pixel format
SelectedPixelFormat =
    ChoosePixelFormat(mydc.m_hdc, &pfd);

ASSERT( 0 != SelectedPixelFormat );

// make that the device context's current pixel format
retVal = SetPixelFormat(mydc.m_hdc,
                SelectedPixelFormat, &pfd);

// make sure it worked
ASSERT( TRUE == retVal );
```

That's it for examining, choosing, and selecting a pixel format. One last function in the Windows OpenGL API deals with pixel formats: the **GetPixelFormat()** function, which is the matching function of **SetPixelFormat()**. As you can imagine, it returns the selected pixel format index, given a DC. The following code fragment illustrates how it works:

```
CClientDC mydc(this);
int SelectedPixelFormat;

// get the current pixel format for this DC
SelectedPixelFormat = GetPixelFormat(mydc.m_hdc);
```

```
// Make sure the call worked
ASSERT( 0 != SelectedPixelFormat );
```

Of course, this all seems like something best handled by a library routine and then best forgotten, and that's exactly how pixel formats are going to be handled in the later chapters. If you examine the COpenGLView class that's discussed in chapter 7, you'll find that suggesting, verifying, and selecting a pixel format are all part of the creation routines of the view class. In fact, you don't have to worry at all about the pixel format if you don't want to, as it's handled as part of the creation of the rendering context required for an OpenGL program running under Windows. When you create an OpenGL window, the rendering context is created along with the pixel format, and each is held inside the class structure. Some optional creation parameters let you have some control over what type of pixel format gets created, but in most cases you'll probably be happy with the defaults.

Rendering Contexts

Every OpenGL command is linked to a *rendering context*. A rendering context is what links OpenGL calls to a Windows window. Every thread of execution must have its own rendering context in order to be able to draw to the window.

If you're a Windows programmer, you are familiar with the concept of a *device context*. In order to draw to a device using Windows' native graphics interface, GDI, you first need to get or create a device context, or DC. When you execute a GDI command, you must first have a DC selected. The DC contains information about the device that GDI uses to render its commands with, as well as the current GDI settings for that DC, such as the current brush, pen color, and so on. An OpenGL rendering context, or RC, plays a similar role. If you fail to select an RC, your OpenGL calls will fail, and nothing will get drawn. A DC is also used when creating an RC. This connects GDI with OpenGL, since in the generic implementation it's really GDI calls that are getting executed. Note that you don't need the exact same DC each time; you just need a DC that matches the one that was used to create the RC initially. For example, you couldn't mix an RC created with a screen DC and then reactivate it with a DC created for a printer. Finally, remember that a thread can have only one current RC (but many *non*current RCs) and that an RC can be current only to one thread (but other threads can have that RC, as long as it's *not* current).

The WGL Context-Rendering Functions

Windows' implementation of OpenGL has a number of routines that are used for managing rendering contexts. These are part of the "Windows GL," or "wgl" (pronounced "wiggle") functions. You'll need to use these in order to have Windows set up a connection between a rendering device and OpenGL calls. Table 2.3 describes all of the context-rendering management functions found in Windows.

Functions	*Description*
`wglCreateContext( )`	Creates a new OpenGL rendering context, suitable for drawing on the device referenced by the DC provided. The RC has the same pixel format as the DC. An application should set the DC's pixel format before creating a rendering context.
`wglMakeCurrent( )`	Makes the specified RC the calling thread's current RC. OpenGL calls made by the thread are then rendered on the device identified by the DC. If the RC specified is NULL, the function deselects the calling thread's current RC and releases the DC used by the RC. In this case the DC is ignored.
`wglDeleteContext( )`	Deletes the RC specified. It's an error to delete an RC that is another thread's current RC. However, if an RC is the calling thread's current RC, the function makes the rendering context not current before deleting it.
`wglGetCurrentContext( )`	If the calling thread has a current RC, the function returns a handle to that RC. Otherwise, NULL is returned.
`wglGetCurrentDC( )`	If the calling thread has a current RC, the function returns a handle to the DC associated with that RC by means of `wglMakeCurrent()` Otherwise, NULL is returned.

Table 2.3   Windows' Context-Rendering Management Functions

The important wgl calls are `wglCreateContext()`, `wglMakeCurrent()`, and `wglDeleteContext()`. As you might expect, they are used to create, select, and delete RCs. Two additional functions deal with RCs: `wglGetCurrentContext()` and `wglGetCurrentDC()`. These functions are used to fetch the current thread's RC and the RC's associated DC.

The usual sequence is to get a DC, use it to create an RC, make the RC current, make your OpenGL calls, deselect the RC, delete it, and then release the DC. A legacy of 16-bit Windows was trying to run on a machine that (initially) only had

640K of memory to work with. Hence resources were very tight, and DCs in particular not only ate up memory but also were very easy to create and then forget about. This led to the practice of using a DC only when a message was passed to your program that told it that it needed to repaint its window, usually in response to a `WM_PAINT` message, which Windows sends when your program needs to redisplay itself. You'd simply wrapper your painting calls with a get DC/release DC pair. And you'd *never* hold on to a DC for the lifetime of your program, since the user might be running other applications, and *they* would need DCs to paint with.

However, with the 32-bit version of Windows, these problems can be dealt with in a less draconian manner. Windows now has a less restrictive architecture than was found in the old 16-bit days, and if a program creates and holds on to a DC, it's no longer the mistake it once was. In fact, if you're interested in high-performance computing, creating and releasing a DC is a time-consuming process, one best done sparingly.

Methods for Creating an RC

That said, I'll show you the two methods of creating an RC from a DC: the resource-penurious approach still habitually performed by old Windows programmers and the more streamlined approach, which favors execution speed at the expense of holding on to a DC for the lifetime of the OpenGL program. If you're new to Windows programming, three messages passed to a program concern us here: `WM_CREATE`, `WM_PAINT`, and `WM_DESTROY`. These messages are passed to a program when it is being created, needs to repaint its display area, and is about to be terminated, respectively.

First, let's examine the resource-penurious approach, illustrated in Figure 2.2. This approach can be done in two ways. One is to create an RC once and hold onto it; the other is to create the RC in response to each `WM_PAINT` message. I'll discuss only the first way, since old Windows programmers using OpenGL are now on a 32-bit platform and so, ideally, won't take resource conservation to the extreme. When a program receives a `WM_CREATE` message, you get a DC, set up your pixel format, create the RC by using `wglCreateContext()`, and then release the DC. When you receive a `WM_PAINT`, you'd get a DC, make the RC you've already created current by means of `wglMakeCurrent()`, perform your OpenGL calls, deselect the RC by using `wglMakeCurrent()` with null parameters, and then release the DC. Finally, when a `WM_DESTROY` message is delivered, you can delete the RC with `wglDeleteContext()`.

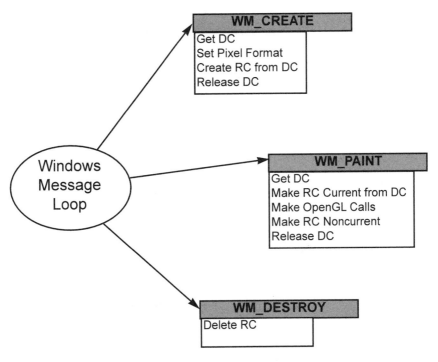

Figure 2.2   The Traditional (and Slow) Method of DC/RC Handling

The optimized approach, illustrated in Figure 2.3, is to get a DC, set the pixel format, create the RC, and make the RC current, all when a **WM_CRE-ATE** is received. This way, when the **WM_PAINT** calls are received—and there will usually be many of them—you need to perform only your OpenGL calls, since your RC is already created and selected. Finally, when the program is terminating, you deselect the RC, delete the RC, and release the DC. By the way, note the terminology: You *delete* the RCs, but you *release* the DCs. The 16-bit Windows had only a fixed number of DCs, so they were returned to Windows for reuse, as opposed to being created from scratch.

Fonts and OpenGL

There's not a whole lot to say about fonts under OpenGL. You'll recall that OpenGL was designed to be a platform-independent, low-level, 3D graphics API. Therefore higher-level things, such as fonts, are left to the operating system to provide to OpenGL, either as bitmapped images or as a sequence of drawing

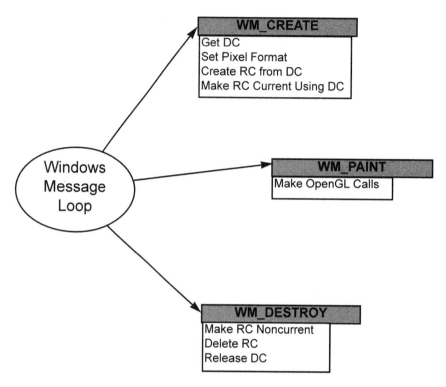

Figure 2.3   The Improved (and Faster) Method of DC/RC Handling

primitives. This brings us to the two functions for converting fonts from Windows' GDI format into an OpenGL-usable format.

First, however, we need a bit of background on how fonts are used natively in Windows. Normally a font is selected into the current GDI device context, and then the appropriate text-rendering functions are called, which render in the selected font. Things work the same way for OpenGL. A font is selected for the DC that's associated with the current OpenGL RC, and then wgl functions are called that render one or more of the font glyphs into either 2D bitmaps or display lists of 3D primitives. Once the glyphs are in this format, you can treat them as any other OpenGL primitive.

The first function is `wglUseFontBitmaps()`. This function takes a DC and the desired glyphs and generates the bitmaps for the glyphs. You then use an OpenGL function with a text string to output the text in the form of bitmaps.

The second function is `wglUseFontOutlines()`; through the same procedure as the previous function, this function generates a series of 3D lines or polygons. The limitation with this function is that the font selected must be a TrueType font.

These functions are too complex to discuss in a paragraph or two, so we'll examine them in depth in chapter 7.

Double Buffering

Double buffering is important in two cases. The first is when you don't want the user to see the rendering being performed but would rather see the entire display updated at one time. The other time is when you need to perform animation or some other rapid updating of the OpenGL display. Since you're reading this book, I'm going to assume that one of your major interests is getting OpenGL to run as fast as possible, so double buffering will be a brief but major part of the techniques we'll use.

If you've selected a pixel format that supports double buffering, you've got an RC that directs OpenGL commands to the "back" buffer. You can think of this buffer as a memory bitmap that sits off screen. In the normal course of processing OpenGL commands, you'd issue your drawing commands and then tell OpenGL to flush any pending commands; this would force any cached rendering commands to be immediately displayed. For single-buffered pixel formats, your OpenGL commands would now be visible on the screen.

Double-buffered pixel formats, however, are rendered to the back buffer. What's displayed on the screen is called the "front" buffer. The Windows API call to swap the front and back buffers is called `SwapBuffers()`. This call exchanges the front and back buffers of the specified DC. What this means to the user is that nothing is displayed on the screen until the buffers are swapped. Then the display appears to be "instantly" updated. If the particular video hardware you are using has enough video memory to support both buffers, this can be as fast as simply resetting the beginning offset of the currently displayed memory, which means that your display change could be as fast as the update frequency of your monitor, usually better than 75 Hz. Considering that if you can get a rate of 15 updates a second or better, your motion can be considered "flicker free," which is pretty good.

You should be aware that double buffering isn't really a method of speeding up your OpenGL program. Rather, it's a method of making it *appear* to run more quickly, simply by letting the user see the individual frames "after" they have been drawn. In some cases—with good video hardware—double buffering will in fact make your programs run a bit faster, although the effect is swamped by the rendering time.

So if double buffering is so wonderful, why shouldn't you use it all the time? There are only two cases in which you can't use double buffering. One is when a double-buffered pixel format isn't available; the other is when you want to use GDI calls in your OpenGL window. GDI and double buffering don't mix; however, you can simulate your own by rendering to a bitmap and BLTing the bitmap with the screen display. However, in most cases you probably can use double buffering, and most of the example programs in this book use it, so if you discover that you can't, you'll have to modify the programs to be single buffered.

 As a final note, if you want to take maximum advantage of an advanced OpenGL feature, you should be aware of the **PFD_SWAP_COPY** and **PFD_SWAP_EXCHANGE** flags mentioned previously. If your program has only certain areas of the OpenGL window that need to be updated or if you want a compromise between the effects of single buffering and double buffering, these flags can give you the ability to judiciously render only those areas of the screen that need it. Refer to the next section and the **glGetString()** function.

Advanced Miscellaneous Functions

We've covered most of the OpenGL calls that you'll need to use when using OpenGL under Windows. However, a few advanced functions should be mentioned to complete our account.

The first function is **wglShareLists()**. This function enables two or more OpenGL rendering contexts to share the same display list address space and textures objects. Normally when an OpenGL RC is created, it has its own unique address space for display lists. However, if your OpenGL threads are cooperative, they might want to share some information. For example, only one thread would need to create a display list for the characters of a particular font common to both threads. You'd want to avoid the overhead of creating and storing the same information for *both* threads, and this function provides a way to do it. You can share display list space only with threads within the same process and threads that use the same OpenGL implementation. Thus you can't have one pixel format using the generic driver and another using a driver-supplied format, for example. As long as both RCs are using the same pixel format, they can always share the same display list address space. This function is available only on OpenGL version 1.01 or later.

The next function, **wglGetProcAddress()**, is a hook into the bowels of the OpenGL implementation you're running. Your particular implementation might support some extensions that aren't in the OpenGL API, and this function provides the ability to get the address of that functionality. This is all dependent on the implementation you are running, but with the original generic version 1.0 of

OpenGL two extensions were originally available. We'll examine how to find out about and use these extensions in chapter 12. You'll need to examine the documentation that accompanied your OpenGL implementation to determine what extensions are available and how to use them.

If your video hardware supports it you can use hardware layer planes (overlay and underlay planes) in your applications. Layer planes are typically used for special visual effects. The pixel format descriptor describes the characteristics of the main plane. At about the time when Windows NT 3.51 shipped, pixel formats were extended to support overlay and underlay planes. Layer planes can look much like the main planes' pixel configurations, and in fact may have more capabilities than the main plane. For example, a layer plane might support stereo while the main plane does not. Layer planes always have a front-left color buffer and also can include front-right and back color buffers. Each layer plane has a specific RC to render into the layer buffers. Layer planes have a transparent pixel color or index that enables any underlying layer planes to show through. Layer planes are beyond the scope of this book, but you can find out more about them by looking up the **LAYERPLANEDESCRIPTOR** in the compiler documentation.

Creating a Simple OpenGL Program with the Windows C API

As with anything else, the difficult part in creating an OpenGL program is learning what has to be done and figuring out how to do it. Once you've done it, repeating the performance is a simple matter. This section examines how to modify a simple Windows API skeleton to draw a simple OpenGL primitive. Its objective is simply to teach you the necessary parts that have to be added to a Windows API program to enable OpenGL calls to work. If you're new to Windows programming, you should have no problem following along with the aid of a good Windows introductory book. If you've already written Windows programs, you should have no problem, since very few new calls are needed to get OpenGL to work.

This is not going to be an exhaustive explanation of how to write OpenGL programs for Windows using the Windows API. I'm going to use straight C API for 32-bit Windows. This is the only time you'll see a straight C program for the Windows API. The rest of the book's examples will be either simple OpenGL programs using the auxiliary library (which contain no Windows calls) or using the Microsoft Foundation Classes (MFC) C++ API as a wrapper to the Windows API. My reasoning is that it's generally easier to write Windows programs using C++ and MFC than it is to use straight C and the Windows API.

The first thing is to go through all the things that you'll have to add to a simple C Windows program in order to get it to be OpenGL ready.

1. Include the OpenGL header files: `gl\gl.h`, `gl\glu.h`, and possibly `gl\glaux.h`.

2. Link with the OpenGL libraries: `opengl32.lib`, `glu32.lib`, and possibly `glaux.lib`.

3. Before the window is created, set the window style to include `WS_CLIPSI-BLINGS` and `WS_CLIPCHILDREN` to prevent OpenGL from trying to draw into any other windows. You do this in the call to `CreateWindow()`, when you process the `WM_CREATE` message. You'll then need to set up a pixel format and get an RC associated with the DC. You'll hold onto this RC for the life of the program.

4. You need to set the size of the OpenGL window according to the size of the window. The `WM_SIZE` message is sent before the window is painted the first time and whenever the user resizes the window.

5. Whenever the `WM_PAINT` message is received, you'll need to associate the RC with the DC (if it's not already) and to do your OpenGL calls. This is where most of your OpenGL calls will occur.

6. When the program is shutting down, you'll receive a `WM_DESTROY` message, and you'll need to free the RC and release the DC.

Listing 2.1 is a simple Windows program that uses OpenGL. You can also find this program on the CD under CH02\Simple. All of the interesting things occur in the processing of the `WM_CREATE`, `WM_SIZE`, `WM_PAINT`, and `WM_DESTROY` messages. The OpenGL-related processing occurs only in these message processes.

Listing 2.1   A Simple Windows OpenGL Program

```
/*
    A Simple OpenGL program using a C interface
    designed to be a quick introduction into the minimal
    settings needed to run OpenGL under Microsoft Windows.
    (Does not hold onto the DC/RC)

    Ron Fosner - Dec. 1996
*/

#include <windows.h>    // standard Windows headers
```

Listing 2.1   A Simple Windows OpenGL Program (continued)

```c
#include <GL/gl.h>       // OpenGL interface
#include <GL/glu.h>      // OpenGL Utility Library interface

LONG WINAPI WndProc( HWND, UINT, WPARAM, LPARAM );
void DrawOpenGLScene( void );
HGLRC SetUpOpenGL( HWND hWnd );

////////////////////////////////////////////////////////
// WinMain - the main window entrypoint,
////////////////////////////////////////////////////////

int WINAPI WinMain (HINSTANCE hInstance,
                    HINSTANCE hPrevInstance,
                    LPSTR lpszCmdLine, int nCmdShow)
{
    static char szAppName[] = "OpenGL";
    static char szTitle[]="A Simple C OpenGL program";
    WNDCLASS wc;   // windows class struct
    MSG      msg;  // message struct
    HWND     hWnd; // Main window handle.

    // Fill in window class structure with parameters that
    // describe the main window.

    wc.style         =
        CS_HREDRAW | CS_VREDRAW;// Class style(s).
    wc.lpfnWndProc =
        (WNDPROC)WndProc;       // Window Procedure
    wc.cbClsExtra    = 0;       // No per-class extra data.
    wc.cbWndExtra    = 0;       // No per-window extra data.
    wc.hInstance     =
        hInstance;              // Owner of this class
    wc.hIcon         = NULL;    // Icon name
    wc.hCursor       =
        LoadCursor(NULL, IDC_ARROW);// Cursor
    wc.hbrBackground =
        (HBRUSH)(COLOR_WINDOW+1);// Default color
    wc.lpszMenuName  = NULL;    // Menu from .RC
    wc.lpszClassName =
        szAppName;              // Name to register as
```

Listing 2.1   A Simple Windows OpenGL Program (continued)

```
// Register the window class
RegisterClass( &wc );

// Create a main window for this application instance.

hWnd = CreateWindow(
            szAppName, // app name
            szTitle, // Text for window title bar
            WS_OVERLAPPEDWINDOW// Window style
              // NEED THESE for OpenGL calls to work!
             | WS_CLIPCHILDREN | WS_CLIPSIBLINGS,
            CW_USEDEFAULT, 0, CW_USEDEFAULT, 0,
            NULL,      // no parent window
            NULL,      // Use the window class menu.
            hInstance,// This instance owns this window
            NULL       // We don't use any extra data
        );

// If window could not be created, return zero
if ( !hWnd )
    {
    return(0);
    }

// Make the window visible & update its client area
ShowWindow( hWnd, nCmdShow );// Show the window
UpdateWindow( hWnd );        // Sends WM_PAINT message

// Enter the Windows message loop
// Get and dispatch messages until WM_QUIT
while (GetMessage(&msg, // message structure
            NULL,       // handle of window receiving
                        // the message
            0,          // lowest message id to examine
            0))         // highest message id to examine
    {
    TranslateMessage( &msg ); // Translates messages
    DispatchMessage( &msg );  // then dispatches
    }

return( msg.wParam );
}
```

Listing 2.1 A Simple Windows OpenGL Program (continued)

```
////////////////////////////////////////////////////////
// WndProc processes messages to our program.
// It's called WndProc because Windows expects it
// to be called that!
////////////////////////////////////////////////////////

LONG WINAPI WndProc( HWND hWnd, UINT msg,
                     WPARAM wParam, LPARAM lParam )
{
    HDC hDC;
    static HGLRC hRC; // Note this is STATIC!
    PAINTSTRUCT ps;
    GLdouble gldAspect;
    GLsizei glnWidth, glnHeight;

    switch (msg)
      {
      case WM_CREATE:
          // Select a pixel format and then
          // create a rendering context from it.
          hRC = SetUpOpenGL( hWnd );
          return 0;

      case WM_SIZE:
          // Redefine the viewing volume and viewport
          // when the window size changes.

          // Make the RC current since we're going to
          // make an OpenGL call here...
          hDC = GetDC (hWnd);
          wglMakeCurrent (hDC, hRC);

          // get the new size of the client window
          // note that we size according to the height,
          // not the smaller of the height or width.
          glnWidth = (GLsizei) LOWORD (lParam);
          glnHeight = (GLsizei) HIWORD (lParam);
          gldAspect =
                (GLdouble)glnWidth/(GLdouble)glnHeight;

          // set up a projection matrix to fill the
          // client window
```

Listing 2.1   A Simple Windows OpenGL Program (continued)

```
            glMatrixMode( GL_PROJECTION );
            glLoadIdentity(); // Clear the projection matrix
            // a perspective-view matrix...
            gluPerspective(
                30.0,     // Field-of-view angle
                gldAspect, // Aspect ratio of view volume
                1.0,      // Distance to near clipping plane
                10.0 );   // Distance to far clipping plane

            glViewport( 0, 0, glnWidth, glnHeight );
            // deselect RC & Release DC
            wglMakeCurrent( NULL, NULL );
            ReleaseDC( hWnd, hDC );
            return 0;

    case WM_PAINT:
            // Draw the scene.

            // Get a DC, then make the RC current and
            // associated with this DC

            hDC = BeginPaint( hWnd, &ps );
            wglMakeCurrent( hDC, hRC );

            DrawOpenGLScene(); // draw our OpenGL scene

            // we're done with the RC, so
            // deselect it
            // (note: This technique is not recommended!)
            wglMakeCurrent( NULL, NULL );

            EndPaint( hWnd, &ps );
            return 0;

    case WM_DESTROY:
            // Clean up and terminate.
            wglDeleteContext( hRC );
            PostQuitMessage( 0 );
            return 0;
    }
```

Listing 2.1   A Simple Windows OpenGL Program (continued)

```
        // This function handles any messages that we didn't.
        // (Which is most messages) It belongs to the OS.
        return DefWindowProc( hWnd, msg, wParam, lParam );
}


//////////////////////////////////////////////////////////
// SetUpOpenGL sets the pixel format and a rendering
// context then returns the RC
//////////////////////////////////////////////////////////

HGLRC SetUpOpenGL( HWND hWnd )
{
    static PIXELFORMATDESCRIPTOR pfd = {
        sizeof (PIXELFORMATDESCRIPTOR), // struct size
        1,                              // Version number
        PFD_DRAW_TO_WINDOW |    // Flags, draw to a window,
            PFD_SUPPORT_OPENGL, // use OpenGL
        PFD_TYPE_RGBA,      // RGBA pixel values
        24,                 // 24-bit color
        0, 0, 0,            // RGB bits & shift sizes.
        0, 0, 0,            // Don't care about them
        0, 0,               // No alpha buffer info
        0, 0, 0, 0, 0,      // No accumulation buffer
        16,                 // 16-bit depth buffer
        0,                  // No stencil buffer
        0,                  // No auxiliary buffers
        PFD_MAIN_PLANE,     // Layer type
        0,                  // Reserved (must be 0)
        0,                  // No layer mask
        0,                  // No visible mask
        0                   // No damage mask
    };

    int nMyPixelFormatID;
    HDC hDC;
    HGLRC hRC;

    hDC = GetDC( hWnd );
    nMyPixelFormatID = ChoosePixelFormat( hDC, &pfd );
    // catch errors here.
    // If nMyPixelFormat is zero, then there's
    // something wrong... most likely the window's
```

Listing 2.1   A Simple Windows OpenGL Program (continued)

```
        // style bits are incorrect (in CreateWindow() )
        // or OpenGl isn't installed on this machine

        SetPixelFormat( hDC, nMyPixelFormatID, &pfd );

        hRC = wglCreateContext( hDC );
        ReleaseDC( hWnd, hDC );

        return hRC;
}


////////////////////////////////////////////////////////////
// DrawScene uses OpenGL commands to draw a triangle.
// This is where the OpenGL drawing commands live
////////////////////////////////////////////////////////////

void DrawOpenGLScene( )
{

    //
    // Enable depth testing and clear the color and depth
    // buffers.
    //
    glEnable( GL_DEPTH_TEST );
    glClear( GL_COLOR_BUFFER_BIT | GL_DEPTH_BUFFER_BIT );
    //
    // Define the modelview transformation.
    //
    glMatrixMode( GL_MODELVIEW );
    glLoadIdentity();

    // move the viewpoint out to where we can see everything
    glTranslatef( 0.0f, 0.0f, -5.0f );

    // Draw a large triangle out of three smaller triangles
    // sharing common vertex colors

    // Upper left triangle
    glBegin( GL_TRIANGLE );
        glColor3f( 0.0f, 0.0f, 0.0f ); // black center
        glVertex3f( 0.0f, 0.0f, 0.0f);
        glColor3f( 0.0f, 1.0f, 0.0f ); // left vertex green
```

Listing 2.1   A Simple Windows OpenGL Program (continued)

```
            glVertex3f(-1.0f, -1.0f, 0.0f);
            glColor3f( 1.0f, 0.0f, 0.0f ); // upper vertex red
            glVertex3f( 0.0f, 1.0f, 0.0f);
    glEnd();

    // bottom triangle
    glBegin( GL_TRIANGLE );
        glColor3f( 0.0f, 0.0f, 0.0f ); // black center
        glVertex3f( 0.0f, 0.0f, 0.0f);
        glColor3f( 0.0f, 0.0f, 1.0f ); // right vertex blue
        glVertex3f( 1.0f, -1.0f, 0.0f);
        glColor3f( 0.0f, 1.0f, 0.0f ); // left vertex green
        glVertex3f(-1.0f, -1.0f, 0.0f);
    glEnd();

    // upper right triangle
    glBegin( GL_TRIANGLE );
        glColor3f( 0.0f, 0.0f, 0.0f ); // black center
        glVertex3f( 0.0f, 0.0f, 0.0f);
        glColor3f( 1.0f, 0.0f, 0.0f ); // upper vertex red
        glVertex3f( 0.0f, 1.0f, 0.0f);
        glColor3f( 0.0f, 0.0f, 1.0f ); // bottom right blue
        glVertex3f( 1.0f, -1.0f, 0.0f);
    glEnd();

    // Flush the drawing pipeline since it's single buffered
    glFlush ();
}
```

Creating a Simple MFC C++ OpenGL Program

For the real Windows programs that we'll be examining, I've chosen to use Microsoft's MFC class library as the platform. Quite a few PC compiler vendors have chosen to provide support for MFC, as well as MFC existing in some UNIX flavors, so it's a fairly popular platform for Windows development. However, most of the important OpenGL information doesn't depend on MFC at all but was covered in the simple C interface program listed previously, and the examples that use MFC can be easily edited to move the OpenGL parts to a simple C program.

I've chosen to use MFC because it's popular, seems to be the emerging standard for writing Windows programs, and, when all is said and done, is a fairly easy interface to hook user interface processing to. The pixel-format enumerator program was written using MFC, and the UI took me about two hours to hook up to the pixel format code. So it's also a reasonably good platform for program development. The only unfortunate part about using MFC is that the programs created by AppWizard (Microsoft's program-template generation utility) are not small by any means. AppWizard has many options, most of which we'll ignore, but even the minimal set of options still leaves us with many files generated.

If you're new to C++ programming you may be confused by the syntax in some of the C++ examples later in this book. I use C++ here because it's the most popular object-oriented language, and MFC in particular since MFC is the most popular and widely supported framework for writing C++ Windows programs. However, since many of the functions in the example C++ classes do similar things to the MFC classes, or to Windows or OpenGL functions, they sometimes have names that are similar; names may even be the same if they meet certain situations. To distinguish between local functions and external Windows or OpenGL functions, I always use the *global scope resolution operator*, ::, (e.g., a double colon), so that both the compiler and the programmer know exactly which function is being called. For example, the line

```
SetPixelFormat( 5 );
```

might be calling a local function in my class, or it might be calling a global Windows function of the same name. For clarity I *always* preface global functions with the global scope resolution operator. Thus, to make sure that I'm calling the global function, the above line of code should read:

```
::SetPixelFormat( 5 );
```

Even though the scope resolution operator doesn't *need* to be used all the time, it's a good habit to get into.

In order to reduce the volume of uninformative source code, only the modified functions of the AppWizard-generated programs will be displayed in the text; however, the entire set of files needed to edit and recompile any of the example programs can be found on the CD. In chapter 6, we'll create the OpenGL MFC platform that we'll base the rest of the examples on, building up functionality and capabilities.

Summary

That pretty much wraps it up for the Windows OpenGL API. You now have enough knowledge on the Windows OpenGL interface to be able to correctly set up a Windows program for OpenGL. In fact, you should also have some ideas as to what to look out for when setting up your program for maximum rendering speed—all before you write your first line of OpenGL code.

Programming OpenGL Windows programs requires a paradigm shift for experienced Windows programmers. You're suddenly faced with unfamiliar function calls, multidimensional values, and a shifting base of basic capabilities. On the other hand, you now have the power to create animated, interactive, 3D graphics programs, knowing that a swarm of hardware manufacturers are currently creating optimized video boards that will make today's OpenGL programs run twenty to fifty times faster! You should take this as a challenge to write the most efficient OpenGL code so that you can fit in as many frames per second of animation as you can, because in two or three years your "top-end" platform will be on the low end of PC platforms selling then. *Now* is the time to start writing 3D applications and to set your sights high, because not only are you writing programs to eke out all possible speed but the new accelerated graphics hardware that is starting to appear will also help speed up your application.

3

Understanding OpenGL

My hope is that the ability to make explanations more natural will
cause more programmers to discover the joys of literate programming because I believe it's quite a pleasure to combine verbal and
mathematical skill. But . . . perhaps I'm hoping for too much.

—Donald Knuth

What Does OpenGL Do?

OpenGL was designed to be *the* easily transportable standard high-end 3D
graphics API for the next decade. OpenGL implementations exist for various X Windows, OS/2, Microsoft Windows 95 and NT implementations running
on Sun, DEC, and SGI platforms. OpenGL provides a standard interface and standard functionality for rendering high-quality 3D graphics—a design intended to
foster the acceptance of OpenGL across a wide variety of platforms, as well as to
provide video board manufacturers with a well-defined collection of functionality on which to build graphics accelerators.

The predecessor to OpenGL was Silicon Graphics Incorporated's (SGI) 3D
graphics language, IRIS GL, designed for SGI's IRIS line of graphics workstations.
SGI was very successful in rapidly dominating the 3D graphics workstation market with a combination of fast hardware platforms and specialized video hardware that implemented many of the IRIS GL routines in the video hardware itself.

Why OpenGL?

One of the deficiencies of Microsoft's Windows platforms has always been their
graphics capabilities, and 3D graphics in particular. With the advent of the 32-bit
Microsoft Windows platforms, Microsoft got together with SGI, and they set
about to create a hardware- and vendor-independent 3D graphics library that

would bring the benefits of an IRIS GL–type library to platforms in addition to SGI's. The benefits to Microsoft were to make Microsoft Windows a serious competitor for the workstation market, and for SGI it was a chance to expand into the PC marketplace.

Of course, Microsoft is hedging its bet with its purchase of RenderMorphics in February 1995. Thus Microsoft acquired the RenderMorphics Reality Lab—a 3D API designed for games—that is, a quick-and-dirty, graphics-object oriented library. However, most of the RenderMorphics API can be considered a superset of OpenGL's, since they both have a vertex-based rendering engine. The polygon- and vertex-based Direct3DRM model requires the application to handle all of the scene management, without requiring a thorough knowledge of how 3D graphics work. It's reasonable to assume that the video hardware manufacturers are working on the common features of the OpenGL/Direct3D API first. D3D is an API that is polygon- and vertex-based, and sounds a lot like OpenGL. Perhaps I'm biased, but I believe that given a choice between a high-level data-hiding API and a lower-level high-access to the underlying data API, graphics programmers will choose the low-level API, since getting as close to the metal as possible usually means getting the most speed possible.

My experience has been that the best graphics programmers usually go for the most flexible, most powerful interface, even if they end up having to do some things for themselves. Although Direct 3DRM may serve to boost the Windows games market and to drive the associated hardware, the applications that really stand out are those that push the envelope. Having absolute control over the scene management, the objects, the textures, the lighting, and so on seems like an excellent payoff for learning a new, complex interface, as opposed to a new, simpler one. You probably think so, too, or else you'd be reading something else!

Enough evangelizing—I'm starting to sound like a Microsoft employee. I don't want to give the impression that you'll have to go back to pixel-by-pixel programming. OpenGL is low level in the sense that it's supposed to sit just above the hardware—it defines the API that the hardware (or, at worst, the emulation software) will provide. The advantage of OpenGL is in the higher-level functionality that it provides. Although it's true that OpenGL is a low-level library, it's a library for creating and rendering surfaces and objects. OpenGL gives you control over the object's coloring, texturing, lighting, and shading. You get hidden-surface removal, modeling and viewing transformations, clipping and stenciling functionality, and object selection—all provided in an interface that can (and eventually will) be hardware resident. This is the dawn of a new age in personal computer programming. Not only our applications but also our very interfaces are going to become rich, textured things. The aesthetic appeal will be such a driving force that soon it will be as impossible to imagine using the flat Windows 3.1 interface as it is for a Mac user to imagine using the DOS prompt.

Who Controls OpenGL?

The OpenGL architecture is designed and maintained by the OpenGL Architecture Review Board. The Board, or "ARB," is a collection of companies interested in seeing that a standard 3D architecture is provided across a variety of hardware platforms and operating systems. Two ARB members—Microsoft and SGI—have been working together on OpenGL since 1991.

The OpenGL standard is maintained by the ARB. Periodic revisions to OpenGL are made on the basis of requests from the OpenGL user community. The OpenGL features and the conformance tests are revised whenever a new version of the OpenGL standard is released. The conformance tests come into play when a vendor licenses OpenGL for a new platform. In order to be called OpenGL compliant, the vendor's implementation must pass the conformance tests. These tests verify correct support for all the OpenGL features that the vendor has implemented. The vendor must implement a certain minimum set of OpenGL features and is free to choose which of the optional features or enhancements it wants to additionally implement. All of the features in the vendor's implementation must pass the conformance tests, ensuring that all versions of OpenGL run code the same way on all platforms. Since OpenGL is designed to be exact in its rendering, a program running on an SGI Indigo workstation should produce nearly the same image, (in some cases pixel-for-pixel), given the same window size, as the program running on a Windows PC. The only differences should be the running time. In reality, an SGI workstation will probably have more features in its OpenGL implementation than a generic Windows implementation, but that hardware limitation can be fixed with the appropriate video hardware.

How OpenGL Works

OpenGL works in much the same way that GDI works. It's just an additional graphics layer that programs can address. GDI's functionality resides in the `GDI32.DLL` (dynamic link library), which gets loaded whenever a program makes a GDI call. OpenGL is similar, in that whenever a program makes an OpenGL call, the `OPENGL32` and `GLU32` DLLs are loaded. Figure 3.1 shows how calls in an application program get processed on their way to becoming pixels on the screen. Windows NT maintains the client/server model that'll be familiar to UNIX OpenGL programmers.

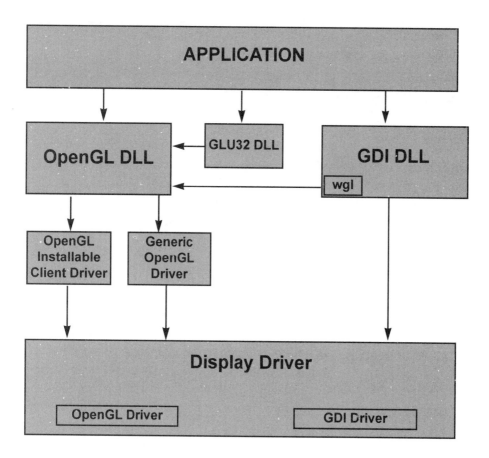

Figure 3.1   OpenGL Architecture

The OpenGL API found in Windows consists of about 150 functions in the API proper, some auxiliary functions, and some new Win32 functions designed to help set up a window for OpenGL rendering. Your particular implementation depends on any drivers that came with your video hardware and their configuration, since one of the benefits of OpenGL is that the hardware interface software can be custom tailored to your video card to provide maximum performance as well as expanded capabilities. Most of this will be almost totally hidden from view, although you should be aware that having a good video software/hardware combination is crucial to having optimized OpenGL performance on your system.

How a Vertex Becomes a Pixel

A vertex specified in OpenGL's model coordinate system goes through quite a few steps before it turns up, if ever, as a pixel on your screen. Figure 3.2 diagrams the steps that a vertex goes through on its way to the screen buffer. A vertex is first run through the *Modelview Matrix*, which is a concatenation of the modeling and the viewing matrices (we'll get into this in chapter 5). Basically these transformations turn the raw model coordinates—the ones that you use to construct your model—into coordinates located as they would be if viewed from that viewpoint.

The next transformation is by the *Projection Matrix*, which allows OpenGL to then clip out vertices that are outside of the specified viewing volume. This is the point at which things that are out of view, or outside of the viewing volume (you specify a finite volume, not something stretching to infinity), are removed from consideration. At this point we have only those objects that are visible on the screen. We then apply the *perspective division*, which means that the w parameter

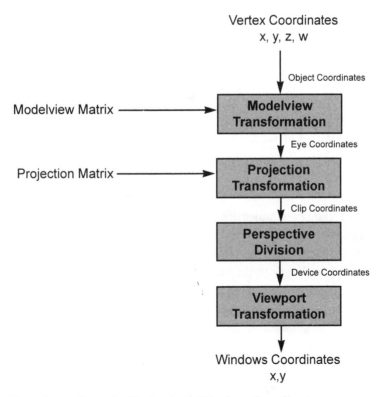

Figure 3.2   Transformation of a Vertex into Window Coordinates

is used to generate what's called *normalized device coordinates*. Most of the time we leave *w* as 1, since you'd change it only under special circumstances. The final step is to apply the *viewport transformation*, which is where the 3D coordinates get turned into 2D framebuffer coordinates for eventual rendering on the screen or bitmap. In this step the depth buffer comes into play for hidden-surface removal.

The *z*-Buffer

You may be familiar with the *Painter's Algorithm* for hidden-surface removal. This technique just draws everything, starting with the things in the back and ending up with the things in the front. The objects in the background get gradually obscured by things drawn in front of them. Although this method is very simple to implement, you still have to render everything in the scene (and rendering is a *very* expensive step), and you have to know about the geometry of the objects you're rendering—a geometry that can't be too complicated. The depth buffer takes care of this for you.

At this point in the rendering pipeline, we're just about to render to the screen at a specific pixel location. The color of the object goes into the color buffer. The *depth* of the object—its distance from the viewpoint—goes into the depth, or *z-buffer*. If we're drawing two objects that have some pixels that overlap, the first object will, after it's rendered, have values in the color and depth buffers. When the next object is rendered, OpenGL will first check to see whether the pixel it's about to draw is in front of (with respect to the viewpoint) any pixel from the first object that's already been drawn. It does this by checking the *z* value of the current pixel with the value of the one already in the *z*-buffer at that particular location. If the new pixel is closer to the viewpoint, OpenGL places the new pixel's color in the color buffer and its depth in the depth buffer. All this is done off in memory somewhere rather than checking the screen pixel, since nothing has been rendered yet; we try to avoid accessing screen memory whenever possible. Thus only those pixels that are in view are drawn, not entire objects. Although this may sound like a variation on the Painter's Algorithm, the important difference is that we don't *render* pixels that shouldn't be rendered. It's always faster to do some calculations than to draw things unnecessarily.

This technique of comparing buffer values to new pixel values is also used for other effects, such as stencil buffers and alpha accumulation values. A stencil buffer allows you to specify a stencil, such as the windows of a StarFighter cockpit, in which to render your OpenGL objects, thus leaving the interior of the cockpit alone. The alpha component is how we get *translucency*—the ability to see one object through another object. Unfortunately the alpha color component is ignored in the generic Windows 95 and NT OpenGL implementation, but you might have hardware that supports it. It works just like the depth buffer, except that if an object in the buffer is translucent but in front of the new pixel, the color of the pixel to be drawn is combined with the color of the pixel already in the color buffer, giving the effect of looking *through* the current object at an object behind it. In the generic implementation colors are always opaque, but when you see the effect of translucency, you'll find the results stunning!

Hardware Accelerators

Figure 3.1 contains an area for an installable client driver. These drivers are hardware-specific methods of accelerating the rendering speed of applications, and are provided by the hardware manufacturers in order to take advantage of their video hardware. Just what capabilities are provided are up to the board manufacturer. It can be nothing at all or just GDI acceleration, if the board has no 3D-specific hardware; or just *some* OpenGL functions in hardware (the Mini Client Driver), up to a full-blown accelerated rendering pipeline that can offer performance orders of magnitude over generic implementation. Despite a lack of clear direction, the majority of board manufacturers seem determined to outdo one another. Standards for measuring OpenGL performance are still emerging, but soon we'll be seeing boards that claim to be able to render so many tens of thousands of 25-pixel, anti-aliased, Gouraud-shaded, mipmapped, textured, lit triangles per second. The biggest advantage is that these will soon be the standard video boards found on PCs. Unlike the slow start on CD-ROMS or sound boards, which usually had to be an additional purchase before they became standard items, video boards are a given for all PCs.

Terminology

A number of terms and phrases pop up frequently. So let's quickly go over them so you'll know what they mean when you see them.

- *Aliasing, antialiasing:* When a line or a curve gets rasterized, you usually end up with a jagged, stepladder effect. That's aliasing. Antialiasing is the effect of using partial pixel intensities to blur the jagged edges so that they appear to be smooth. As you might expect, antialiasing is computationally expensive. Aliasing effects decrease with higher-resolution screens, so if you're considering turning antialiasing on, you might want to do this depending on the resolution of the screen your program's currently running on.

- *Buffers:* Computer memory is set aside for some purpose in buffers to denote color, z-value, stencils, textures, and so on. Generally the more and deeper the buffer, the better (and more expensive and slower to execute—all else being equal).

- *Depth:* Depending on the context, this can refer either to a distance along the z-axis or, less restrictively, the distance away from the viewpoint or to the number of bits available in a buffer. For example, we can speak of depth of color (32K colors is deeper that 256 colors, that is, 15 bits deep as opposed to 8 bits) or of the z-buffer, in which case we're referring to the magnitude of the values that can be stored. Depth is another word for granularity.

- *Lighting:* This term refers to the effects of a light source on the colors that an object displays. These effects include *ambient* lighting, the omnidirectional light everywhere in a room; *diffuse* lighting, the lightening of surface colors due to a light source shining on the surface; and *specular* lighting, the effects of the "shininess" of a surface. Lighting and texture mapping are the two most important methods that OpenGL has for making rendered scenes appear rich and complex.

- *Matrix:* Usually we mean a 4 × 4 matrix that can perform scaling, rotation, and translation when applied to a vertex. OpenGL, however, also uses some internal matrices that we can access and modify.

- *Model, object:* An object is usually a "piece" that's generally rendered as an entity. A model is just a collection of objects that go together somehow. A car might be a model, made up of a body object, four wheel objects, and so on. Since OpenGL doesn't have any native objects, this usually becomes a project-specific term. In this book it means whatever we happen to be rendering.

- *Normal, or surface normal:* Given any plane, the surface normal is a vector that extends perpendicularly from the plane. This is used in lighting calculations to compute the angle at which light is reflected from the surface.

- *Plane:* A mathematically flat surface, extending into infinity, a plane can also be thought of as a boundary used to define OpenGL's viewing area and clipping effects. If you have three points in space that don't coexist or lie on the same line, you can define a plane from them.

- *Polygon:* Generally a polygon is a closed, flat surface bounded by three or more line segments. OpenGL has a slightly more restrictive definition for the polygons that it can render. See chapter 4. A polygon, the basic building block of OpenGL objects, is a flat, non-convex surface bounded by three or more vertices. You make everything out of these flat surfaces, usually ending up with hundreds or thousands of them (frequently machine or database generated, so don't worry).

- *Primitive:* Both native OpenGL primitives and user-defined primitives are any collection of polygons created as a whole. An object, on the other hand, is usually a collection of one or more primitives.

- *Quadrilateral:* This term refers to a polygon of four sides, or a *quad.*

- *Rasterization:* The last step in rendering is rasterization, the reduction of 3D primitives into 2D images.

- *Red Book, Blue Book:* These are the standard OpenGL reference guides, the *OpenGL Programming Guide,* which has a red cover, and the *OpenGL Reference Manual,* which has a blue cover, respectively. The Microsoft online documentation has excerpts from these books, but by themselves the books are invaluable resources for both the novice and the expert OpenGL programmer. See the bibliography at the end of this book.

- *Rendering:* This is the process of taking one or more *objects* specified in an abstract object model and turning them into shaded, textured, illuminated objects in a raster image. By contrast, *drawing* means writing directly to the raster image. If you want to change the scene in 3D graphics, you change the objects and let the rendering process draw the results.

- *Shading:* This is the interpolation of color (usually after lighting effects have been calculated) across an object, usually from the vertices. OpenGL supports two shading models. *Flat* shading uses only one vertex to calculate shading for the entire polygon, which sometimes results in each polygon standing out from its neighbors (but it's fast!). *Smooth* shading, which in OpenGL is called *Gouraud* shading (rhymes with Thoreau), linearly interpolates the lighting effects from each vertex. It looks great but is computationally expensive. Another popular interpolation method, called *Phong* shading, achieves even better results but was deemed too computationally expensive for the initial release of OpenGL.

- *State machine:* OpenGL is a state machine; you change a current parameter by direct action—setting the color, for example. That state remains in effect until it's changed. This means that your program has to be state-aware.

- *Tessellate:* This refers to the act of decomposing a complicated, usually curved, surface into a collection of simpler shapes, the objective being to simplify rendering those shapes. Sometimes done with pencil and paper, tessellation is more frequently done by handing a description of a curved or complicated surface to a function that breaks the surface down into component polygons.

- *Texture mapping:* The effect of applying a texture bitmap, usually a 2D bitmap, onto a 3D object is to give the appearance of having a highly textured surface, like painting a picture on the surface. Texture mapping is a highly efficient way to give a realistic look to an otherwise simple object. A picture of a building placed onto a square makes the square look like a building, and it's a heck of a lot faster to render than all those door and window objects if you added them to your model.

- *Transformation:* OpenGL has many transformation steps, or the mathematical act of applying some form of scaling, rotation, or translation. Transformation involves going from model coordinates to viewing coordinates, through projection, and on to rasterization. Transformation generally means that we're applying some matrix calculations to our model's vertices to get them into another state.

- *Vertex:* In this book the term *vertex* of a polygon refers to the intersection of two edges—the corner of a polygon. I'll be referring to a vertex as either a particular corner of an object or the location of that corner as a two-, three-, or four-element coordinate. All objects, at their lowest level, are defined by their vertices.

- *Windows, windows:* In this book *Windows* refers to Microsoft Windows— either Windows NT or Windows 95—unless specifically noted. The term *windows*, on the other hand, refers to an on-screen window, the kind that the operating system opens up and that we render to.

Constructing Primitives

Programming OpenGL usually means creating some type of primitive. Most of the examples in the next section will be using OpenGL commands that are new to you, simply because you need to make a variety of OpenGL calls before anything can be seen on the screen. This section is a quick introduction to the basics of OpenGL commands and how to set up for and describe vertices.

The `glBegin( )`/`glEnd( )` Wrappers

In order to further optimize the rendering of primitives, OpenGL restricts the time that you can describe primitives to be wrapped between two calls to the API, `glBegin()` and `glEnd()`. This is similar to the Windows requirement of wrappering drawing code with a fetch and release of a DC (drawing context) when preparing to draw to a window. All OpenGL descriptions of primitives start with **glBegin(xxx)**, where **xxx** is an OpenGL-defined constant that identifies the OpenGL primitive you're about to describe. In order to further simplify the API interface, only a restricted set of OpenGL functions may be called between a **glBegin()**/**glEnd()** pair. These calls are the ones that describe vertices or their attributes.

OpenGL Command Notation

OpenGL has an abundance of function calls that differ only in the type of arguments they take. These functions result in the same commands being executed but with a variety of ways of initiating the function call. (Remember, this is a C interface, not a C++ one!) Following with the tradition started in the Red and Blue Books, I'll use a generic notation for those calls that have multiple formats. For example:

```
void glSomeFunction{3}{bsifd}{v}(arguments);
```

The first optional term in curly braces indicates that this particular function is the one that takes three arguments. Some groups of functions take two, three, and four arguments. The second set of braces indicates that this function can take five (of eight) possible argument types: b = byte, s = short, i = integer, f = float, d = double. The last term in curly braces indicates that a vector form of the command also exists. Instead of passing in the required number of parameters, in this case you'd pass in a vector containing the proper amount. Thus the following commands for describing a 3D vertex are all functionally equivalent:

```
GLdouble v[3] = { 1.0, 2.0, 3.0 }; // create a vector

glVertex3i(1,2,3); // ints
glVertex3f(1.0f,2.0f,3.0f); // floats
glVertex3d(1.0,2.0,3.0); // doubles
glVertex3dv( v ); // the 3 element double vector
```

Rather than type in function calls with items in curly braces, any function being generically talked about in the text but having a multitude of interface formats will be referenced as **glSomeFunction*()**, so don't be confused when you see this; it's just a reminder that there are many ways to call this function.

Vertex Commands

As we've seen, the `glVertex*( )` function is used to construct a primitive in OpenGL. The arguments are the vertex's **x**, **y**, and (optionally) **z**, and **w** coordinates. We'll be using the two-argument and three-argument forms for most of the book. The two-argument form uses **z** = 0, placing the vertices on the *x-y* plane. The three-argument form accepts a **z** coordinate. The fourth argument, the **w** parameter, allows you to play with the normalized coordinate values. Generally we just leave this as a value of 1.0 and ignore it. The full format of all the 2D and 3D versions of the `glVertex*()` command are listed next; as you can see, we save a lot to space by using the generic format.

```
glVertex2s( GLshort, GLshort ); // two shorts
glVertex2i( GLint, GLint ); // two ints
glVertex2f( GLfloat, GLfloat ); // two floats
glVertex2d( GLdouble, GLdouble ); // two doubles
glVertex2sv( GLshort[] ); // vector of two shorts
glVertex2iv( GLint[] ); // vector of two ints
glVertex2fv( GLfloat[] ); // vector of two floats
glVertex2dv( GLdouble[] ); // vector of two doubles

glVertex3s( GLshort, GLshort, GLshort ); // three shorts
glVertex3i( GLint, GLint, GLint ); // three ints
glVertex3f( GLfloat, GLfloat, GLfloat ); // three floats
glVertex3D(GLdouble, GLdouble, GLdouble ); // three doubles
glVertex3sv( GLshort[] ); // vector of three shorts
glVertex3iv( GLint[] ); // vector of three ints
glVertex3fv( GLfloat[] ); // vector of three floats
glVertex3dv( GLdouble[] ); // vector of three doubles
```

OpenGL and DLLs

How does all this functionality become available? There are two ways that OpenGL might be on your system. If you have Microsoft Windows NT 3.5 or later, or you've recently obtained Windows 95 on a new machine then you're all set—all the functionality is already in your system. OpenGL is part of Windows NT, and beginning in late 1996, machines that come with Windows 95 will come with OpenGL installed. Be aware, though, that prior to the release of Windows NT 4.0, there were different versions of OpenGL floating around. Windows NT 3.51 had an updated version of OpenGL from NT 3.5, and Microsoft made a set of DLLs available for Windows 95. You should have your programs carefully check out the current system's capabilities before making any assumptions about the capabilities of the version of OpenGL they are running. If you are running an early version of Windows 95 and don't have the OpenGL DLLs, you can either use the DLLs on the CD-ROM that came with this book, or you can check the on-line resource listed in chapter 12 for the latest versions.

OpenGL is made available in your system through a system DLL. A DLL, or dynamic-link-library, is a library that resides separately from your program but is an integral part of it. At program run time the operating system will load the DLLs your program requires. One advantage of the DLL system is that your executable is smaller and faster to load, especially if other programs already have the DLLs loaded for you, since DLLs are loaded only once and then shared. The biggest advantage is that by using a DLL, you'll get the benefit whenever any other program or new operating system brings in an updated DLL. For example, when Microsoft released OpenGL 1.1 with its speed enhancements, any program that used only OpenGL 1.0 features will still benefit from the improvements in OpenGL 1.1. This will be just as true when some future OpenGL version 6.0 becomes available.

OpenGL's Main Library

On Microsoft Windows platforms the *main library* is the `opengl32.dll`. This library is the main repository of all the `gl*()` routines. If your program uses nothing more than the main OpenGL routines, this is the only library you'll need to link to.

OpenGL's Utility Library

The *utility library*—`glu32.dll`—is the repository of all the `glu*()` routines. The utility routines contain several collections of commands that complement the main OpenGL routines. These commands provide such things as rendering spheres and other geometric shapes, manipulating bitmaps, performing surface tessellation, creating projection matrices, and handling errors. The utility library is considered part of a standard OpenGL implementation.

OpenGL's Auxiliary Library

The *auxiliary library*, `glaux.lib`, is only a library, since it's a system-dependant wrapper about some of the operating system. As the repository of all the `aux*()` routines, the auxiliary library is not an official part of OpenGL per se. However,

it's such a valuable learning aid that it accompanies most, if not all, OpenGL implementations. The auxiliary library is designed to insulate you from having to
know much about the windowing system that you're experimenting on. You can
use the auxiliary library to create an entire, running OpenGL program that can re-
act to mouse and keyboard events with fewer than fifty lines of code. Of course,
it won't be able to do a whole lot with such insulation from the operating system.
However, it's very useful for examining the behavior of OpenGL commands
without having to worry about getting a framework set up beforehand.

The source code for this library is distributed as part of the WIN32 SDK and
the Microsoft Developer Network (MSDN) Level 2 membership. If you examine
the source code, you'll readily find evidence of an even *earlier* toolkit, called the
TK toolkit, which was originally part of the OpenGL toolkit found on X Windows
systems. Examining the sources for the AUX library, the other OpenGL examples
found on the MSDN CD, and the sources that accompanied your compiler is a
good way to see how OpenGL programs are written and to get an idea of other
things that you can do with OpenGL.

Installing OpenGL on Windows 95 is straightforward. If you have an early release of Windows 95 and don't have the `glu32.dll` or the `opengl32.dll` on your
system, simply copy them to the system subdirectory of your Windows directory.
That's all.

Summary

Learning OpenGL is a lot like learning a new programming language; you can
get as much out of it as you care to invest. I don't want to give you the impression
that OpenGL is particularly easy—it *is* easy. It just does complicated things that
sometimes require some head scratching to figure out. And of course the advanced features will require some thought before you can use them, but that's
true of any powerful language.

The nice thing about OpenGL is that it's pretty easy to get started with, building up your knowledge to a point where you're ready to take on something more
complex. I find that when I have a new toy, such as the Visual C++ updates I seem
to keep getting, I'll peruse the manual, looking for new things or things that I
don't know much about yet. I find that frequently I'll run across some problem or
implementation that will tickle the back of my mind and something I'll have read
will pop up, and I'll have a flash of insight into how to use some feature I haven't
tried yet.

OpenGL is conducive to this method of learning, since you can *always* achieve
some effect you thought was impossible, just by applying a feature that you don't

know or haven't thought much about. And the best way of learning is to jump right in and start programming!

The next chapter will cover all the necessary but boring details of implementing OpenGL on a Windows platform. Then you'll be ready to start writing your own OpenGL programs.

4

Rendering with OpenGL

Once you understand the universe at the *atomic* level everything else is easy.

—Richard P. Feynman

OpenGL was designed to provide two things: a portable yet powerful 3D graphics API and a narrow interface portal between the high-level calls and the low-level hardware interface routines. Although we're interested mostly in the first item, it's the second one that's driving a lot of our actions. For OpenGL to be wildly successful, there's got to be a synergy among the software developers (you!), the hardware platforms (mostly the video card manufacturers), and the operating systems (Windows 95, Windows NT, OS/2, and the UNIX flavors).

The operating systems have provided us with OpenGL implementations that we can work with. OpenGL was designed so that the generic implementation that comes with the operating system could be easily superseded by drivers provided for specific video hardware. This is a key issue. After all, Windows 3.x didn't really become the largest GUI operating system on the face of the planet simply because it was better than anything else. Hardly! It became that way (despite Microsoft's considerable marketing efforts) because the platform that it ran well on—a 16 MHz Intel 80286 with 1M of memory and a VGA display screen—not only was the current standard but also ran *adequately* on that platform. Slapping a multitasking GUI on the front of an application program means that you can expect about a 50 percent degradation in performance. The greatest bottleneck is usually just waiting around for all the graphics commands of the GUI to be executed. This led to the rapid development of specialized hardware on video cards that would install their own video drivers to take advantage of their hardware to speed up graphics commands. The result was many, many different hardware interfaces as these so-called *super*-VGA, or SVGA, cards came out. This was a nightmare for applications developers, who either had to get each hardware card's specifications and write a driver (for writing a DOS program, for example), or else programmed only for Windows and let the user install the driver provided for the particular video card.

It was quite a painful period for nascent Windows programs, since the hardware manufacturers didn't really understand that if they sent out slow or buggy software drivers, it made their hardware nearly useless. What good is fast hardware if it's misprogrammed by a buggy driver?

Fortunately OpenGL was designed to avoid these problems, through the combination of a well-defined API and a test suite. This enables the video hardware manufacturers to choose what hardware enhancements to implement and to have their software drivers tested through the standard OpenGL test suite. Since the low-level API that calls can come through is so small, there isn't a lot of room to make mistakes in the interface code, and the test suite will catch the majority of implementation problems. With the hardware manufacturers writing their own optimized driver code and with a test suite to catch most of the bugs, OpenGL applications can be written with good assurance that they will work better than average on anything other than generic implementations.

Primitives

What does this have to do with drawing primitives? You might be surprised to see how limited the number of primitives is that OpenGL supports. After all, ten seems like such a small number! Ten? Yes! One type of point, three types of lines, and six types of polygons: OpenGL contains the barest minimum for creating objects. It's a very powerful graphics interface with built-in effects, such as hidden-surface removal, shading, lighting, and texture mapping, but it's very limited in the *things* that you can draw. This is by design, since the objective of a limited set of drawing primitives is to provide as clean and concise an API as possible and, in effect, to get as many hardware graphics accelerators manufactured as possible.

The other things that you usually want after you get basic drawing functionality, the lighting, the texture mapping, and so on are even more difficult to do than primitive creation, but that's provided by the OpenGL API. By limiting you to the ten primitives in the API, you're forced to write your own or to use the ones in the auxiliary library. This allows the graphics pipeline to be optimized for speed at the expense of forcing you to write your own macros to construct the objects you want. Once you get over the shock of having to create your own circle-drawing routine, you'll be thankful that you don't have to write your own texture-mapping code as well.

OpenGL has three basic types of primitives: points, lines, and polygons. Let's start with the simplest.

OpenGL Points

Despite its one point primitive, OpenGL gives you a great deal of control over how the point looks. You control the size of a point, and you control the antialiasing of the point. This gives you great control over how a point is displayed. The default rendering of a point is simply a pixel. However, you can control the size to make points any number of pixels in diameter, even fractional pixels. If antialiasing is enabled, you're not going to get half a pixel displayed, but OpenGL will "blur" the point across the pixels, or *antialias* the pixel, which gives the point the perceived effect of being located fractionally.

As with any OpenGL commands to create an object to render, we must wrapper the commands between a call to **glBegin()** and **glEnd()**, with the single argument for **glBegin()** being one of the ten enum values for the primitive you're creating. A single argument to **glBegin()** creates a set of points.

That argument, **GL_POINTS**, draws a point at each vertex, for as many vertices as are specified. For example, if we wanted to draw four points in a diamond pattern about the origin, we might have the following code:

```
glBegin( GL_POINTS )
    glVertex2f( 0.0f, 2.0f ); // note 2D form
    glVertex2f( 1.0f, 0.0f );
    glVertex2f( 0.0f,-2.0f );
    glVertex2f(-1.0f, 0.0f );
glEnd();
```

The pixels that get drawn on the screen depend on a number of factors. Normally the locations of a point are reduced to a single pixel on the screen. If antialiasing is turned on, you might get a group of pixels of varying intensity instead, with the sum of their location representing a single pixel located across a couple of pixel boundaries. If you change the default pixel size with the **glPointSize()** command, the pixels drawn will then correspond to that size. If antialiasing is also turned on, the edges of the point might be slightly "fuzzed," as OpenGL attempts to represent a point that doesn't fall exactly on pixel boundaries.

You can query the maximum and minimum sizes that your implementation allows for pixels by using the **glGetFloatv()** function with the

GL_POINT_SIZE_RANGE argument. Check the *OpenGL Reference Manual* for the exact calling procedure. Figure 4.1 shows the entire collection of ten primitives that can be created in a call to **glBegin()**.

OpenGL Lines

OpenGL has a bit more latitude with the ability to manipulate lines. In addition to controlling line width, you can also specify stipple patterns. Lines are the first primitive we've seen that are really effected by lighting calculations. Unlike the points primitive, the order in which both lines and polygons have their vertexes given is important. When you construct your primitives, make sure that the order the vertexes are specified in is correct for the primitive you're creating. Three different line primitives can be created:

- **GL_LINES** draws a line segment for each pair of vertices. Vertices v_0 and v_1 define the first line, v_2 and v_3 the next, and so on. If an odd number of vertices is given, the last one is ignored.

- **GL_LINE_STRIP** draws a connected group of line segments from vertex v_0 to v_n, connecting a line between each vertex and the next in the order given.

- **GL_LINE_LOOP** draws a connected group of line segments from vertex v_0 to v_n, connecting each vertex to the next with a line, in the order given, then closing the line by drawing a connecting line from v_n to v_0, defining a loop.

To draw the diamond pattern we used for the points, we'd just change the primitive specified in the **glBegin()** call. This will result in a parallelogram being draw.

```
glBegin( GL_LINE_LOOP )// make it a connected line segment
    glVertex2f( 0.0f, 2.0f ); // note 2D form
    glVertex2f( 1.0f, 0.0f );
    glVertex2f( 0.0f,-2.0f );
    glVertex2f(-1.0f, 0.0f );
glEnd();
```

Just as with points, the default size is one pixel, but you can control both the line size, using **glLineWidth()**, and the smoothness of the lines drawn with antialiasing. And again, just as with points, you can get the maximum and minimum line sizes by using the **glGetFloatv()** call with the appropriate arguments.

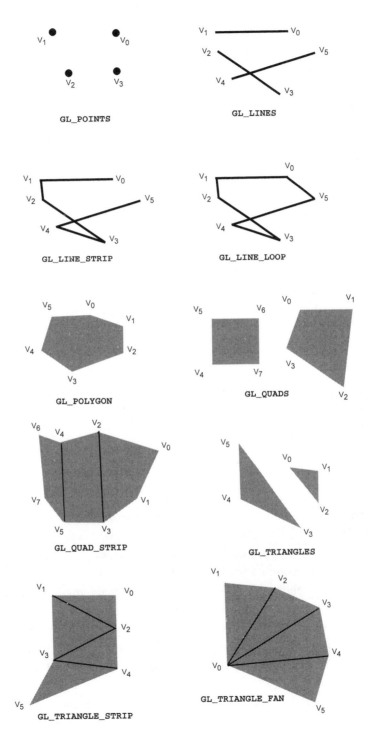

Figure 4.1   The Ten OpenGL Primitive Types

You can also specify patterned, or *stippled,* in the OpenGL vernacular, lines. These patterns are essentially a series of 0s and 1s specified in a 16-bit variable. For every 1 appearing in the pattern, drawing is turned on; a 0 turns drawing off. You can also increase the size of the pattern by specifying a multiplying factor. This allows you to make the patterns appear larger. When the full 16 bits have been used to draw with, the pattern is restarted. For example, a pattern of 0xFFFF renders a solid line, whereas 0xFF00 renders a dashed line, with the drawn and undrawn parts being of equal length.

If you are rendering a series of connected lines (that is, they are all in the same `glBegin()`/`glEnd()` sequence), the pattern continues across the connecting vertices. This is useful if you're plotting data on a graph and want the pattern to continue along the entire length of the line or if you're plotting a curved shape and want the pattern to flow along the curve, as the curve is really nothing more than a series of connected straight lines of very small intervals.

You can also control the width of stippled lines just as you would for solid lines. The width is independent of the pattern, so you have complete control over the line. If you need a line that contains a pattern in two or more colors, you can create patterns that draw only in the appropriate locations and then use those patterns to create multiple, overlapping lines. As long as you use the exact same vertices, you should get the effect you want, with only the occasional overlapping pixel being drawn in both colors; so use only opaque colors, and you'll never notice.

OpenGL Polygons

Unlike the more comprehensive mathematical definition of a polygon, a polygon that OpenGL can render correctly is a simple, convex polygon of three or more unique points that all lie on the same plane. A polygon is *simple* if its edges don't intersect; that is, two edges can't cross without forming a vertex. A polygon is *convex* if it's never dimpled inward—or mathematically speaking, that for any two vertices of the polygon, a line drawn between them remains on the interior of the polygon. By definition, the polygon must have three or more points; anything less is either a line or a point. Finally, all of the polygon's points must lie on the same plane—any arbitrary plane, not just the three planes formed by intersections of the x-, y-, and z-axes. Figure 4.2 shows examples of simple and nonsimple polygons.

An example of a simple polygon with four vertices is a square of cloth with all four corners pinned to a tabletop. If you pull up one corner of the cloth, you have a curved surface—a nonsimple polygon.

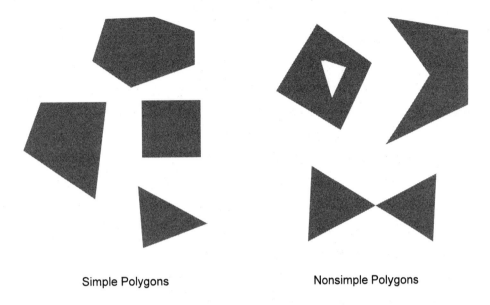

Simple Polygons   Nonsimple Polygons

Figure 4.2   Simple and Nonsimple OpenGL Polygons

OpenGL will be perfectly willing to attempt to render any nonsimple polygons; it's up to *you* to make sure that you give it accurate information. There'll be no warning if you enter a nonsimple polygon; what happens when you try to render one is undefined. Frequently OpenGL will do a creditable job of rendering polygons that are only slightly out of true; however, at certain angles the polygon will look inaccurate, and it's agonizing trying to figure out what's wrong. This is why triangles are so popular; with only three points, they *have* to lie on a plane. That's why so many routines in OpenGL degenerate objects into groups of triangles, since triangles meet all the requirements of being simple, convex polygons.

Polygons are also the most fulfilling primitives, since they are the building blocks from which all the *satisfying* things are constructed. Polygons let you have a *surface*. A surface gives you the ability to specify fun things, such as color, opacity, the appearance of material it's constructed from, and how light reflects off it. (Note that lines and points also share some of these attributes.) And *these* capabilities, combined, give you the ability to create realistic-looking objects.

You construct polygons just as you would a line segment. The following code constructs a filled-in parallelogram on the *x-y* plane.

```
glBegin( GL_POLYGON )
    glVertex2f( 0.0f, 0.0f ); // note 2D form
    glVertex2f( 1.0f, 1.0f );
```

```
    glVertex2f( 0.0f, 1.0f );
    glVertex2f( -1.0f, 0.0f );
glEnd();
```

Note that the *order* of the vertices is very important, since the order tells OpenGL which side of the polygon is the "front." This is important when constructing enclosed objects or when only one side of an object will be visible. By judiciously constructing objects so that you need to render only the front faces, you can significantly increase performance at no expense to the rendering quality. The face of a polygon that's rendered to the screen and that has a counterclockwise vertex order around the perimeter of the polygon is—by default—considered the front face of the polygon; a clockwise order denotes the back face.

Front Faces, Back Faces, and Rendering Modes

By default both faces of a polygon are rendered. However, you can select which faces get drawn and how front faces are differentiated from back faces. This is another of those subtle points that can bite you if you aren't paying attention. If you mix the order in which you draw your polygons, rendering becomes problematic, since you frequently don't want the back-facing polygons to be displayed. For example, if you're constructing an astounding 3D texture–mapped game in tribute to your favorite TV series, you probably don't want the interior of the Romulan ships drawn. In fact, you probably don't want OpenGL to bother with worrying about any of the faces of the objects that aren't visible, so you specify that the back faces (or front faces if you like) can be ignored when rendering your scene, in order to boost performance.

How do you tell whether the polygon is going to be clockwise or counterclockwise in screen coordinates? After all, you can always move your viewpoint to the other side! Well, technically it's complicated, but in practical terms just make sure that if the object has an "outside" or a "front," that that side's vertex order is counterclockwise.

You can control whether front-facing or back-facing polygons are rendered by the command `glCullFace()`, with a value indicating front or back faces. This will allow you to select which faces get culled. You toggle culling by using `glEnable()` with the appropriate arguments. You can swap the clockwise or counterclockwise designation of a "front" face by using the `glFrontFace()` command.

Note that you can easily control the culling for an object by prefacing the modeling commands for it by the appropriate commands. Don't forget to restore the attributes you'll need later.

It's also possible to individually control how the front and back faces are rendered. The `glPolygonMode()` command takes two parameters. The first parameter selects which side of the polygon we want to select: front facing, back facing, or both. The second parameter, the rendering mode, indicates that the polygon should be rendered as only vertex points, lines connecting the vertexes (a wire frame), or filled polygons. This is useful if your user may end up inside a model; you want to provide a hint that the user *is* inside. If the mode were filled polygons, the user would just see a screen full of color. If the mode were points (or back-face culling enabled), the user would probably see nothing recognizable. If the wire-frame mode were on, the user would probably quickly get the feeling of being inside the model. You can control which edges in a polygon are rendered and thus eliminate lines in the wire frame. This is discussed in the section on controlling polygon edge boundaries.

Polygon Types

OpenGL can construct six types of polygon primitives, each optimized to assist in the construction of a particular type of surface. The following list describes the polygon types you can construct:

- `GL_POLYGON` draws a polygon from vertex v_0 to v_{n-1}. The value of n must be at least 3, and the vertices must specify a simple, convex polygon. These restrictions are not enforced by OpenGL. In other words, if you don't specify the polygon according to the rules for the primitive, the results are undetermined. Unfortunately OpenGL will attempt to render an ill-defined polygon without notifying you, so you must construct *all* polygon primitives carefully.

- `GL_QUADS` draws a series of separate four-sided polygons. The first quad is drawn using vertices v_0, v_1, v_2, and v_3. The next is drawn using v_4, v_5, v_6, v_7, and each following quad using the next four vertices specified. If n isn't a multiple of 4, the extra vertices are ignored.

- `GL_TRIANGLES` draws a series of separate three-sided polygons. The first triangle is drawn using vertices v_0, v_1, and v_2. Each set of three vertices is used to draw a triangle.

- `GL_QUAD_STRIP` draws a strip of connected quadrilaterals. The first quad is drawn using vertices v_0, v_1, v_2, and v_3. The next quad reuses the last two vertices (v_2, v_3) and uses the next two, in the order v_5 and v_4. Each of the following quads uses the last two vertices from the previous quad. In each case n must be at least 4 and a multiple of 2.

- **GL_TRIANGLE_STRIP** draws a series of connected triangles. The first triangle is drawn using vertices v_0, v_1, and v_2; the next uses v_2, v_1, and v_3; the next v_2, v_3, and v_4. Note that the order ensures that they all are oriented alike.

- **GL_TRIANGLE_FAN** draws a series of triangles connected about a common origin, vertex v_0. The first triangle is drawn using vertices v_0, v_1, and v_2; the next uses v_0, v_2, and v_3; the next v_0, v_3, and v_4.

As you can see, OpenGL is geared toward providing a rich, albeit limited set of primitives. Since this pipeline is so regulated, it provides a closed set of functionality for hardware manufacturers to implement. In other words they'll be providing OpenGL hardware implementations that will be optimized in a standard way—in this case optimized rendering of just ten primitive types. As we'll see later, having a hardware assist results in a huge improvement in speed.

Patterned Polygons

In addition to stippling an OpenGL line, you can stipple a polygon. Instead of the default filled-polygon style, you can specify a pattern 32 bits by 32 bits that will be used to turn rendering off and on. The pattern is window aligned so that touching polygons using the same pattern will appear to continue the pattern. This also means that if polygons move and the viewpoint remains the same, the pattern will appear to be moving over the polygon!

The pattern can be placed in any consecutive 1024 bits, with a 4-by-32 **GLubyte** array being a convenient format. The storage format of the bytes can be controlled so that you can share bitmaps between machines that have different storage formats, but by default the storage format is the format of the particular machine your program is running on. The first byte is used to control drawing in the lower-left corner, with the bottom line being drawn first. Thus the last byte is used for the upper-right corner.

Complex Polygons—Controlling Polygon Edge Boundaries

Suppose that you'd like to make a routine that draws a circle. It's relatively easy to make a routine that draws a circle out of triangles—it's just a matter of connecting a bunch of triangles that share a common center and have edge vertices spaced around the perimeter of the circle. However, although OpenGL handles the case of overlapping edges and vertices, with only one edge drawn even though two polygons share an edge, there is *still* an edge shared by two polygons. If the polygons are drawn as wire frames, both edges become visible. This might not be a problem if both polygon edges are the same color and are fully opaque. However, if they are translucent, the color of the shared edge will be calculated twice. Or, you might simply not want the underlying structure of a complex shape to be visible. In these cases you can turn edges on and off for each vertex by preceding that vertex (and any others that follow it) by prefacing the `glVertex*()` command with the `glEdgeFlag*()` command with the appropriate arguments. Using this argument, you can construct what appears to be a nonsimple polygon. The edge boundaries are automatically set for polygon strips and fans, so you can control the edge flag only for individual polygons you are constructing. Thus this command effects only the edges of individual triangles, individual quadrilaterals, and individual polygons, not any of the shared vertex primitives.

Rectangles—A Special Case

Since rectangles are frequently called in graphics applications, OpenGL contains a specialized call, `glRect*()`, that draws a rectangle. This call takes arguments that specify two opposing corner points and renders a rectangle on the *x-y* plane. You should note that `glRect*()` should *not* be called in a `glBegin()/glEnd()` sequence, since this command essentially encapsulates its own `glBegin()/glEnd()` pair. For example, the following line of code:

```
glRectf( 0.0f, 0.0f, 1.0f, 1.0f );
```

is precisely the same as the following sequence of commands:

```
glBegin( GL_QUADS );
    glVertex2f( 0.0f, 0.0f );
    glVertex2f( 1.0f, 0.0f );
    glVertex2f( 1.0f, 1.0f );
    glVertex2f( 0.0f, 1.0f );
glEnd();
```

The reason behind this command is, of course, speed. Rectangles render quickly, especially if the viewpoint is perpendicular, or nearly perpendicular, to the screen. So if you're strictly interested in 2D rendering or in simple business graphics, you might get a big performance boost by using rectangles wherever possible.

Rendering Primitives

Now that you've been exposed to the basic primitives, let's go over what you need to do to try out some of them in your own code. In addition to specifying the type of primitive and the vertices that make up the primitive, you'll need to specify colors for the vertices. If you're interested in lighting for your model, you'll also have to specify additional information with each vertex or polygon.

Specifying a Color

OpenGL is a state machine, and nowhere is it more obvious than in setting the color of a vertex. Unless explicitly changed, a state remains in effect. Once a color is selected, for example, all rendering will be done in that color. The `glColor*()` function is used to set the current rendering color. This family of functions takes three or four arguments: three RGB values and an (optional) alpha value. The `gl-Color3f()` function takes three floating-point values for the red, blue, and green color to select. A value of 0 means zero intensity; a value of 1.0 is full intensity, and any value in between is a partial intensity. Note that if you're using a 256-color driver, you'll probably get a dithered color.

Selecting a color is done for each vertex, but it's also effected by the current shading model selected. If flat shading is currently selected, only one vertex is used to define the shaded color for the entire polygon. (Note that *which* vertex defines the shaded color depends on the primitive type. See the following section for more information.) If, however, we have smooth shading enabled (in OpenGL's case, this means *Gouraud* shading), each vertex can have a unique shaded color (which depends on the vertex's *unshaded* color—the color assigned that particular vertex and the current light falling on the vertex). What happens between vertices of different shaded colors is that the intermediate pixel's colors are interpolated between the shaded colors of the vertices. Thus OpenGL will smoothly blend from the shaded color at one vertex to the shaded color of other vertices, all with no intervention from us. You can see the effects of lighting by examining Color Plate 9-1.

Calculating Normal Vectors

A *normal* vector is a vector that is perpendicular to a line or a polygon. A normal vector is shown in relationship to a polygon in Figure 4.3. Normal vectors are used to calculate the amount of light that's hitting the surface of the polygon. If the normal vector is pointing directly at the light source, the full value of the light is hitting the surface. As the angle between the light source and the normal vector

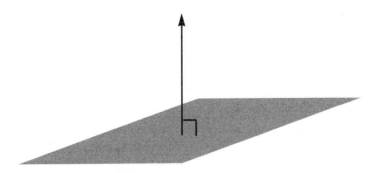

Figure 4.3   A Surface and its Normal Vector

increases, the amount of light striking the surface decreases. Normals are usually defined along with the vertices of a model. You'll need to define the normals of a surface if you're going to use one of the lighting models that OpenGL provides.

You'll need to define a normal for each vertex of each polygon that you'll want to show the effects of incident lighting. The rendered color of each vertex is the color specified for that vertex, if lighting is disabled. If lighting is enabled, the rendered color of each vertex is computed from the specified color and the effects of lighting on that color. If you use the *smooth*-shading model, the colors across the surface of the polygon are interpolated from each of the vertices of the polygon. If *flat* shading is selected, only one normal from a specific vertex is used. If all you're going to use is flat shading, you can significantly speed up your rendering time by not only selecting a faster shading model but also by not having to calculate any more than one normal for each polygon. For a single polygon the first vertex is used to specify the color. For all the other primitives it's the last *specified* vertex in each polygon or line segment.

Calculating Normals for Flat Surfaces

Calculating normals is relatively easy, especially if we're restricted to simple polygons, as we are when using OpenGL primitives. Technically we can have a normal for either side of a polygon. But by convention normals specify the outside surface. Since we need at least three unique points to specify a planar surface, we can use three vertices of a simple polygon to calculate a normal. We take the three points and generate two vectors sharing a common origin. We then calculate the *vector*, or *cross product*, of these two vectors. The last step is to *normalize* the vector, which simply means making sure that the vector is a *unit* vector, meaning that it has a length of one unit. Listing 4.1 is some working code to calculate a unit normal vector. OpenGL will normalize *all* normal vectors for you, if you tell it to. But we can use this routine to provide only unit normals automatically. The following routine takes three vertices specified in counterclockwise order and calculates a unit normal vector based on those points.

Listing 4.1 Code for Calculating a Unit Normal Vector

```
// Pass in three points, and a vector to be filled

void NormalVector( GLdouble p1[3], GLdouble p2[3],
                   GLdouble p3[3], GLdouble n[3] )
{
    GLdouble v1[3], v2[3], d;
    // calculate two vectors, using the middle point
    // as the common origin
    v1[0] = p2[0] - .p1[0];
    v1[1] = p2[1] - p1[1];
    v1[2] = p2[2] - p1[2];
    v2[0] = p2[0] - p0[0];
    v2[1] = p2[1] - p0[1];
    v2[2] = p2[2] - p0[2];

    // calculate the cross-product of the two vectors
    n[0] = v1[1]*v2[2] - v2[1]*v1[2];
    n[1] = v1[2]*v2[0] - v2[2]*v1[0];
    n[2] = v1[0]*v2[1] - v2[0]*v1[1];

    // normalize the vector
    d = ( n[0]*n[0] + n[1]*n[1] + n[2]*n[2] );
    // try to catch very small vectors
    if ( d < (Gldouble)0.00000001)
        {
        // error, near zero length vector
        // do our best to recover
        d = (GLdouble)100000000.0;
        }
    else // take the square root
        {
        // multiplication is faster than division
        // so use reciprocal of the length
        d = (GLdouble)1.0/ sqrt( d );
        }
    n[0] *= d;
    n[1] *= d;
    n[2] *= d;
}
```

If you use this approach, you'll get reasonably good results, with lighting effects that look good. However, you'll get an artifact called *faceting,* which means that the shading on adjacent polygons is discontinuous, in some cases clearly showing the individual polygons that make up the surface. If this is unacceptable, you can switch to smooth shading. However, smooth shading, although interpolating between the vertices of a polygon, does nothing to make sure that the interpolygon shading is smooth. In this case you'll need to either use a larger number of polygons to define your surface or modify the normals to *simulate* a smooth surface.

Calculating Normals for Analytic Surfaces

Analytic surfaces are defined by one or more equations. The easiest way of getting surface normals for such a surface is to be able to take the derivative of the equation(s). If the surface is being generated from a sampling function—one that provides interpolated values taken from a database—you'll have to estimate the curvature of the surface and then get the normal from this estimate. Both of these approaches are beyond the scope of this book. An appendix in the *OpenGL Programming Guide* gives a very quick overview of what you'll need to do if you're interested in it.

An alternative is to take the information you've got and interpolate your own surface normals. To reduce faceting of all the vertices that are touching, you'll need to make all those vertices have the same normal. The easiest way is to simply average all the normals of each vertex and to use this averaged value for all of them. For n polygons that share a common point, there are n vertices, and n individual normals. You need to add up all the normal values, $n_0 + n_1 + n_2 + ... + n_n$. Then normalize this vector and replace the original normal values with this one.

Clearing the Rendering Window

Another important item you'll need to know is how to clear the rendering window. For simple 3D scene rendering, you'll usually clear both the color buffer and the depth buffer. The color buffer is the current color of a pixel on the screen, whereas the depth buffer is the "distance" of that pixel from the viewpoint. See the discussion of the z-buffer in chapter 3. For now understand that we need to set the clear values for both the color and depth buffers, usually the color black for the color buffer and a value of 1.0 for the depth buffer. That's done with the following commands:

```
glClearColor( 0.0f, 0.0f, 0.0f ); // set to black
glClearDepth( 1.0f );                // set to back of buffer
```

Once the clear color and clear depth values have been set, both buffers can be cleared with the following call:

```
// clear both buffers simultaneously
glClear( GL_COLOR_BUFFER_BIT | GL_DEPTH_BUFFER_BIT );
```

This command is usually issued just before you begin to render a scene, usually as the first rendering step in your response to a **WM_PAINT** message.

Summary

Creating primitives is the heart of 3D programming. It doesn't matter if it's a car widget or a Velociraptor; the really interesting things usually consist of one complicated thing made up of less complicated parts, made up of still simpler parts. Once you get a feel for creating your own primitives that you can file away for later reuse, you're well on your way to creating your own "toolbox" of primitives that you'll be able to reuse in a number of ways.

Of course, it's not just creating primitives that make up those spectacular scenes from movies and flight simulators that you've seen. OpenGL still has some tricks to divulge about display lists (essentially an interpreted, replayable string of drawing commands) and texture mapping. Texture mapping is the ability to make a cube look like a five-story building, down to doors, windows, and bricks, with almost no extra effort (and almost no time penalty)! But that's a subject for a later chapter. You should have a good idea about how to go about designing your own primitives. Start small and work your way up. Pick an object that's pretty complicated and break it down into parts that you can model. Once you have all the parts, it's a simple matter to put them together to form something spectacular!

5

Matrix Transformations Are Your Friends!

Life must be understood backwards. But it must be lived forwards.
—Søren Kierkegaard

One of the most daunting aspects of 3D graphics is that you can no longer simply apply pen to screen, as it were, but must construct a mathematical entity that, to 3D novices, seemingly has no relationship with what's to appear on the screen. With 2D there is a direct one-to-one relationship between what your drawing commands are and what appears on your screen. Not so in 3D! After first using a lot of math and mathematical constructs to assemble your object, you must then essentially toss it into rapids of the graphics pipeline, swept away with the hope of seeing some related form emerge on your rendering window. And what if you are rewarded with a blank screen? Reexamine your code and try again. However, rather than blindly groping for success, the better you understand the process of 3D transformations, the better your chances are for satisfaction. In order to avoid wasting a lot of time trying to figure out why the screen is blank no matter what you try, you need to understand just how the matrices interact with the model's coordinates. Trial and error won't save you here!

In order to realize why it's so important to understand how transformation matrices work, let's consider two important transformations—*translation*, or moving along an arbitrary axis, and *rotation*, or spinning about an arbitrary axis—and how they work together. Figure 5.1 shows the organization of the 3D axes that OpenGL uses: a *right-handed coordinate system.*

If you take your thumb and the first two fingers of your right hand and hold them out at right angles to each other, the arrangement is similar to the one shown for the right-handed system. The other coordinate system

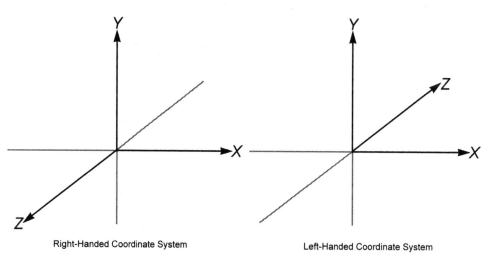

Figure 5.1   Coordinate Systems Used for 3D Graphics

shown is a left-handed coordinate system and is sometimes used in graphics texts. You have to be aware of what coordinate system you are using when performing calculations. A consequence of using the right-handed coordinate system is that the negative z-axis goes *into* the screen, which sometimes seems to be counterintuitive to what you'd naturally expect, namely, increasing z should move *away* from the viewer. However, right-handed coordinate systems are

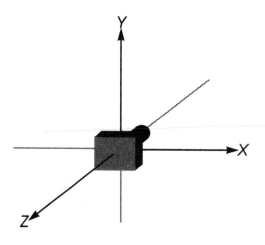

Figure 5.2   The Default Viewpoint Location and Orientation

found in most 3D graphics languages and in all math texts, so it seems like a small point to have to accept in order to avoid general confusion.

When you start specifying coordinates for models, everything is specified in relation to the origin. By default the viewpoint is also located at the origin and is looking down the negative *z*-axis. Figure 5.2 uses a drawing of a camera to indicate the default viewpoint settings. Since it's easier to conceptually construct your model using a common reference point, most people use the origin as that reference. However, there's nothing preventing you from choosing another location for the origin for your objects. Since the viewpoint is also centered at the origin, you need to move the model or move the viewpoint; otherwise, they'll coexist at the origin, and you'll be looking out from inside your model.

Elementary Transformations

Rotation and Translation

Understanding how transformations *work* is relatively easy. But understanding how transformations *interact* is one of the single most difficult concepts for people new to 3D graphics to understand. As an example, let's take a wire-frame cube, as can easily be specified by the auxiliary library routine `auxWire-Cube(1.0f)`. This routine draws a wire cube of size 1.0 centered at the origin. Now suppose that we want to take our viewpoint, which is also centered at the origin, and position it to look on the top of the cube from a short distance away. Two transformations are required: rotation of the viewpoint to tilt it down and translation to move the viewpoint back from the cube. Let's examine the OpenGL commands for rotation and translation.

The command for rotation is `glRotate*(angle,x,y,z)`, where `angle` is the angle of counterclockwise rotation in degrees, and `x`, `y`, and `z` are the coordinates of the end point of a vector (originating at the origin) to rotate about. Typically we rotate about only one of the major axes, which simplifies `x`, `y`, and `z` to be a unit vector, as in `x` = 0, `y` = 1, and `z` = 0 for rotation about the *y*-axis.

The command for translation is `glTranslate*(x,y,z)`, where `x`, `y`, and `z` are the values to move along that particular axis. For example, to move back from the origin, we might set `z` to –5 units and let `x` and `y` remain at 0 (to signify no translation in the `x` or `y` directions).

Since we now have enough knowledge to start changing things, we might issue the following commands to place the viewpoint in front of, above, and looking down at the cube:

```
// rotate about the x axis by 30 degrees
glRotatef( 30.0f, 1.0f, 0.0f, 0.0f );
// now translate back 5
glTranslatef( 0.0f, 0.0f, -5.0f );
// use the auxiliary library's cube routine to
// draw a cube centered (by default) at the origin
auxWireCube( 1.0f );
```

Figure 5.3 shows our cube and our viewpoint, illustrated by a camera. As you can see, we've pointed the viewpoint down and moved the camera back, but it's looking *under* the cube. This is not what we wanted at all! What's happening is one of the most common mistakes that you'll make as a 3D graphics programmer. Once you understand the interaction of transformation matrices, you'll be well on your way to becoming a skilled 3D graphics programmer.

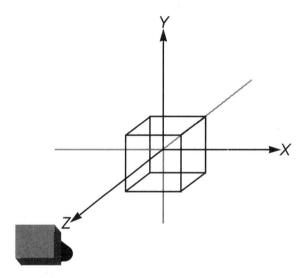

Figure 5.3   Results of Rotation Followed by Translation

Since our first try didn't work, let's switch the translation and rotation calls and try again. Now the code looks like this:

```
// first translate back 5
glTranslatef( 0.0f, 0.0f, -5.0f );
// then rotate about the x axis by 30 degrees
glRotatef( 30.0f, 1.0f, 0.0f, 0.0f );
// use the auxiliary library's cube routine to
// draw a cube centered (by default) at the origin
auxWireCube( 1.0f );
```

Figure 5.4 shows the results of this code; *this* sequence produces the expected results. The problem was in the order of our transformation calls, but exactly why are the results different?

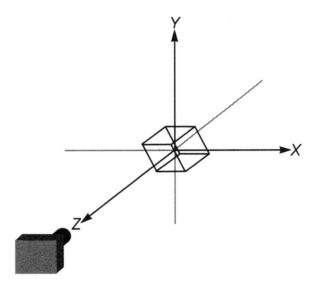

Figure 5.4   Results of Translation Followed by Rotation

To understand what happened, imagine that we have a global coordinate system that's fixed to the camera and that it's originally aligned with a local coordinate system used by the model. Using this analogy, let's examine what happens to the local coordinate system as we issue our OpenGL commands. We can perform the matrix calculations that OpenGL performs. The viewpoint is described by three parts: the viewpoint's origin and its direction and orientation vectors (see Figure 5.5). The direction vector is the direction we're looking toward, and the orientation vector is the direction we consider "up."

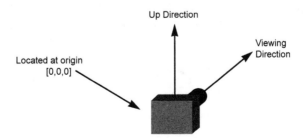

Figure 5.5.   Parts of the Viewpoint

Let's first observe the translation transformation, which effects where the local origin is. If the model is originally located at the origin, this is described by the coordinate $[0,0,0]^T$. This is the notation of a column vector, where the "T" superscript means *transpose*, or swap, the displayed rows and columns. It's easier to read (and write) $[x,y,z]^T$ than the form it represents:

$$\begin{bmatrix} x \\ y \\ z \end{bmatrix}$$

As an aside, you'll frequently see $[x,y,z]$ (without the transpose) written in computer graphics texts as a simpler method of writing a 3D coordinate. However, in order to do the math, it has to be a column vector, not a row vector. The transformation of a 3D coordinate in matrix notation looks like this:

$$\begin{bmatrix} x' \\ y' \\ z' \end{bmatrix} = \begin{bmatrix} x \\ y \\ z \end{bmatrix} + \begin{bmatrix} 0 \\ 0 \\ -5 \end{bmatrix}$$

The primed values are the translated coordinate. Thus the viewpoint's origin, $[0,0,0]^T$, becomes the point $[0,0,-5]^T$. After this step, the local model origin is located five units away from the global origin along the negative z-axis. The viewpoint is still looking directly back, parallel to the z-axis, directly at the cube. That seems a reasonable result of simply moving the model origin.

Let's place the local origin back to the global origin and consider what happens when we just rotate the local coordinate system about the x-axis by 30 degrees. By convention positive rotations are performed *counterclockwise* when viewed *from a positive axis toward the origin*. In other words, if we want to rotate about the x-axis so that the top of the cube is visible, the rotation is counterclockwise rotation about the x-axis, so our rotation will be specified by a positive angle. This is shown in Figure 5.6. Thus specifying a rotation of +30 degrees will have the effect of tilting the top of the cube up so that it's visible to the viewpoint's direction vector.

To rotate about a vector, we need a *rotation matrix*, the generic format of which is as follows:

$$\begin{bmatrix} r_{11} & r_{12} & r_{13} \\ r_{21} & r_{22} & r_{23} \\ r_{31} & r_{32} & r_{33} \end{bmatrix}$$

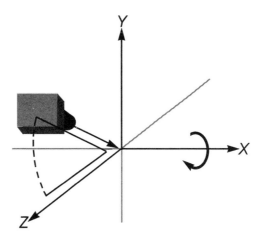

Figure 5.6   Positive Rotation about the *X*-Axis

Each element refers to the values calculated to rotate our vector about an arbitrary vector. The *r* indicates an element made up of a function that depends on the component *x*, *y*, or possibly *z* of the vector about which we're rotating. In order to keep things simple, usually counterclockwise rotation about only one of the primary axes is considered. This reduces the rotation matrix to one of three forms:

- rotation about the *x-axis* by α degrees, described by the matrix:

$$
\begin{bmatrix}
1 & 0 & 0 \\
0 & \cos(\alpha) & \sin(\alpha) \\
0 & -\sin(\alpha) & \cos(\alpha)
\end{bmatrix}
$$

- about the *y*-axis by

$$
\begin{bmatrix}
\cos(\alpha) & 0 & -\sin(\alpha) \\
0 & 1 & 0 \\
\sin(\alpha) & 0 & \cos(\alpha)
\end{bmatrix}
$$

- about the *z*-axis by

$$
\begin{bmatrix}
\cos(\alpha) & \sin(\alpha) & 0 \\
-\sin(\alpha) & \cos(\alpha) & 0 \\
0 & 0 & 1
\end{bmatrix}
$$

Thus for rotation about the x-axis by 30 degrees, the rotation matrix is

$$\begin{bmatrix} 1 & 0 & 0 \\ 0 & \cos(30) & \sin(30) \\ 0 & -\sin(30) & \cos(30) \end{bmatrix} = \begin{bmatrix} 1.000 & 0.000 & 0.000 \\ 0.000 & 0.866 & 0.500 \\ 0.000 & -0.500 & 0.866 \end{bmatrix}$$

To see how the rotation effects the cube, we'll use a direction vector that originates at the cube's center and is pointing down the negative z-axis. Multiplying this direction vector, $[0,0,-1]^T$, by the rotation matrix yields the new direction vector $[0,-0.5,-0.866]^T$. This new direction vector points slightly in the positive y direction and mostly down the negative z-axis, which again is about what we expected—a vector that's tilted up slightly. The effect of this rotation matrix on the direction vector is the same as its effect on the vertices of the cube; they are all rotated counterclockwise about the x-axis, as illustrated in Figure 5.7.

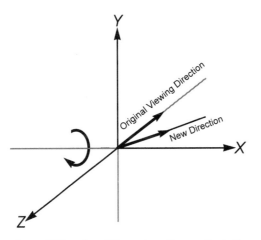

Figure 5.7   Reorientation of Viewing Direction due to Rotation about the X-Axis

Individually, both transformations look correct, so let's examine what happens when we perform them in sequence. First, let's introduce a compact form of specifying translations and rotations in matrix format. This matrix notation concatenates translation and rotation into one matrix format. If you're new to matrix math, check out one of the 3D graphics books mentioned in the bibliography, as a good understanding of matrix math is essential to understanding how to construct transformation matrices. You can use the following section as a quick, but by no means thorough, introduction.

A Quick Overview of Matrix Multiplication

Matrix math is simply a method of expressing a set of equations succinctly. For example, suppose that you have the following two equations:

$$x' = a \times x + b \times y$$
$$y' = c \times x + d \times y$$

They can also be expressed in matrix notation as

$$\begin{bmatrix} x' \\ y' \end{bmatrix} = \begin{bmatrix} a & b \\ c & d \end{bmatrix} \times \begin{bmatrix} x \\ y \end{bmatrix}$$

Not just any matrices can be multiplied together, however. The dimensions of the matrices must be such that the number of columns of the matrix on the left of the multiplication sign is the same as the number of rows of the matrix on the right. For example, for matrix A_{ik} (dimensions i,k) you need a matrix B_{kj} (dimensions k,j) in order to multiply them together. The result is a matrix of dimensions i,j. This is where the requirement that we use the notation $[x,y,z]^T$ enters, since in order to obtain a three-dimensional result, we must multiply the translation matrix by the vector. In other words, to pass a 3D coordinate, point b, through translation matrix A, and to get a 3D coordinate, b', back out, the equation must be of the form $b' = Ab$. Doing it the other way, b^TA, yields a single element, or scalar, not a 3D coordinate vector. This is stated mathematically as the matrix multiplication and is not *commutative*. For the two matrices, A and B, $AB \neq BA$. The meaning of this is discussed in the next section.

Homogeneous Coordinates

Adding a fourth coordinate to our three-coordinate system gives us $[x,y,z,w]^T$, where w can be considered a scaling factor (and never equal to zero), with the representation of our original three-coordinate system being $[x/w,y/w,z/w,1]^T$. This converts from three dimensions into four dimensions. The benefit of this is that in this new 4D coordinate system, translations (and scaling, as we'll get to later) can be treated the same as a rotation, which requires a matrix multiplication. If w is always left as 1, the values for x, y, and z in this 4D coordinate system are the same as in the 3D coordinate system, and we can ignore the fact that we're really using 4D coordinates. Our new generic matrix representation becomes

$$\begin{bmatrix} s_x r_{11} & r_{12} & r_{13} & t_x \\ r_{21} & s_y r_{22} & r_{23} & t_y \\ r_{31} & r_{32} & s_z r_{33} & t_z \\ 0 & 0 & 0 & 1 \end{bmatrix}$$

The r values are the rotational components, the t elements the translational, and the s elements the scaling factors. Thus with this slightly more complicated idiom, we can express any combination of transformations that we'll need. Although it may seem as though we've added to the complexity, we now have a single operation (matrix multiplication) that can perform scaling, rotation, or translation; the benefit is that these operations can be folded into one matrix, as we'll soon see.

Now, to return to our example, let's perform the original translation in matrix notation. Whenever we are starting a matrix operation, we start out with the *identity* matrix, a matrix with 1s along the diagonal, which is equivalent to multiplying a number by 1; it results in no change to the original vector. When we plug our translational values into the identity matrix, we get the matrix we need for the translation, as shown next. The translation calculation in matrix format looks like this:

$$\begin{bmatrix} 0 \\ 0 \\ -5 \\ 1 \end{bmatrix} = \begin{bmatrix} 1 & 0 & 0 & 0 \\ 0 & 1 & 0 & 0 \\ 0 & 0 & 1 & -5 \\ 0 & 0 & 0 & 1 \end{bmatrix} \times \begin{bmatrix} 0 \\ 0 \\ 0 \\ 1 \end{bmatrix}$$

Note that the origin is specified by $[0,0,0,1]^T$ in homogenous coordinates. As you can see, the effect of this matrix multiplication has the same results as before, which is reassuring.

Now let's perform both transformation operations on the origin of the local coordinate system. The first operation will be to translate, then rotate to the origin. The format of the calculation will be $v' = RTv$, where R and T are the rotation and translation matrices, respectively, and v' and v are the transformed and original local coordinate system origin. The values for the matrices on right-hand side of the equals sign are as follows:

$$\begin{bmatrix} 1.000 & 0.000 & 0.000 & 0.000 \\ 0.000 & 0.866 & -0.500 & 0.000 \\ 0.000 & 0.500 & 0.866 & 0.000 \\ 0.000 & 0.000 & 0.000 & 1.000 \end{bmatrix} \times \begin{bmatrix} 1.000 & 0.000 & 0.000 & 0.000 \\ 0.000 & 1.000 & 0.000 & 0.000 \\ 0.000 & 0.000 & 1.000 & -5.000 \\ 0.000 & 0.000 & 0.000 & 1.000 \end{bmatrix} \times \begin{bmatrix} 0 \\ 0 \\ 0 \\ 1 \end{bmatrix}$$

Performing the operations from the left, the first multiplication reduces the equation to

$$\begin{bmatrix} 1.000 & 0.000 & 0.000 & 0.000 \\ 0.000 & 0.866 & -0.500 & 0.000 \\ 0.000 & 0.500 & 0.866 & 0.000 \\ 0.000 & 0.000 & 0.000 & 1.000 \end{bmatrix} \times \begin{bmatrix} 0 \\ 0 \\ -5 \\ 1 \end{bmatrix}$$

The final multiplication yields

$$\begin{bmatrix} 0.000 \\ 2.500 \\ -4.330 \\ 1.000 \end{bmatrix}$$

This places the center of the cube 2.5 units up the y-axis and 4.33 units along the negative z-axis. This explains Figure 5.3; the rotation occurred about the global coordinate system (centered at the viewpoint), not the local one (centered at the cube). Thus when the translation moved the local coordinate system away from our global coordinate system, the rotation swung the cube up by 30 degrees. Another way of looking at it is the fixed coordinate system, in which the cube moves in relation to the viewpoint. These equivalent approaches are shown in Figure 5.8.

Now we'll swap the rotation and translation matrices to get $v' = TRv$.

$$\begin{bmatrix} 0.000 \\ 0.000 \\ -5.000 \\ 1.000 \end{bmatrix} = \begin{bmatrix} 1.000 & 0.000 & 0.000 & 0.000 \\ 0.000 & 1.000 & 0.000 & 0.000 \\ 0.000 & 0.000 & 1.000 & -5.000 \\ 0.000 & 0.000 & 0.000 & 1.000 \end{bmatrix} \times \begin{bmatrix} 1.000 & 0.000 & 0.000 & 0.000 \\ 0.000 & 0.866 & -0.500 & 0.000 \\ 1.000 & 0.500 & 0.866 & 0.000 \\ 0.000 & 0.000 & 0.000 & 1.000 \end{bmatrix} \times \begin{bmatrix} 0 \\ 0 \\ 0 \\ 1 \end{bmatrix}$$

In this case the origin of the cube remains on the z-axis. The vertices of the cube are rotated by 30 degrees, about the origin of both the local coordinate system and the global one. You can verify this by examining what happens to a unit vector pointing away from the origin that's multiplied by the same transformation matrices. The translation then moves this rotated cube away from us, down the negative z-axis, thus bringing into view the front and top of the cube.

Thus we can see that when two matrices are multiplied together, **AB** will yield different results than **BA**. Because matrix math is not commutative, you must remain aware of the order in which transformation matrices are applied. The order

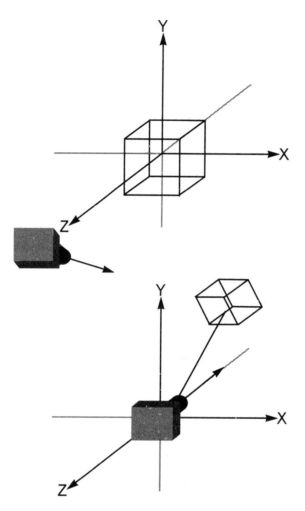

Figure 5.8   Two Different Results of the Same Transformations

of these transformation calculations is crucial and is a key part of understanding
how to set up transformations.

Scaling Transformations

A scaling transformation allows a transformation matrix to change the dimensions of an object (or the local coordinate system) by shrinking or stretching along
the major axes. Refer back the generic matrix representation; the scaling values
run down the diagonal. Usually these values are implicitly assumed to be 1.0,
which is interpreted to mean no scaling along any of the axes.

Now the Earth is drawn in the correct position, but we've omitted one detail. Since the Earth rotates about its axis once a day, we need to account for this effect as well. Since you can't see a solid sphere spinning about its axis, we'll make the Earth a wire-frame sphere, using another auxiliary library command. An alternative to creating a wire-frame sphere would be to use a texture map of the Earth and to texture the sphere with that, but texture mapping's a topic for a later chapter.

The rotation of the Earth about its axis is calculated just as is its rotation about the Sun. In this case we'll use a variable that indicates the current hour of the day to compute the fractional part of a full rotation about the axis. Since we need the Earth to be rotated about its axis before it's rendered, the rotation command must come before the command to draw the sphere. This places it just after the translation command. If you've been envisioning the transformations that the local coordinate system has been going through as we've been going along, you've probably noted that just after the translation out to the Earth orbital position, the coordinate system is still rotated about by the rotation we needed to compute where along its orbital path the Earth is located. If we were worried about a more exacting representation, we would now unrotate the orbital path rotation. The overall effect is small compared to the speed of the daily axial rotation, so we'll leave this step out. The following code now rotates the Earth about its axis according to the hour of day:

```
// select white as the color
glColor3f( 1.0f, 1.0f, 1.0f );
// draw the sun
auxSolidSphere( 1.0f );
// rotate the Earth in its orbit
glRotatef( (GLfloat)(360.0*DayOfYear/365.0),
        0.0f, 1.0f, 0.0f );// rotate about the y axis
glTranslatef( 4.0f, 0.0f, 0.0f );
// Rotate the Earth in its orbit
glRotatef( (GLfloat)(360.0*HourOfDay/24.0),
        0.0f, 1.0f, 0.0f );
// draw the Earth
glColor3f( 0.2f, 0.2f, 1.0f );
auxWireSphere( 0.2f );
```

The commands to add the Moon should be fairly obvious by now. We'll need to rotate to calculate where the Moon is in its orbital path about the Earth and to then translate it out by its orbital distance from the Earth. Remember that rotations occur about the current origin, so the rotation has to come first, before the translation. The lunar month is about 29 and a half days, which we'll approximate by using a twelfth of the year, which lets us calculate the orbital position based on the day of the year. (However, this introduces a discontinuity in the moon's orbit at the beginning of every year. Oh, well.)

The Moon's rotational rate is much slower than the rotation of the Earth about its axis, so in this case we can't ignore the previous effects of a rotation of the local coordinate system. However, we can temporarily save and restore the current matrix by using two OpenGL commands designed for just this purpose, `glPush-Matrix()` and `glPopMatrix()`. These commands store and restore the current matrix, respectively, and they'll be discussed in detail in a following section. For now we'll use them and take their effects on faith. The final addition to our model of the solar system looks like this:

```
// select white as the color
glColor3f( 1.0f, 1.0f, 1.0f );
// draw the sun
auxSolidSphere( 1.0f );
// rotate the Earth in its orbit
glRotatef( (GLfloat)(360.0*DayOfYear/365.0),
         0.0f, 1.0f, 0.0f );// rotate about the y axis
glTranslatef( 4.0f, 0.0f, 0.0f );
glPushMatrix(); // save matrix state
// Rotate the Earth in its orbit
glRotatef( (GLfloat)(360.0*HourOfDay/24.0),
         0.0f, 1.0f, 0.0f );
// draw the Earth
glColor3f( 0.2f, 0.2f, 1.0f );
auxWireSphere( 0.2f );
glPopMatrix(); // restore matrix state

glRotatef( (GLfloat)(360.0*12.5*DayOfYear/365.0),
         0.0f, 1.0f, 0.0f );
glTranslatef( 0.5f, 0.0f, 0.0f );
glColor3f( 0.3f, 0.3f, 0.3f );
auxWireSphere( 0.01f );
```

If you were following along, you are probably nodding your head right now. The tricky part is understanding the relationship between the order of rotations and translations. You might be wondering whether you could avoid all these translations and rotations and just compute the position of the Earth by using sines and cosines to position it on a circle; that way you'd get it in unrotated, untranslated Cartesian coordinates that stayed the same throughout the modeling process. The answer is yes, but it's a lot more work than is necessary. OpenGL can almost always perform rotations and translations more quickly than you can. You really don't want to avoid using a powerful part of the language just because it's difficult to grasp at first. Becoming proficient with modeling transformations is a skill required of anyone hoping to become an expert in 3D graphics.

Viewing Transformations

You use viewing transformations to get your viewpoint positioned and aligned to get the desired view of your model. As with modeling transformations, you'll use some combination of `glScale*()`, `glRotate*()`, and `glTranslate*()`, along with any of the other matrix manipulation routines that can be used to alter the current matrix. Typically you'll need only two or three translations to position your viewpoint. The cleanest way of thinking about transforming the viewpoint is to picture the viewpoint fixed to the global coordinate system. If your model is also based at the origin, you'll want to translate the model's coordinate system in relationship to the global. For example, you've seen the following translation used to give our viewpoint a view of what's at the origin:

```
glTranslatef( 0.0f, 0.0f, -5.0f );
```

This line says to translate five units in the negative z direction. Assuming that the viewpoint is fixed at the global coordinate system, this command translates all coordinates (and coordinate systems) that follow it in the flow of the program.

Alternatively you can think about viewing transformations as moving the viewpoint in an opposite manner as the modeling transformations. Using this methodology, we'd need to translate –5 units in order to move the viewpoint to the +5 position on the z-axis. This is the same result as the global coordinate approach. If you wanted to look at the left side of your model, you could rotate the model counterclockwise (looking down from above). This is the local coordinate method. Alternatively, you could move the viewpoint around the model in a clockwise direction, using the fixed coordinate method. Figure 5.9 shows both methods. But it gets tricky when we add rotations.

Let's return to our solar system example. Now we'd like to view the solar system from outside the Earth's orbit and just a little bit above the plane of rotation. Using the local coordinate method, we'd first move the local coordinate system's origin down the negative z-axis by 5 units and then rotate that coordinate system about its origin by 5 degrees. If you're having trouble, just hold your hand out flat and place it under your chin. Let your hand be the x-z plane and your head be the viewpoint. Initially both your hand and your head are identically located and ori-

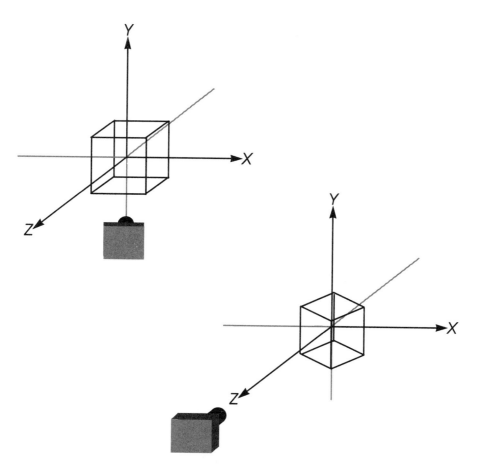

Figure 5.9   The Local and Fixed Approaches to a Rotation

ented. Now translate your hand out in front of you, which is down the negative z-axis; the local coordinate system origin is now positioned correctly. Now we'll rotate the coordinate system about its origin. Simply tilt your fingers up slightly; this is the rotation that we'll give the local coordinate system. Note that this rotation is counterclockwise (looking down the x-axis), so the rotation is positive. The code to perform this orientation would look like this:

```
glTranslatef( 0.0f, 0.0f, -5.0f );
glRotatef( 5.0f, 1.0f, 0.0f, 0.0f );
DrawTheModel();
```

Now let's perform the same operation, using the fixed coordinate method. Again start with your hand under your chin. Your hand represents our model in global coordinates. Since there is only one coordinate system, our current state is that the viewpoint and the model are both centered at the origin. In the fixed coordinate method we're going to move the viewpoint and leave the model behind, so the first thing we do is to tilt our head down to give us the correct viewing angle and incidentally to rotate the global coordinate system. It helps to consider the solar system as already rendered and fixed at your hand; we're now trying to position the viewpoint so that we can view it correctly. Next, we move our head back and up, which is translating on the newly rotated z-axis.

How does this approach get coded? Remember that in the fixed coordinate approach, the order is reversed. The first thing that has to occur is a rotation about the x-axis *just* before we render our solar system. Since the *next* thing to occur is the translation, the rotation command has to come between the modeling commands and the translation. The modeling commands come last in the program, the rotation precedes it, and the translation precedes the rotation. The orientations are also opposite. For example, when we translated the global coordinate system backwards, that was a translation down the positive z-axis (remember, the viewpoint is looking down the *negative* z-axis). However, since the fixed coordinate method requires us to reverse the orientation, this means that the actual translation command is for a negative translation. Similarly, tilting our head down is a clockwise rotation (negative rotation); however, we code it as a counterclockwise rotation. Thus the code becomes

```
glTranslatef( 0.0f, 0.0f, -5.0f );
glRotatef( 5.0f, 1.0f, 0.0f, 0.0f );
DrawTheModel();
```

That is what the local coordinate approach gave us. You might be scratching your head and wondering what's really going on. The next section explains why we're going through all these gyrations. If you don't understand it right away, don't worry. It will eventually become clear. Listing 5.1 is the complete program as it appears on the CD. This example uses the auxiliary library to avoid the Windows interface bulk.

Listing 5.1   A Simple OpenGL Solar System Program in C

```
#include "glos.h" // MS specific stuff

#include <GL/gl.h> // system OpenGL includes
```

Listing 5.1   A Simple OpenGL Program in C (continued)

```c
#include <GL/glu.h>
#include <GL/glaux.h>

static GLenum spinMode = GL_TRUE;

void OpenGLInit(void);

static void CALLBACK Animate(void );
static void CALLBACK Key_a(void );
static void CALLBACK Key_up(void );
static void CALLBACK Key_down(void );
static void CALLBACK ResizeWindow(GLsizei w, GLsizei h);

static int HourOfDay = 0, DayOfYear = 0;
static int AnimateIncrement = 24;  // in hours

static void CALLBACK Key_a(void)
{
    spinMode = !spinMode;
}

static void CALLBACK Key_up(void)
{
    AnimateIncrement *= 2;
    if ( 0 == AnimateIncrement )
        AnimateIncrement = 1;
}

static void CALLBACK Key_down(void)
{
    AnimateIncrement /= 2;

}

static void CALLBACK Animate(void)
{
    // clear the rendering window
    glClear(GL_COLOR_BUFFER_BIT | GL_DEPTH_BUFFER_BIT);

    if (spinMode)
        {
```

Listing 5.1   A Simple OpenGL Program in C (continued)

```
            // calc animation parameters
            HourOfDay += AnimateIncrement;
            DayOfYear += HourOfDay/24;

            HourOfDay = HourOfDay%24;
            DayOfYear = DayOfYear%365;
            }

    // clear current matrix (Modelview)
    glLoadIdentity();
    // back off six units
    glTranslatef ( 0.0f, 0.0f, -5.0f );
    // rotate the plane of the elliptic
    // (rotate the model's plane about the
    // x axis by five degrees)
    glRotatef( 5.0f, 1.0f, 0.0f, 0.0f );

    // draw the sun as a wireframe for speed.
    glColor3f( 1.0f, 1.0f, 1.0f );
    auxWireSphere( 1.0f );

    // draw the Earth
    glRotatef( (GLfloat)(360.0*DayOfYear/365.0),
          0.0f, 1.0f, 0.0f );
    glTranslatef( 4.0f, 0.0f, 0.0f );
    glPushMatrix(); // save matrix state
    glRotatef( (GLfloat)(360.0*HourOfDay/24.0),
          0.0f, 1.0f, 0.0f );
    glColor3f( 0.2f, 0.2f, 1.0f );
    auxWireSphere( 0.2f );
    glPopMatrix(); // restore matrix state

    glRotatef( (GLfloat)(360.0*12.5*DayOfYear/365.0),
          0.0f, 1.0f, 0.0f );
    glTranslatef( 0.5f, 0.0f, 0.0f );
    glColor3f( 0.3f, 0.3f, 0.3f );
    auxWireSphere( 0.05f );

    // flush the pipeline, swap the buffers
    glFlush();
    auxSwapBuffers();
    }
```

Listing 5.1   A Simple OpenGL Program in C (continued)

```c
// initialize OpenGL
void OpenGLInit(void)
{
    glShadeModel( GL_FLAT );
    glClearColor( 0.0f, 0.0f, 0.0f, 0.0f );
    glClearDepth( 1.0f );
    glDepthFunc( GL_LEQUAL );
    glEnable( GL_DEPTH_TEST );
}


// called when the window is resized
static void CALLBACK ResizeWindow(GLsizei w, GLsizei h)
{
    h = (h == 0) ? 1 : h;
    w = (w == 0) ? 1 : w;
    glViewport( 0, 0, w, h );
    glMatrixMode( GL_PROJECTION );
    glLoadIdentity();
    gluPerspective( 45.0f, (GLfloat)w/(GLfloat)h, 1.0f,
    20.0f );
    // select the Modelview matrix
    glMatrixMode( GL_MODELVIEW );
}


// main routine
// set up OpenGL, hook up callbacks
// and start the main loop
int main( int argc, char** argv )
{
    // we're going to animate it, so double buffer
    auxInitDisplayMode(AUX_DOUBLE | AUX_RGB );
    auxInitPosition( 0, 0, 620, 160 );
    auxInitWindow( "Solar System Example" );

    // Initialize OpenGL as we like it..
    OpenGLInit();

    // set up callback functions
    auxKeyFunc( AUX_UP, Key_up ); // faster
    auxKeyFunc( AUX_DOWN, Key_down ); // slower
    auxKeyFunc( AUX_a, Key_a ); //animate
    auxReshapeFunc( ResizeWindow );
```

Listing 5.1   A Simple OpenGL Program in C (continued)

```
    // call this when idle
    auxIdleFunc( Animate );
    // call this in main loop
    auxMainLoop( Animate );

    return(0);
}
```

The gluLookAt( ) *Function*

The gluLookAt() helper function is provided by the utility library to make getting the right viewpoint transformations easier. This function takes two 3D coordinates: the viewpoint location and the location that you want to look at, which is typically the center of your model. The last parameter passed in is the "up" vector, which is typically the same as the positive y-axis. This function doesn't require you to calculate the rotation or translation distance; rather, you provide a "from" point and a "to" point, and the utility library does the rest for you. In fact, the utility library is calculating how to translate the viewpoint to the "from" point and how to rotate about this viewpoint location to look toward the "to" point. Figure 5.10 shows how the parameters relate to the coordinate system.

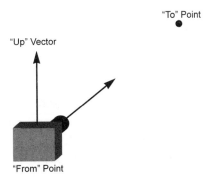

Figure 5.10   Physical Relationship of Parameters for gluLookAt()

The gluLookAt() function makes it particularly easy to move both the "from" and the "to" points in a linear manner. For example, if you needed to pan along the wall of a building located away from the origin and aligned along no axes in particular, you could simply take the "to" point to be one corner of the building and calculate the "from" as a constant distance from the "to" point. To pan along the building, just vary the "to" point; *presto!* One thing to be wary of is whether you've made any nonlinear scaling transformations, since these can cause uneven movement if the scales of the axes are different. Don't forget to select **GL_MOD-ELVIEW** mode.

How to Look at Anything from Anywhere

The **gluLookAt()** routine provides a hint of what you need to do to achieve any viewpoint you want. You have to move the viewpoint to a location, swing the viewpoint to point toward the model, and twist along the line of sight to get the correct "up" vector. This is how the **gluLookAt()** command works.

Since all rotations occur about the origin, you first need to move the "from" point (our viewpoint) onto the origin. This is a simple translation in all three coordinates and the first OpenGL command to effect the viewpoint (and the *last* one to be executed in the code). If our "from" point is at **fromX**, **fromY**, and **fromZ**, the translation looks like this:

```
glTranslatef( -fromX, -fromY, -fromZ );
DrawTheModel();
```

Note that these values are negative, as expected when manipulating the viewing part of the Modelview matrix. After this step, the viewpoint is at the origin and directed as before the translation.

The next step is to translate the "to" point onto the negative z-axis. After this rotation, the viewpoint will be looking at the "to" point. After the initial translation, the location of the "to" point is also translated; however, the values passed in need to be "translated" as well. Thus the translated "to" point simply has the "from" point subtracted from it. If we look down the positive y-axis, we can see where the "to" point is in relationship to the new viewpoint origin. This is illustrated in Figure 5.11. The x and z values can be used to calculate the angle Φ in the illustration. The code to calculate the rotation about the y-axis would thus look like this:

```
GLdouble newX = toX - fromX; // translate to
GLdouble newY = toY - fromY; // the new origin
GLdouble newZ = toZ - fromZ;
GLdouble theta;

// use arc cotangent or arc tangent depending
// on the quadrant of the angle. This prevents
// division by zero except when from == to
```

```
if ( abs(newX) > abs(newZ) )
     theta = arctan( newZ/newX );
else
     theta = arccos( newX/newZ );

// convert from radians to degrees
theta = 360.0*(theta/(2.0*3.14159265));
```

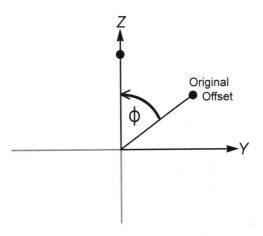

Figure 5.11   Rotating the Point about the Y-Axis to Align It with the Z-Axis

This procedure is repeated to get the corresponding rotations about the x-axis. We need rotations only about the x- and y-axes to place the "to" point onto the negative z-axis. Once these angles are calculated, it's a simple matter to perform the rotations about each corresponding axis.

```
// from and to are entered in above

.. calculations here to get thetaX,
.. and thetaY go here

glRotate(thetaY, 0.0f, 1.0f, 0.0f ); // y rotation
glRotate(thetaX, 1.0f, 0.0f, 0.0f ); // x rotation
glTranslatef( -fromX, -fromY, -fromZ );
DrawTheModel();
```

This sequence of transformations correctly aims our viewpoint at the "to" point. (Note that you'd never program this way if it were going to be done frequently; the inverse trigonometric functions would prove to be too expensive.)

The last step is to calculate the "up" direction. You can think of this as a twist or roll about the z-axis, since we're looking down the negative z-axis. This angle of rotation is calculated as the other angles were. You'll need to perform a translation of this vector to align it with the positive y-axis. This turns out to be a single rotation about the z-axis. Thus the final sequence of rotations and translation is

```
// angle calculations go here
glRotate(twistZ, 0.0f, 0.0f, 1.0f ); // z rotation
glRotate(thetaY, 0.0f, 1.0f, 0.0f ); // y rotation
glRotate(thetaX, 1.0f, 0.0f, 0.0f ); // x rotation
glTranslatef( -fromX, -fromY, -fromZ );
DrawTheModel();
```

The Components of the Modelview Matrix

All this confusion over modeling and viewing transformations stems from the fact that OpenGL uses *one* matrix to contain *all* the transformation matrices, both modeling and viewing. Not too surprisingly, this matrix is called the *Modelview* matrix. The transformations used to describe the model and the transformations used to describe the viewpoint's location and orientation coexist in one matrix, called the Modelview matrix in OpenGL. This matrix results in a simpler set of calculations in the graphics pipeline. Remember that matrix multiplication is not commutative but rather *associative*, which means that the product of ((AB)C) is the same as (A(BC)). Thus OpenGL's Modelview matrix is the product of a viewing matrix and a modeling matrix.

$$M_{Modelview} = M_{Viewing} M_{Modeling}$$

IMPORTANT What this means in terms of programming the Modelview matrix is that your viewing transformations must be entered into the Modelview matrix *before* your modeling transformations. This is a bit unnatural, since we usually construct the model before we think about viewing it. However, it's quite easy to place all viewing calculations into a viewing subroutine and all modeling calculations into a rendering subroutine. When it's time to render to the screen, you just call the viewing subroutine before the rendering subroutine. As long as you follow this convention, you'll avoid getting the modeling and viewing calculations mixed up.

Why this concatenation works is simple to understand mathematically. But conceptually it's one of the most difficult ideas to comprehend, especially if you don't regularly work with 3D graphics. To understand why it's possible to combine modeling and viewing transformations, it helps to use an example to visualize the different approaches.

Let's say that we want to view a model we've created and that both the model and the viewpoint are centered on the origin. In order to view the model, you can move either the viewpoint away from the model or the model away from the viewpoint. By the time the vertices are transformed to raster coordinates, the results are the same. In other words, it doesn't really matter whether you move the model or the viewpoint; the end result is the same.

Suppose that we'd like to view the object from the side. Our previous examples have demonstrated the importance of the order in which we issue translations. Since the viewpoint and the model share the origin initially, we can achieve the effect we want by first rotating the object about the fixed origin, then translating it away from the origin. This is the global, or fixed coordinate system, approach. The model is moved and rotated in relation to it. If you use this method of thinking about translations, you must remember to issue the translation commands in *reverse* order, since the vertices must be multiplied by the transformations in order. For example, if we wanted to translate vertex v first by rotation matrix R and then by translation matrix T, the first multiplication would be Rv, and the next would be to take the product of the first translation (Rv) and multiply it by the translation matrix, resulting in $T(Rv)$. We know that because matrix multiplications are associative, $T(Rv) = (TR)v$. Thus it's possible (and this is the way that OpenGL's Modelview matrix works) to precompute these translations *before* we get to enter in a vertex.

If many vertices are to be transformed, which is the normal state of things, we get quite a savings by precomputing the matrix containing all the viewing and modeling transformations beforehand and then using the resulting matrix for all the vertices. Thus the correct order for our example is

```
glTranslate*(...);
glRotate*(...);
DrawTheModel();
```

The vertices are effected first by the rotation transformation before the translation (its order in the Modelview matrix). Using the global coordinate approach will almost always yield the results you want, but it's difficult to conceptualize sometimes.

A different approach is to think of a local coordinate system that's fixed on the model. We'll be manipulating this local coordinate system when we use transformation matrices. Using this approach, we can easily visualize moving the model and its local coordinate system away from us and rotating it about its origin. In this case the commands we'd issue are

```
glTranslate*(...);
glRotate*(...);
DrawTheModel();
```

These commands are not only in the same order as we visualize them but also in the same order as the global coordinate system. However, if you have multiple objects, organizing multiple local coordinate systems can be quite overwhelming if you're not careful.

The approach that you use depends on which one is convenient. If you're constructing a huge monolithic model in which the user can move around, the fixed coordinate system will probably be the easiest to visualize. If, however, your model is something that's animated, particularly if some objects depend on the location of other objects, the local coordinate system is usually easier to use. Take whichever approach makes it easier to visualize your system. If you can, take both approaches and make sure that the results agree. This kind of mental exercise will help to make you adept at visualizing transformations.

You may be wondering why we have different ways of looking at modeling and viewing transformations. The reason is that in reality there is no such thing as a local coordinate system but rather just one global coordinate system. However, every transformation modifies vertices in the model in relationship to that coordinate system. The effects of all these transformations are in the reverse order that they are entered into the Modelview matrix, so those last few transformations—the ones that we consider the viewing transformations—essentially have to twist, turn, and move all of the vertices in our model to position them in relationship to the viewpoint, which sits immobile as the origin, and from there, through the projection transformation and onto the rasterization transformation. It's difficult to visualize such a convoluted sequence of events, especially since they're entered in backward. So we make the job easier on ourselves by breaking the task into smaller, more easily visualized steps.

Although it all sounds incredibly confusing, it's not that bad. Go ahead and write the modeling transformations first, and get your model constructed. You won't be able to see it, but you can at least use your imagination to visualize how it's laid out. Then simply insert the viewing transformation code so that it comes just after the Modelview matrix initialization but before the modeling transformations. For Windows programs this typically means that in your **WM_PAINT** or **WM_SIZE** message routines, before where you'd normally be doing all of the rendering, you call a routine to initialize and set up the Modelview matrix. This routine performs the correct viewing transformations and then does the modeling transformations to leave the matrix at the model origin. Then you call another function to render the scene, and this function does some local transformations from the modeling requirements (however, these still have to be in the "reverse" order). Stick with it. Taking 3D programming in small, digestible bites is the best way to grasp what's going on.

Manipulating the Matrix Directly

Whichever method you use, you'll almost always make use of the three OpenGL matrix manipulation commands **glLoadIdentity()**, **glPushMatrix()**, and **glPopMatrix()**. The first command replaces the current matrix with the identity matrix, which is usually the first matrix command issued before starting any transformations, since you'll usually want to start out with a known state. The next two commands are used to push and pop the current matrix, which is useful if you need to temporarily move the local coordinate system and then return it to a previous state. When modeling a car, for example, you might temporarily translate to each of the wheel wells and then render each of the wheels, pushing the matrix before the translation and popping it afterward. You *could* reverse the translation. However, pushing and popping is generally a fast operation, and repeatedly manipulating a matrix without eventually resetting it is an invitation to accumulate round-off error.

Both **glPushMatrix()** and **glPopMatrix()** are used to temporarily store matrices on a stack. OpenGL has three matrix modes: one for the Modelview matrix, one for the texture, and one for the projection. For the generic implementation you can count on a stack depth of at least 32 for the Modelview matrix. Pushing a matrix pushes the current matrix stack down and duplicates the current matrix. Popping a matrix replaces the current matrix with the matrix on the top of the stack and removes that matrix from the stack. You'll find that when your models get to be complex, you'll be making heavy use of these commands. If you ever find yourself performing a transformation to get back to a previous state, stop and reexamine your code to make use of these commands, as they're certain to be faster than any transformation calculations.

Three OpenGL commands let you directly manipulate the current matrix: `glLoadIdentity()`, `glMultMatrix*()`, and `glLoadMatrix*()`. The first replaces the current matrix with the identity matrix, as follows:

$$\begin{bmatrix} 1 & 0 & 0 & 0 \\ 0 & 1 & 0 & 0 \\ 0 & 0 & 1 & 0 \\ 0 & 0 & 0 & 1 \end{bmatrix}$$

The second is used to perform any matrix manipulations that you want. Its argument is a vector of sixteen values of the form shown next:

$$\begin{bmatrix} m0 & m4 & m8 & m12 \\ m1 & m5 & m9 & m13 \\ m2 & m6 & m10 & m14 \\ m3 & m7 & m11 & m15 \end{bmatrix}$$

There are two important things to note when using `glMultMatrix*()`. The first is that these elements are stored in *column* order, whereas multidimensional arrays in C or C++ are stored in *row* order. Thus you'll probably want to simply allocate a vector of length 16 and access them directly. The second is understanding just what `glMultMatrix*()` does. If we allocate and populate matrix A and if the current matrix on the stack is M, the result on the stack is MA after we pass matrix A to the function.

The `glLoadMatrix*()` function is used to directly replace the top stack matrix. Like `glMultMatrix*()`, it takes a vector of sixteen elements and loads them into the current matrix. The storage of these elements is the same as for `glMultMatrix*()`.

In order to demonstrate just how the Modelview matrix effects the scene, I've written a demo program to take advantage of OpenGL's ability to have multiple viewports of the same scene. That is, you can create a scene and then have it rendered twice, in two different viewports. (See the next section, on the Viewport transformation.) The program does this by using two different Modelview matrices for the two different views and then adding a final (hardcoded) transformation to both scenes so that you can "step outside" of the transformation you specified to see what you've done—sort of a superviewpoint. This allows you to view the results of different transformations on the same modeling code. When running the program, you'll see the OpenGL window containing the two viewports and a modeless dialog box that displays the values of the 4×4 Modelview matrix. See Plate 5.1. The view on the left is the reference view; the view on the right is effected by the matrix in the dialog box, which you use to modify the Modelview matrix.

The dialog box has three buttons. The Load button clears out any previous Modelview matrix and applies the values you have entered to the scene, which is then rendered in the right view; that is, it takes a fresh Modelview matrix and applies the values in the dialog box before displaying the view. The Append button multiplies the current Modelview matrix by the values you entered in the dialog box. Thus you can see the effects of cumulative transformation matrices on the scene. For example, you'd use this button to see the cumulative effects of the same matrix, such as slowly rotating the model about the y-axis. The Reset button simply resets the dialog box matrix to the identity matrix without effecting or recalculating the Modelview matrix.

Unless you're a mathematical savant with intuitive comprehension about how matrices interact, you'll benefit from expanding your understanding with the Modelview matrix manipulator. What usually happens to me is that I envision the viewpoint I want to look at my model from, program it in, and then stare at a blank screen—or worse, peer out from inside one of the parts of the model. I then sit back and scratch my head wondering where I messed up. Usually it's because I've done a rotation or translation out of order for the results I wanted. It's imperative that you get the transformations in the correct order, and the best way of becoming skilled in programming the Modelview matrix is to program, program, program! You need to gain experience in coordinating the transformations, and to do that you need to practice. Try working out a few examples on paper, say, looking directly down the negative y-axis onto the top of the origin, with the positive x-axis pointing to the left, and then programming the Modelview matrix manipulator to see whether you can achieve the desired results. Finally, try some of the suggestions at the end of the chapter. When you can intuitively (or at least flawlessly) get the correct sequence of transformations to complete the exercise, you can consider yourself a master of viewing transformations.

Viewport and Projection Transformations

Once you've mastered Modelview transformations, the next step is to understand projection modes and the Projection matrix. All of the preceding sections dealt with manipulating the Modelview matrix. As was mentioned previously, OpenGL has three matrices, any one of which may be the currently active matrix. Remember, OpenGL is a state machine, commands operate on the current conditions, and you need to explicitly set these conditions if necessary.

In this case you need to select the Projection matrix as the current matrix before you use any of its functions. The function `glMatrixMode()` takes one of three enumerated parameters to select the Modelview matrix, the Projection matrix, or the Texture matrix. This section deals with manipulating the Projection matrix using functions specialized for the job.

Viewport Transformations

Although one of the last steps in the graphics pipeline, the viewport transformation is the one that determines where the 3D view will be located on your screen. Keeping with OpenGL's complete innocence of operating system particulars, you have to tell the OpenGL subsystem the size of the window into which it's rendering. The OpenGL command `glViewport()` takes four parameters, which are used to specify the lower-left corner coordinates and the width and height of the viewport. For an OpenGL scene as large as the window itself, you'd just pass in 0,0 for the lower-left corner and the height and width of the window. If you want your OpenGL view to take only part of the window you'd adjust the parameters accordingly. Note that you'll need to keep track of the aspect ratio (the width/height ratio) when the window is resized, in order to keep things from getting distorted.

Since Windows sends a **WM_SIZE** message (indicating that the window size has changed) before it sends a **WM_PAINT** message (telling the application to repaint its display area), the **WM_SIZE** handler is the ideal place to set the viewport parameters and the projection transformation parameters, which are covered in the following section. In the MFC class structure the current view class has an **OnSize()** member that's ideal for handling the viewport configuration. Listing 5.2 shows a short **OnSize()** member function that shows how you might set up the member function to pass the new size onto OpenGL.

Listing 5.2   Connecting the Viewport to the Window

```
void CSomeOpenGLView::OnSize(UINT nType, int cx, int cy)
{
        // OnSize might be called with cx or cy == 0
        // during startup, so catch it and return.
        if ( 0 == cx || 0 == cy )
           {
           return;
           }

        // select the whole window as the viewport
        ::glViewport(0, 0, cx, cy);
}
```

One of the interesting features of OpenGL is its ability to have multiple viewports open simultaneously. This allows you to have multiple scenes or even the same scene with different viewpoints being displayed simultaneously. This is how the Modelview matrix manipulator program works. In this case you can't set the viewport in the `OnSize()` member function, because you need to set one viewport, set its transformation matrix, and then render the model. Then you can set up the other viewport, set *its* transformation matrix, and then render the model. For multiple viewports you'll need to save the client window's dimensions when the `OnSize()` member function is called and then use those values to calculate the dimensions of each of your viewports in the `OnDraw()` member function.

Projection Transformations

Orthographic Projection

OpenGL provides two methods of converting 3D images into 2D ones. The first is called *orthographic*, or *parallel*, projection and is illustrated in Figure 5.12. You use this style of projection to maintain the scale of objects and their angles without regard to their apparent distance. This is particularly useful for architectural drawings and for charting data; in both instances you need to retain lengths and sizes regardless of the distance from the viewpoint. As you can see from the figure, no matter how far distant the objects are from the viewing plane, their relative sizes do not change.

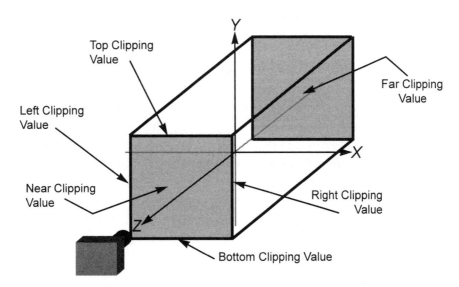

Figure 5.12 Orthographic Viewing Volume and Its Parameters

The OpenGL command for orthographic projection is `glOrtho()`. The six parameters to this command are used to define the *viewing volume*. Figure 5.12 shows how these parameters relate to one another. Each is used to define a rectangular clipping box that surrounds the viewing volume. Nothing is shown outside of this volume. Generally you'll pick values for the top, left, bottom, and right that are centered about your objects (usually at the origin). The size should be just large enough to encompass the model. For example, if your model is centered about the origin and extends about 4 units out, values of –5, 5 for left and right, and –5, 5 for bottom and top should provide a good starting place. The values of the front and back are a bit less critical for orthographic, and values of 0.5 and 10 for front and back should suffice. These values assume that you're looking down the negative z-axis, so these values are converted to negative z-values. Objects to be drawn should lie between the values specified on the negative z-axis. Thus the objects in the example should all be rendered between 0.5 and 10 units away from the viewpoint's location along the negative z-axis.

 If you move the model around, you may pass it entirely out of the viewing volume, especially if you allow a wide range of values in the distance that the viewpoint may move in relation to the model. It's a good idea to limit how small and how large you allow the viewpoint-to-model distance to become. If you're allowing the user to modify this distance, you should have something like a "reset" button that will return the viewpoint and model to a known state.

Perspective Projection

The second transformation is called *perspective*, or what most people consider the characteristic signature of 3D graphics—the effect of *foreshortening*, or the apparent effect of distance on the size of objects. This is by far the most popular choice in 3D graphics, and not too surprisingly, it's the one used throughout the examples in this book. Figure 5.13 shows perspective projection. The characteristic of perspective projection is the center of projection, the point to which all lines converge. The viewing volume for a perspective projection is called a *frustum*, or a truncated pyramid.

OpenGL's perspective projection is created by a couple of commands. The first and more powerful (and the more difficult to use) is `glFrustum()`. Like is `glOrtho()`, `glFrustum()` takes six parameters that are used to define the viewing volume, as shown in Figure 5.13. These parameters are the same and are used the same way as in `glOrtho()`. The difference here is that the near and far values are

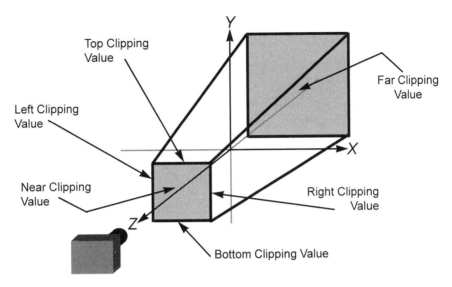

Figure 5.13 Perspective Viewing Volume and the `glFrustum()` Parameters

used to alter the size of the values placed in the depth buffer. There were no restrictions on the near and far values used by `glOrtho()`, but `glFrustum()` requires that they both be positive. If you use a very small value for near, you might discover that surfaces near the same depth might be incorrectly rendered, because you lose precision with very small near values. The *OpenGL Reference Manual* has a good explanation of how each of the input values effects the Projection matrix.

Another aspect of the power of `glFrustum()` is the ability to have nonsymmetric viewing volumes. Typically you'll leave the frustum centered on your model, but in certain cases you might want a special effect. If you're designing the interior of a cockpit that has two windows split by a vertical support, for example, you could simulate this perspective by providing two viewports and using an off-center frustum for each. The left frustum would specify a distance, say, **-x**, as the left parameter and **0** as the right, whereas the right frustum would specify **0** as the left and **x** as the right. This is called a false perspective and in effect moves the vanishing point of the rendered image from the middle of the viewing volume.

As you can see, `glFrustum()` is a powerful command. Although it seems simple to use, it's not very intuitive. OpenGL programmers generally use a much simpler perspective command, called `gluPerspective()`. Like `glFrustum()` it generates a perspective viewing volume but in a much simpler way. The four parameters provided to it are a near and far clipping value, just as for `glOrtho()` and `glFrustum()`, and an aspect ratio value of the width to height. This allows you to maintain the aspect ratio of objects on the screen with the dimensions of the viewport. When the viewport size changes, you recalculate the aspect ratio. The last parameter is called the field of view. Figure 5.14 shows what the parameters mean.

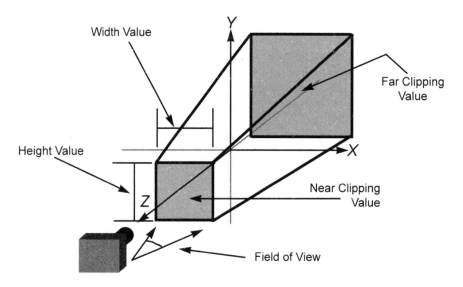

Figure 5.14   Perspective Viewing Volume and the gluPerspective Parameters

The field of view is the angle, in degrees, that the viewport encompasses. What this means depends on how you'd like the scene to look. Typically the field-of-view angle is the angle that your monitor (or the window devoted to the viewport) takes up. Typical values range from 60 to 30 degrees. The larger the value, the greater the apparent depth effect. You can achieve some nifty special effects by experimenting with the field-of-view parameter. What's happening is that we're essentially changing the lens on the virtual camera. A wide-angle lens means a wide field of view. Figure 5.14 shows the relationship between the viewing volume and the **gluPerspective()** parameters. Listing 5.3 shows the **OnSize()** member function implementing a full-window viewport with a perspective view that'll keep the aspect ratio correct.

Listing 5.3   How to Modify the Perspective When the Window is Resized

```
void CSomeOpenGLView::OnSize(UINT nType, int cx, int cy)
{
        // OnSize might be called with cx & cy == 0
        // during startup, so catch it and return.
        if ( 0 == cx || 0 == cy )
```

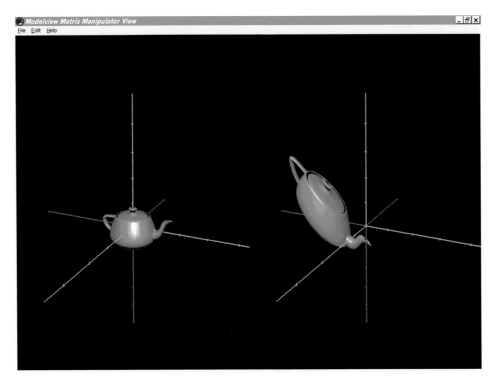

Plate 5.1 An Example of Two Scenes in a Single Window

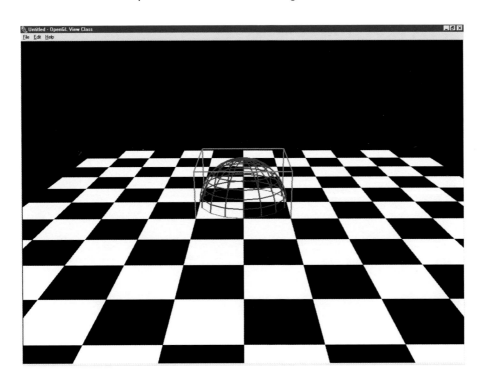

Plate 6.1 The Default View for the `COpenGLView` Class

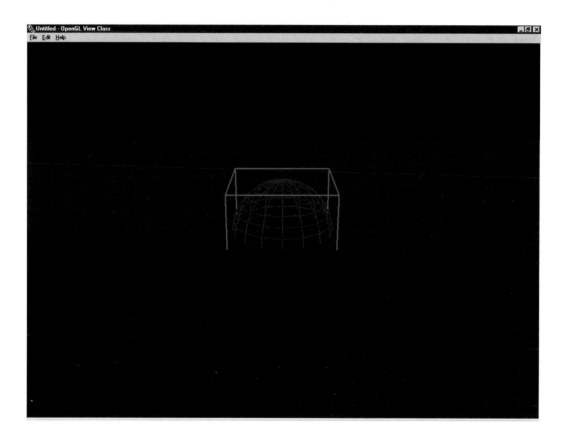

Plate 6.2 The `COpenGLView` class with the Red and Blue Triangle Stock Scene Selected

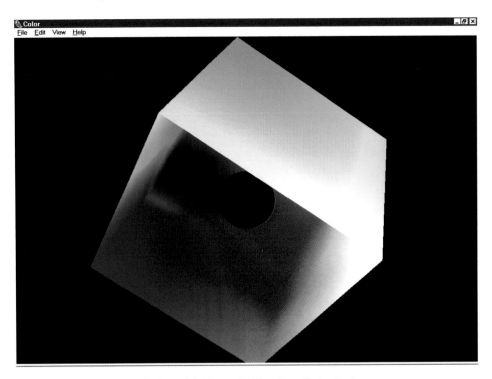

Plate 9.1 The Color Cube with Smooth Shading Selected

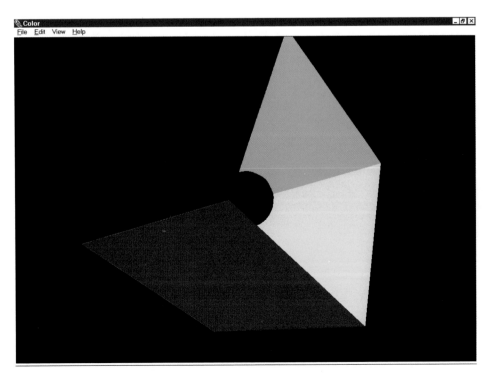

Plate 9.2 The Color Cube with Flat Shading Selected

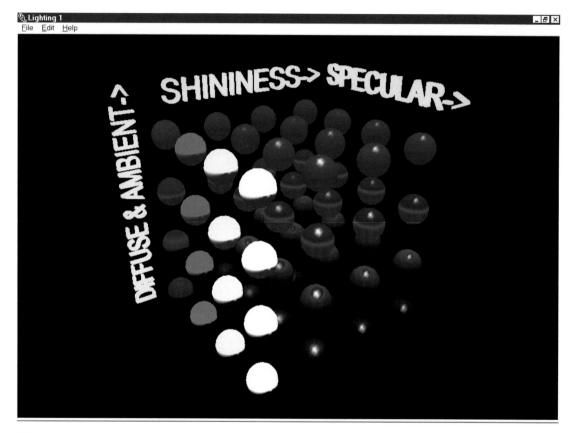

Plate 9.3   A Matrix of Spheres Showing the Range of Materials Properties

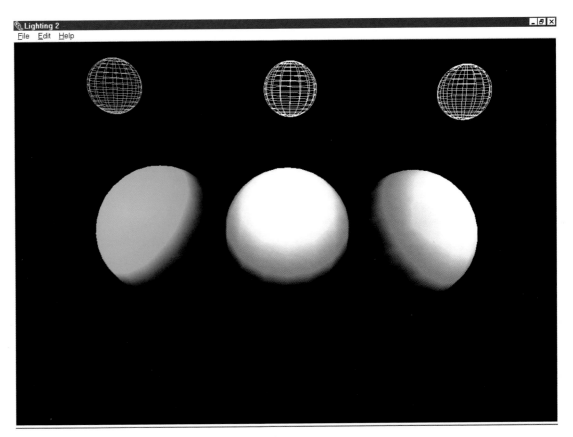

Plate 9.4 Three Spheres with Different Ambient and Reflective Properties

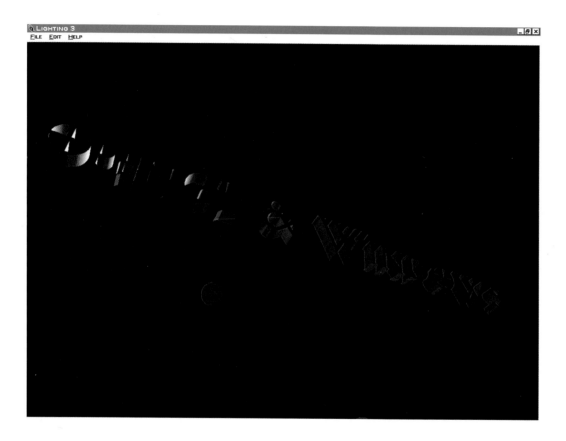

Plate 9.5 3D Text Demonstrating Chrome Text with Colored Lights

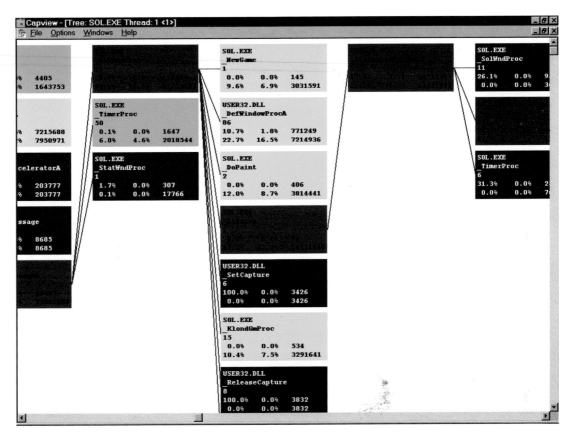

Plate 12.1 The CAPVIEW Program's Graphical View of Execution Times

Plate 12.2   The SGI Logo Demonstrating Shadows

Listing 5.3   How to Modify the Perspective When the Window is Resized (continued)

```
    {
    return;
    }

    // select the whole window as our canvas
    ::glViewport(0, 0, cx, cy);

    GLdouble theAspectRatio;

    // use the new dimensions to calculate
    // the new aspect ratio
    theAspectRatio = (GLdouble)cx/(GLdouble)cy;

    // select the projection matrix
    ::glMatrixMode(GL_PROJECTION);
    // initialize it
    ::glLoadIdentity();
    // transform it with a perspective matrix
    ::gluPerspective( 45.0f, // FOV is 45 degrees wide
                theAspectRatio, // newly calculated
                3.0f, // near clipping plane
                7.0f); // far clipping plane

    // since we hardly ever use the projection matrix
    // except in this case, let the default return
    // back to the projection matrix, saving us from
    // selecting it before each redraw
    ::glMatrixMode(GL_MODELVIEW);
}
```

You'll probably be using **gluPerspective()** in most of your programs, so you should get a firm understanding of exactly what it does. You might be wondering why we bother with the near and far clipping planes: Why not just have everything at or behind the viewpoint clipped and everything else rendered? The answer is in the depth buffer. If the objects that have to be rendered have a large range in depth values, the range of values to be represented in the depth buffer is large, and hence the granularity of the depth buffer is necessarily coarse. Values in the depth buffer are normalized to the range [0–1]. Thus the smaller the distance between the near and far clipping planes, the better differentiation there will be in the depth of objects. If you don't keep the far/near ratio small, you may occasionally start to see round-off errors in z values, so-called *z-fighting*, in which random pixels from polygons with similar z values start popping in and out. If you see this effect, reducing the far/near ratio usually helps.

On the other hand, if you seem to have correctly set up the Modelview matrix yet can't see anything, set the near and far planes to a small and a large value, respectively. It's pretty easy to miscalculate and push your model out past the far clipping plane if you're not careful.

Summary

If you've made it this far, only the exciting parts are in front of you. If you've gotten through this chapter, programmed the examples, and tackled the problems at the end, you're ready to get to the fun part of OpenGL programming. In the next chapters we'll start putting to use all this information that we've been patiently collecting. So whether your goal is to write a virtual reality program, the next killer business charting package, or your own version of DOOM, where the exploding barrels leave a dense, translucent fog you can see through (yes, you can do that with OpenGL!), stay tuned, because the fun is about to begin!

Try This

- In the solar system program the `auxWireSphere()` routine draws the wire sphere with the "poles" aligned with the z-axis. Add one more rotation before each sphere to align the poles with the y-axis instead.

- Add a satellite that rotates the moon in a polar orbit, on either the x-y plane or the y-z plane.

- Use the `glScale*()` routine to compress the z-axis by a factor of 2. Use this to effect the orbit of the Earth and nothing else. In other words, the orbit of the Earth about the Sun will now be an oval, not a circle. Don't let it effect any other orbits or spheres.

- Modify the viewpoint location of the solar system program so that it looks from the center of the Earth toward the Sun. Then move it to the Moon so that it looks toward the Earth. Finally, move it to the satellite so that it points toward the Moon.

6

Creating a Windows OpenGL View ————————

To a programmer, it's never concrete 'til they see code.

—John Vlissides

Encapsulating OpenGL

So far we've covered the basic OpenGL operations and have learned how to create an OpenGL window under Windows. The simplest way to *use* OpenGL is to encapsulate and keep all this functionality in one place. After all, the process of creating an OpenGL window when using the Microsoft Foundation Classes (MFC) is going to be the same, no matter what the objective of your OpenGL program is going to be. Thus we can encapsulate all this initialization and setup, using C++ as a reusable class for viewing OpenGL scenes. If you've never used MFC before or if you use another framework, the next section will give you a quick overview of how MFC works. If you're an old hand at MFC programming, you'll recognize what's going on. In any event, the class structure we create will be used throughout the rest of the book, in order to simplify the creation of OpenGL programs. If fact, you might want to use the class for your own OpenGL programs.

Architecture of the Model–View–Controller

In the mid-1970s, Smalltalk was the ultimate object-oriented programming language. Smalltalk came with its own operating environment. You didn't run a program on your PC; you first ran the Smalltalk environment, which in turn ran your program. While this made it very handy for things like garbage collection, it also meant that the program was intimately tied to the input system, since a running program was, in essence, part of the operating system.

Program design entailed breaking your program into three parts. The first part was the *Model,* or database. All the data that was unique to your program resided there. The next part was the *View* of the data. If your model consisted (in some internal form) of a table of data, a possible view might have been a spreadsheet or a graph. In other words, a view was just a way of displaying some or all of the data to the user. The third part of the architecture was the *Controller,* or the methods for the user to manipulate the model or the view. All user input and gestures came from the controller. All display items belonged to a view. All data associated with the current program was stored in the model.

This architecture was very successful and spawned many imitations, such as the Microsoft Foundation Classes. MFC programs consist of a *Document* and a *View,* which correspond to the Smalltalk Model and View. The Controller aspect is shared between Windows and the message processing of your program's windows and frames. Thus when your program starts, you usually inform the frame window (where all the normal commands, such as File or Edit, are processed) to open a document. When the document is read in, it usually opens up a default view. If your program has multiple views, you can switch between them or open up additional windows. All these windows contain views of the same document.

The base view class in MFC is called the `CView` class. When you use the Developer Studio to create a new MFC Windows–executable project (the Developer Studio's term for the source code and make files to produce an executable or library), the Developer Studio will create an application framework, consisting of an application file (the main window stuff), a document file (the default single-document-interface file), and a view file (containing the default view file). You can then compile and execute this program. It won't do anything, but it will run. Both the document and the view will be empty, but the messaging loops are in place, the window gets resized when it should, and you have an excellent starting place for the construction of a program.

One reason for my focusing on MFC is its popularity. Of course, the other major reason is that Microsoft is ultimately responsible for supporting OpenGL under Windows. If you're serious about OpenGL programming, you may not use the Microsoft compiler, but its collection of examples, source code, and documentation for OpenGL is unequaled.

The `CView` class provides the basic functionality for programmer-defined view classes. A view is attached to a document and acts as an intermediary between the document and the user. The purpose of the view is to render an image of the document on the screen and to interpret user input as operations on the document or changes to the view. In the next section I'll take you through the step-by-step creation of `COpenGLView`, an OpenGL-aware view class derived from the `CView` class. Unfortunately Microsoft deemed it unessential to add an OpenGL view class to MFC when updating to version 4.0, perhaps due in part to the problems of printing and GDI drawing associated with OpenGL 1.0 rendering contexts. Therefore we must not only live with these limitations but also create OpenGL views from scratch. Thus creating the `COpenGLView` class will enable us to create default OpenGL windows by simply using it. As we go along, we'll add to the basic functionality of the class. You'll see that we can encapsulate quite a few things once for later reuse.

The first step is to create a framework for the OpenGL viewing class. We'll let the Developer Studio create a Windows executable using MFC. This will create a framework in which we can build and test the `COpenGLView` class. When we're done, it's a simple matter to move the source code and header to another subdirectory, where we can either use the class directly or create a library or DLL.

Building the OpenGL View Class Framework

The first step is to create a new project, using the Developer Studio. You'll need to perform the following steps:

1. Select the new file as Project Workspace.
2. Select the target as an MFC AppWizard exe.
3. Name the project "OpenGL" in the location of your choice.
4 Select Single-Document-Interface (SDI).
5 Turn off all other options (no OLE, ODBC, 3D controls, and so on).
6. If necessary, edit the view class file names to make them "COpenGLView" for both the source and header files.

When you're done you should see the screen indicated in Figure 6.1.

Continue through the last dialog box. By then Developer Studio will have created the `COpenGLView` class file skeleton and a framework where we can test it. At this point you might want to compile the application just to make sure that there are no errors in your build process. If the project builds successfully, you're ready to proceed to the next step: incorporating all of the steps necessary to make the view class capable of displaying OpenGL images.

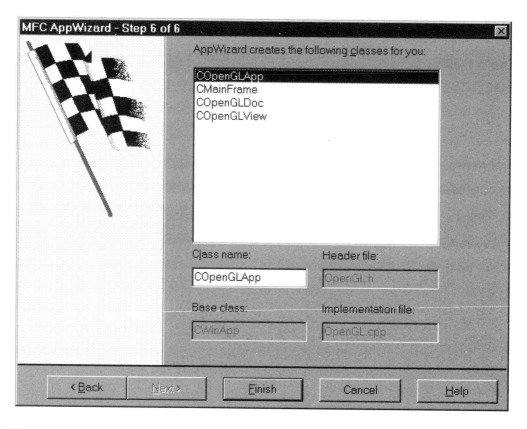

Figure 6.1   Creating an OpenGL Framework using MFC

Customizing the View for OpenGL

If you open up the ClassWizard and select the `COpenGLView` class, you'll see that
the message handlers for `OnDraw()` and `PreCreateWindow()` are already passed
onto the class. We'll need to add functions for the following additional messages:

- `WM_CREATE` (for `OnCreate`)
- `WM_DESTROY` (for `OnDestroy`)
- `WM_ERASEBACKGROUND` (for `OnEraseBkground`)
- `WM_SIZE` (for `OnSize`)

You add functions by selecting the message and then clicking on the Add Function button. Listing 6.1 shows you what you should have in your `COpenGLView`
when you're done: the CPP file for the framework for the `COpenGLView` class.

Listing 6.1   The COpenGLview Framework

```
// COpenGLView.cpp : implementation of the COpenGLView class
//

#include "stdafx.h"
#include "OpenGL.h"

#include "OpenGLDoc.h"
#include "COpenGLView.h"

#ifdef _DEBUG
#define new DEBUG_NEW
#undef THIS_FILE
static char THIS_FILE[] = __FILE__;
#endif

/////////////////////////////////////////////////////////////
// COpenGLView

IMPLEMENT_DYNCREATE(COpenGLView, CView)

BEGIN_MESSAGE_MAP(COpenGLView, CView)
    //{{AFX_MSG_MAP(COpenGLView)
        // NOTE—the ClassWizard will add and remove
        // mapping macros here.
        //    DO NOT EDIT what you see in these blocks
        // of generated code!
    //}}AFX_MSG_MAP
END_MESSAGE_MAP()

/////////////////////////////////////////////////////////////
// COpenGLView construction/destruction

COpenGLView::COpenGLView()
{
    // TODO: add construction code here

}
```

Listing 6.1   The `COpenGLView` Framework (continued)

```
COpenGLView::~COpenGLView()
{
}


BOOL COpenGLView::PreCreateWindow(CREATESTRUCT& cs)
{
    // TODO: Modify the Window class or styles here
    // by modifying the CREATESTRUCT cs

    return CView::PreCreateWindow(cs);
}


/////////////////////////////////////////////////////////////
// COpenGLView drawing

void COpenGLView::OnDraw(CDC* pDC)
{
    COpenGLDoc* pDoc = GetDocument();
    ASSERT_VALID(pDoc);

    // TODO: add draw code for native data here
}


/////////////////////////////////////////////////////////////
// COpenGLView diagnostics

#ifdef _DEBUG
void COpenGLView::AssertValid() const
{
    CView::AssertValid();
}


void COpenGLView::Dump(CDumpContext& dc) const
{
    CView::Dump(dc);
}


COpenGLDoc* COpenGLView::GetDocument()
  // non-debug version is inline
{
```

Listing 6.1   The COpenGLView Framework (continued)

```
        ASSERT(m_pDocument->IsKindOf(
                    RUNTIME_CLASS(COpenGLDoc)));
        return (COpenGLDoc*)m_pDocument;
}
#endif //_DEBUG

/////////////////////////////////////////////////////////////
// COpenGLView message handlers
int COpenGLView::OnCreate(LPCREATESTRUCT lpCreateStruct)
{
    if (CView::OnCreate(lpCreateStruct) == -1)
        return -1;

    // TODO: Add your specialized creation code here

    return 0;
}

void COpenGLView::OnDestroy()
{
    CView::OnDestroy();

    // TODO: Add your message handler code here

}

BOOL COpenGLView::OnEraseBkgnd(CDC* pDC)
{
    // TODO: Add your message handler code here and/or
    // call default

    return CView::OnEraseBkgnd(pDC);
}

void COpenGLView::OnSize(UINT nType, int cx, int cy)
{
    CView::OnSize(nType, cx, cy);

    // TODO: Add your message handler code here

}
```

The first step is to add the include statements for the OpenGL header files. I've added mine to the **COpenGLView.h** file because whenever I'll be using the class, I'll also be needing these headers. Placing them in the header for the view class means that I don't have to add them to my file. If you have religious convictions that prevent you from nesting header files, place them wherever you like. In any event you'll need to add something that looks like the following:

```
// Include the OpenGL headers
#include "gl\gl.h"
#include "gl\glu.h"
#include "gl\glaux.h"
```

We'll be adding some routines that will make use of the auxiliary library; hence the **glaux.h** include. If you're using a compiler that doesn't provide the auxiliary library, you can skip this include.

The next step is to add the OpenGL libraries to the link step. Select Build-Settings, and then select the Link tab. Select the Category of Input. Add the following line to the Object/Library Modules edit control:

```
opengl32.lib glu32.lib glaux.lib
```

Again, if you don't have the auxiliary library, you won't be able to add the **glaux.lib**. This is again a good point at which to try rebuilding the program. If you build successfully, you're all set to start editing the functions.

Editing PreCreateWindow()

In chapter 2 we said that you can't create an OpenGL window without setting the **WS_CLIPSIBLINGS** and **WS_CLIPCHILDREN** style. In addition, you *can't* set the **CS_PARENTDC** bit. Make these changes to your **PreCreateWindow()** member function. When it's done, it should look like this:

```
BOOL COpenGLView::PreCreateWindow(CREATESTRUCT& cs)
{
    // TODO: Add your specialized code here and/or call
    // the base class
    // An OpenGL window must be created with the following
    // flags and must not include CS_PARENTDC for the
    // class style.
```

```
    cs.style |= WS_CLIPSIBLINGS | WS_CLIPCHILDREN;

    return CView::PreCreateWindow(cs);
}
```

After each change, it's good practice to try a test compile to make sure that everything is compiling correctly. Don't try to execute the program yet, because we're in the intermediate stages of bringing OpenGL up. The next step is to modify the `OnEraseBkgnd()` member function.

Editing `OnEraseBkgnd()`

Although it's not really necessary, we'll edit the `OnEraseBkgnd( )` member function simply to turn it off. We'll do this by returning TRUE immediately from the function. Since OpenGL will be erasing its own window, there's no reason for Windows to do it as long as your OpenGL viewport takes up the entire client area. The edited code should look like this:

```
BOOL COpenGLView::OnEraseBkgnd(CDC* pDC)
{
    // TODO: Add your message handler code here and/or
    // call default

    // comment out original call
    // return CView::OnEraseBkgnd(pDC);
    return TRUE; // tell Windows not to erase the background
}
```

Editing `OnCreate()` and Setting up a Pixel Format and a Rendering Context

We're about to get into the meat of the Windows OpenGL interdependent code. At this point I'd like to introduce some error-checking code. There are many, many things that you may forget to do correctly when setting up a window for OpenGL rendering, and it's good to have all the help possible.

The first step is to stick in some diagnostic error messages that we'll make use of when something goes wrong when setting up a window for OpenGL. An alternative is to stick in Asserts, but with this method it's possible to put in some code that checks for an error message. While we're doing this, we'll also add some code we'll use for the `OnCreate()` function. In the `COpenGLView.h` file, add the following code before the last brace:

```
public:
    virtual BOOL SetupPixelFormat( void );
    virtual BOOL SetupViewport( int cx, int cy );
    virtual BOOL SetupViewingFrustum( GLdouble );
    virtual BOOL SetupViewingTransform( void );
    virtual BOOL RenderScene( void );

private:
    void SetError( int e );
    BOOL InitializeOpenGL();

    HGLRC m_hRC;
    CDC* m_pDC;

    static const char* const _ErrorStrings[];
    const char* m_ErrorString;
```

This adds some member function prototypes that we'll use later on, some RC and DC variables, and some error string pointers. To initialize these variables, we'll modify the default constructor by adding initializers:

```
COpenGLView::COpenGLView()  :
    m_hRC(0), m_pDC(0), m_ErrorString(_ErrorStrings[0])
{
    // TODO: add construction code here
}
```

The last step is to set the static error codes in the CPP file. I've made them static strings rather than resource them, since we'll be copying the source files around a bit. Since these are static, they must be in the implementation and not in the header. This means that the following lines are added to the CPP file:

```
const char* const COpenGLView::_ErrorStrings[]= {
    {"No Error"}, // 0
    {"Unable to get a DC"}, // 1
    {"ChoosePixelFormat failed"}, // 2
    {"SelectPixelFormat failed"}, // 3
    {"wglCreateContext failed"}, // 4
    {"wglMakeCurrent failed"}, // 5
    {"wglDeleteContext failed"}, // 6
```

```
{"SwapBuffers failed"}, // 7
};
```

These errors cover the general problems that can occur when setting up an OpenGL window. To set the error, we've got a special function that stores only the first error specified:

```
void COpenGLView::SetError( int e )
{
    // if there was no previous error,
    // then save this one
    if ( _ErrorStrings[0] == m_ErrorString )
        {
        m_ErrorString = _ErrorStrings[e];
        }
}
```

That covers recording errors as they occur. The next step is to initialize OpenGL by selecting a pixel format, a DC, and an RC. We'll simplify this task by breaking it into parts. We'll add a function call to OnCreate() to the new private member function InitializeOpenGL(). It's a small change to OnCreate() and looks like this:

```
int COpenGLView::OnCreate(LPCREATESTRUCT lpCreateStruct)
{
    if (CView::OnCreate(lpCreateStruct) == -1)
        return -1;

    // TODO: Add your specialized creation code here

    InitializeOpenGL();

    return 0;
}
```

Of course, the real functionality is hidden inside the new member function, InitializeOpenGL(). This function needs to create a DC, select a pixel format for this DC, create an RC associated with this DC, and select the RC. (You might note that we're using the faster method of holding onto both the RC and the DC for the life of the viewing window.)

Like most of the helper functions, **InitializeOpenGL()** returns a Boolean. A TRUE value signals that the function succeeded; a FALSE value signals failure. This is one of the points where the error messages come into play. Let's examine the OpenGL setup step by step.

```
BOOL COpenGLView::InitializeOpenGL()
{
    m_pDC = new CClientDC(this);

    if ( NULL == m_pDC ) // failure to get DC
        {
        SetError(1);
        return FALSE;
        }

    if ( !SetupPixelFormat() )
        {
        return FALSE;
        }
    if ( 0 == (m_hRC =
        ::wglCreateContext( m_pDC->GetSafeHdc() ) ) )
        {
        SetError(4);
        return FALSE;
        }

    if ( FALSE ==
        ::wglMakeCurrent( m_pDC->GetSafeHdc(), m_hRC ) )
        {
        SetError(5);
        return FALSE;
        }

    // specify black as clear color
    ::glClearColor( 0.0f, 0.0f, 0.0f, 0.0f );
    // specify the back of the buffer as clear depth
    ::glClearDepth( 1.0f );
    // enable depth testing
    ::glEnable( GL_DEPTH_TEST );

    return TRUE;
}
```

This function gets a DC for our client area, which comes from the client area of the frame window. If this fails, we set the error variable and return FALSE. This is how the error function is used throughout the **COpenGLView** class.

 The next step is to select a pixel format, which is such a complicated process that we've delegated it to its own function. The next two steps are to create a rendering context and then to make that RC current. Problems in setting up OpenGL windows usually occur during one of these three steps, so if you're having problems, such as an OpenGL window that never gets painted, this should be the first place you look.

The next step is to select the pixel format. We're eventually going to allow customization of this function later on, since selecting the optimum pixel format depends entirely on what the program is intended for. In this case we're going to use the OpenGL view class to examine various models. Thus this default pixel format will be for a double-buffered RGB window for animated 3D rendering. Note that we need only a temporary **PIXELFORMATDESCRIPTOR**, since we'll use it only once. (If you need to get the current pixel format, you can always query it.) Thus our initial pixel function looks like this:

```
BOOL COpenGLView::SetupPixelFormat()
{
    PIXELFORMATDESCRIPTOR pfd =
        {
        sizeof(PIXELFORMATDESCRIPTOR),// size of this pfd
        1,                          // version number
        PFD_DRAW_TO_WINDOW |        // support window
          PFD_SUPPORT_OPENGL |      // support OpenGL
          PFD_DOUBLEBUFFER,         // double buffered
        PFD_TYPE_RGBA,              // RGBA type
        24,                         // 24-bit color depth
        0, 0, 0, 0, 0, 0,           // color bits ignored
        0,                          // no alpha buffer
        0,                          // shift bit ignored
        0,                          // no accumulation buffer
        0, 0, 0, 0,                 // accum bits ignored
        16,                         // 16-bit z-buffer
        0,                          // no stencil buffer
        0,                          // no auxiliary buffer
        PFD_MAIN_PLANE,             // main layer
        0,                          // reserved
        0, 0, 0                     // layer masks ignored
        };
    int pixelformat;
```

```
    if ( 0 == (pixelformat =
        ::ChoosePixelFormat(m_pDC->GetSafeHdc(), &pfd)) )
        {
        SetError(2);
        return FALSE;
        }

    if ( FALSE == ::SetPixelFormat(m_pDC->GetSafeHdc(),
        pixelformat, &pfd) )
        {
        SetError(3);
        return FALSE;
        }

    return TRUE;
}
```

After the **PIXELFORMATDESCRIPTOR** is set, **ChoosePixelFormat()** is called, followed by **SetPixelFormat()**. As always, if there is an error, we call the error function and return FALSE. And that completes the initialization and setup of the Windows portion of the OpenGL processing. Since we just created our window, let's examine what we need to do when the window is destroyed.

Editing OnDestroy()

Unlike **OnCreate()**, destroying an OpenGL view is relatively easy. The code looks like this:

```
void COpenGLView::OnDestroy()
{
    CView::OnDestroy();

    // TODO: Add your message handler code here

    if ( FALSE == ::wglMakeCurrent( 0, 0 ) )
        {
        SetError(2);
        }

    if ( FALSE == ::wglDeleteContext( m_hRC ) )
        {
        SetError(6);
        }
```

```
if ( m_pDC )
    {
    delete m_pDC;
    }
}
```

The steps are to first make the current RC noncurrent, delete it, and then delete the DC. Note that you don't *need* to make the RC noncurrent if you are going to delete it, since `wglDeleteContext()` will do that for you. Also note that we call the error function but don't return FALSE, since at this point it's more important to clean up than to immediately return. Besides, if the rest of the program ran, we'd rather clean up all the RCs and DCs if we can figure out any other problems separately.

Editing `OnSize()`

`OnSize()`, one of the more interesting functions, is where you usually set up the viewport and the viewing frustum. We also set the viewing transformations here simply because it's convenient. You don't want to set up the viewing transformations in the painting routine unless you're going to be modifying the viewing transformation as your program runs—when translating or rotating the viewpoint as the program animates, for example. This is the reason for the numerous member functions that get called: to enable you to easily override the default behavior.

The basic operations that occur in the `OnSize()` member function are setting up the viewport (by means of a member function), then selecting the projection matrix, initializing it, and setting up the viewing frustum (also by means of a member function). The last operations are selecting the Modelview matrix, initializing it, and then setting up the viewing transformations by calling another member function. This use of member functions gives us great flexibility in tailoring the `COpenGLView` class to our needs without rewriting a great deal of code. The edited `OnSize()` member function follows:

```
void COpenGLView::OnSize(UINT nType, int cx, int cy)
{
    CView::OnSize(nType, cx, cy);

    // TODO: Add your message handler code here
    GLdouble aspect_ratio; // width/height ratio

    if ( 0 >= cx || 0 >= cy )
```

```
        {
        return;
        }

    SetupViewport( cx, cy );

    // compute the aspect ratio
    // this will keep all dimension scales equal
    aspect_ratio = (GLdouble)cx/(GLdouble)cy;

    // select the projection matrix and clear it
    ::glMatrixMode(GL_PROJECTION);
    ::glLoadIdentity();

    // select the viewing volume
    SetupViewingFrustum( aspect_ratio );

    // switch back to the Modelview matrix and clear it
    ::glMatrixMode(GL_MODELVIEW);
    ::glLoadIdentity();

    // now perform any viewing transformations
    SetupViewingTransform();
}
```

In order to make the **COpenGLView** class as easy to use as possible, I've taken the approach that it should provide a default everything, including a default view. This allows the **COpenGLView** class easy incorporation into other programs; if it's hooked up correctly, you'll get a default working view with no more effort than just connecting the **COpenGLView** class into your program. This allows easy customization, since you can be assured that if your program suddenly fails to display correctly after editing a member function, it's due to your editing, not to some other source. With that explanation in place, let's examine the default view that the **COpenGLView** class sets up.

The first thing that **OnSize()** sets up is the default viewport. In this case it's probably going to be exactly what you want—the OpenGL window to take up the entire client area.

```
BOOL COpenGLView::SetupViewport( int cx, int cy )
{
    // select the full client area
    glViewport(0, 0, cx, cy);
```

```
    return TRUE;
}
```

The next step is to set up the default viewing frustum. Again this is probably exactly what you want—a perspective view centered on the middle of the screen. If you'll be using an orthographic or a custom perspective view, you'll have to override this member function, but if you're interested mostly in simple 3D perspective views, the default viewing frustum is probably just what you need.

```
BOOL COpenGLView::SetupViewingFrustum(GLdouble aspect_ratio)
{
    // select a default viewing volume
    gluPerspective(40.0f, aspect_ratio, .1f, 20.0f);
    return TRUE;
}
```

Finally, we set up the default viewing transform, which places the viewpoint down the positive z-axis and elevates it slightly. The viewpoint is directed at the origin. The viewpoint is set up here for simplicity; you could also set it up anywhere between the OpenGL RC selection and the model rendering. For static viewpoints you'd want it set up outside the OnDraw( ) command, since the viewpoint needs to be entered into the Modelview matrix only once.

If you wanted a dynamic viewpoint, you'd have to set it up every time the model was about to be rendered. The code for the default viewing transform looks like this:

```
BOOL COpenGLView::SetupViewingTransform()
{
    // select a default viewing transformation
    // of a 20 degree rotation about the X axis
    // then a -5 unit transformation along Z
    ::glTranslatef( 0.0f, 0.0f, -5.0f );
    ::glRotatef( 20.0f, 1.0f, 0.0f, 0.0f );
    return TRUE;
}
```

Note how the OnSize() member function selects the appropriate matrix before each operation and that when it ends, the Modelview matrix is selected by default. This is by design, since usually the OnDraw() member function will be called next, which means that we'll be setting up further modeling transformations.

Editing `OnDraw()`

For this function we depart from the normal methodology of overriding base-class member functions to change their behavior, because there's usually a sequence of events that occurs in OpenGL programs when it's time to rerender a scene. These steps are as follows:

1. Clear the buffer(s).
2. (Optional) Set up the dynamic viewpoint or other custom viewports or viewing frustums.
3. (Optional) Render the static portion of your model. This usually means that you render the background of your scene. Static models can be optimized for display, as we'll see in the next chapter.
4. Render the dynamic parts of your model.

The `COpenGLView` class provides additional member functions, each designed to handle one of these particular subtasks. The first subtask is the `PreRenderScene()` member function. The default implementation is empty, since we've already set up our viewing volume and have selected a viewpoint. The next subtask is the `RenderStockScene()` member function, which takes care of rendering the static, or "stock," part of the view. We'll provide a simple stock scene of a checkerboard surface on the *x-z* plane as a default stock scene.

Finally, we'll call the last subtask, the `RenderScene()` member function, where you'll be spending most of your time. This function is intended to provide you with a location to construct your model. In the default `RenderScene()` we'll provide a simple default scene consisting of a blue wire-frame cube with a red wire-frame sphere inside it. Since the sphere and the cube are centered at the origin, they'll show up as being embedded into the checkerboard's surface. Now let's take a look at the code.

```
void COpenGLView::OnDraw(CDC* pDC)
{
    COpenGLViewClassDoc* pDoc = GetDocument();
    ASSERT_VALID(pDoc);

    // TODO: add draw code for native data here

    ::glClear( GL_COLOR_BUFFER_BIT | GL_DEPTH_BUFFER_BIT );
```

```
PreRenderScene();

::glPushMatrix();
RenderStockScene();
::glPopMatrix();

::glPushMatrix();
RenderScene();
::glPopMatrix();

::glFinish();

if ( FALSE == ::SwapBuffers( m_pDC->GetSafeHdc() ) )
    {
    SetError(7);
    }
}
```

Note that we clear the color and depth buffers first. If you're interested in hidden-surface removal, you'll need to enable depth testing (which we did at the end of the **InitializeOpenGL()** member function) and also clear the depth buffer, which we do here. We also wrapper the scene-rendering member functions with calls to push and pop the current matrix state, to save you from having to do it yourself. Finally, we call **glFinish()**, which makes sure that all OpenGL rendering calls are completed, and then we swap the buffers. We created a double-buffered pixel format when we set up our RC, and this is the spot where we make use of them.

As you can see, a lot of coordination is going on here, which is why there's a multitude of member functions to take care of the various subtasks that you might want to modify. With this basic structure you should never have to override the **OnDraw()** member function; all you'll need to do is write your own **RenderScene()** function to draw your scene and optionally override the other member functions to modify the program as you require. The subtask functions (except for **PreRenderScene()**, which is an empty member function at this point) are coded like this:

```
BOOL COpenGLView::RenderScene()
{
    // draw a red wire sphere inside a
    // light blue cube
```

```
    // rotate the wire sphere so it's vertically
    // oriented
    ::glRotatef( 90.0f, 1.0f, 0.0f, 0.0f );
    ::glColor3f( 1.0f, 0.0f, 0.0f );
    ::auxWireSphere( .5 );
    ::glColor3f( 0.5f, 0.5f, 1.0f );
    ::auxWireCube( 1.0 );
    return TRUE;
}
// Draw a square surface that looks like a
// black and white checkerboard
void COpenGLView::StockScene( )
{
    // define all vertices X Y Z
    GLfloat v0[3], v1[3], v2[3], v3[3], delta;
    int color = 0;

    delta = 0.5f;

    // define the two colors
    GLfloat color1[3] = { 0.9f, 0.9f, 0.9f };
    GLfloat color2[3] = { 0.05f, 0.05f, 0.05f };

    v0[1] = v1[1] = v2[1] = v3[1] = 0.0f;

    ::glBegin( GL_QUADS );

    for ( int x = -5 ; x <= 5 ; x++ )
        {
        for ( int z = -5 ; z <= 5 ; z++ )
            {
            ::glColor3fv( (color++)%2 ? color1 : color2 );

            v0[0] = 0.0f+delta*z;
            v0[2] = 0.0f+delta*x;

            v1[0] = v0[0]+delta;
            v1[2] = v0[2];

            v2[0] = v0[0]+delta;
            v2[2] = v0[2]+delta;

            v3[0] = v0[0];
            v3[2] = v0[2]+delta;
```

```
        ::glVertex3fv( v0 );
        ::glVertex3fv( v1 );
        ::glVertex3fv( v2 );
        ::glVertex3fv( v3 );
        }
    }
  ::glEnd();

}
```

The `RenderScene()` member function makes use of the auxiliary library functions to render a wire cube and a wire sphere. If your implementation doesn't have the auxiliary library, you can use the utility library's more complex routines to draw a cube and a sphere.

The `RenderStockScene()` member function is probably more interesting to you. This is the first real example we've seen of creating a model out of polygons. There are two **for** loops. The first draws a strip of touching squares (quads), and the second simply moves the origin over. You might be wondering why I'm not using a quad strip as opposed to constructing individual quads. The reason is that vertices that are shared between two polygons can't have different colors when using smooth shading. Quad strips (and all the other strips and fans) are made for constructing a homogeneous surface, and thus we're going to create our checkerboard out of individually colored squares. Plate 6.1 shows what you get when you run the program with the default member functions. The source code in this initial form of the `COpenGLView` class can be found in the "Chapter 6/Creating the OpenGL View Class" subdirectory. The Developer Studio files are all in this subdirectory, so you can edit and rebuild the files if you like or run the executable.

Using the `COpenGLView` Class

Having the view class directly hooked into our application is not the final intent of the `COpenGLView` class. We now need to remove the direct linkages of the `COpenGLView` class in the application and to create our own subclass, based on the `COpenGLView` class. As it turns out, this is relatively simple. The first step is to create a subclass from our `COpenGLView` class and to modify it. Let's create a subclass called `MyView` and override the stock-scene member function. The code to do this looks like this:

```
class CMyView : public COpenGLView
{
private:
    DECLARE_DYNCREATE(CMyView)
protected:
    virtual void RenderStockScene( void );
};
```

In addition to the **RenderStockScene()** member function that we're going to override, we'll need to add the **DECLARE_DYNCREATE(CMyView)** macro, which is required to enable objects derived from the **CObject** base class to be created dynamically at run time. MFC uses this ability to create new objects dynamically—for example, when it reads an object from disk during serialization. All view classes should support dynamic creation, because the framework needs to create them dynamically. The **DECLARE_DYNCREATE** macro is placed in the **.h** module for the class, and this header file is then required for all **.cpp** files that need access to objects of this class. If **DECLARE_DYNCREATE** is part of the class declaration, **IMPLEMENT_DYNCREATE** macro must be included in the class implementation. The source code for **MyView** class looks like this:

```
IMPLEMENT_DYNCREATE(CMyView, COpenGLView)


void CMyView::RenderStockScene ( )
{
    . . . . details in next section
}
```

As you can see, there's not much to it—which is exactly how we want it.

The final step is to connect up our **MyView** class instead of the **COpenGLView** class. This occurs in the "app" source code, which is in the **COpenGLViewClass-App.cpp** file. Your particular "app" implementation file will depend on what you tell the Developer Studio to call it. A section in the **InitInstance()** member function of the app source dynamically creates the document from a template that includes the view class to use. We can simply change the name of the view class to use in the template to **MyView** and recompile. The section of the **InitInstance()** member function that needs to change looks like this:

```
...
    // Register the application's document templates.
    // Document templates serve as the connection between
```

```
        // documents, frame windows, and views.
        CSingleDocTemplate* pDocTemplate;
        pDocTemplate = new CSingleDocTemplate(
            IDR_MAINFRAME,
            RUNTIME_CLASS(COpenGLViewClassDoc),
            RUNTIME_CLASS(CMainFrame),
            RUNTIME_CLASS(CMyView)); // <- Where it changes
            AddDocTemplate(pDocTemplate);
    ...
```

The last thing to do is implement the `RenderStockScene()` member function in the `MyView` class. Instead of a checkerboard pattern, let's create a new pattern that consists of several triangles in red and blue that share a common vertex at the origin. The code for this function is as follows:

```
// Draw a square surface of red and blue triangles
// all touching the origin.
void CMyView::RenderStockScene( )
{
    // define all vertices    X       Y       Z
    GLfloat surface0[3] = { 0.0f,  0.0f,  0.0f };
    GLfloat surface1[3] = {+5.0f,  0.0f,  0.0f };
    GLfloat surface2[3] = {+5.0f,  0.0f, -5.0f };
    GLfloat surface3[3] = { 0.0f,  0.0f, -5.0f };
    GLfloat surface4[3] = {-5.0f,  0.0f, -5.0f };
    GLfloat surface5[3] = {-5.0f,  0.0f,  0.0f };
    GLfloat surface6[3] = {-5.0f,  0.0f, +5.0f };
    GLfloat surface7[3] = { 0.0f,  0.0f, +5.0f };
    GLfloat surface8[3] = {+5.0f,  0.0f, +5.0f };
    GLfloat surface9[3] = {+5.0f,  0.0f,  0.0f };

    // define the two colors
    GLfloat color1[3] = { 0.5f, 0.0f, 0.0f };
    GLfloat color2[3] = { 0.0f, 0.0f, 0.5f };
    ::glBegin( GL_TRIANGLES );
        ::glColor3fv( color1 );
        ::glVertex3fv( surface0 );
        ::glVertex3fv( surface1 );
        ::glVertex3fv( surface2 );
        ::glColor3fv( color2 );
        ::glVertex3fv( surface0 );
        ::glVertex3fv( surface2 );
        ::glVertex3fv( surface3 );
```

```
    ::glColor3fv( color1 );
    ::glVertex3fv( surface0 );
    ::glVertex3fv( surface3 );
    ::glVertex3fv( surface4 );
    ::glColor3fv( color2 );
    ::glVertex3fv( surface0 );
    ::glVertex3fv( surface4 );
    ::glVertex3fv( surface5 );
    ::glColor3fv( color1 );
    ::glVertex3fv( surface0 );
    ::glVertex3fv( surface5 );
    ::glVertex3fv( surface6 );
    ::glColor3fv( color2 );
    ::glVertex3fv( surface0 );
    ::glVertex3fv( surface6 );
    ::glVertex3fv( surface7 );
    ::glColor3fv( color1 );
    ::glVertex3fv( surface0 );
    ::glVertex3fv( surface7 );
    ::glVertex3fv( surface8 );
    ::glColor3fv( color2 );
    ::glVertex3fv( surface0 );
    ::glVertex3fv( surface8 );
    ::glVertex3fv( surface9 );
  ::glEnd();

}
```

We've defined all the vertices in an array and then created each triangle, using these shared vertices. When we run this customized implementation of our OpenGL view class, we get the scene shown in Plate 6.2, which shows the default scene from COpenGLView with our new stock scene from MyView.

Summary

After all these changes to our original COpenGLView class, the modified version and the implementation of the MyView class can be found in the "Chapter 6/Using the OpenGL View Class" subdirectory. Listing 6.2 is the declaration of the original COpenGLView class, in the header file. Listing 6.3 is the implementation of the COpenGLView class, as found in the COpenGLView.cpp file.

Listing 6.2 The COpenGLView Header File

```
// COpenGLView.h : interface of the COpenGLView class
/////////////////////////////////////////////////////////
// Include the OpenGL headers
#include "gl\gl.h"
#include "gl\glu.h"
#include "gl\glaux.h"

class COpenGLView : public CView
{
protected: // create from serialization only
    COpenGLView();
    DECLARE_DYNCREATE(COpenGLView)
// Attributes
public:
    COpenGLViewClassDoc* GetDocument();
// Operations
public:

// Overrides
    // ClassWizard generated virtual function overrides
    //{{AFX_VIRTUAL(COpenGLView)
    public:
    virtual void OnDraw(CDC* pDC); // overridden to draw
                                   // this view
    virtual BOOL PreCreateWindow(CREATESTRUCT& cs);
    //}}AFX_VIRTUAL

// Implementation
public:
    virtual ~COpenGLView();
#ifdef _DEBUG
    virtual void AssertValid() const;
    virtual void Dump(CDumpContext& dc) const;
#endif

// Generated message map functions
protected:
    //{{AFX_MSG(COpenGLView)
    afx_msg int OnCreate(LPCREATESTRUCT lpCreateStruct);
    afx_msg void OnDestroy();
```

Listing 6.2 The COpenGLview Header File (continued)

```
    afx_msg BOOL OnEraseBkgnd(CDC* pDC);
    afx_msg void OnSize(UINT nType, int cx, int cy);
    //}}AFX_MSG
    DECLARE_MESSAGE_MAP()

    // The following was added to the COpenGLView class
    virtual BOOL SetupPixelFormat( void );
    virtual BOOL SetupViewport( int cx, int cy );
    virtual BOOL SetupViewingFrustum(GLdouble aspect_ratio);
    virtual BOOL SetupViewingTransform( void );
    virtual BOOL PreRenderScene( void ) { return TRUE; }
    virtual void RenderStockScene( void );
    virtual BOOL RenderScene( void );

private:
    BOOL InitializeOpenGL();
    void SetError( int e );

    HGLRC m_hRC;
    CDC* m_pDC;

    static const char* const _ErrorStrings[];
    const char* m_ErrorString;
};

#ifndef _DEBUG // debug version in COpenGLView.cpp
inline COpenGLViewClassDoc* COpenGLView::GetDocument()
    { return (COpenGLViewClassDoc*)m_pDocument; }
#endif
/////////////////////////////////////////////////////////////
```

Listing 6.3 The COpenGLview Source File

```
// COpenGLView.cpp : implementation of the COpenGLView class
//

#include "stdafx.h"
#include "OpenGL View Class.h"
```

Listing 6.3   The COpenGLView Source File (continued)

```
#include "OpenGL View ClassDoc.h"
#include "COpenGLView.h"

#ifdef _DEBUG
#define new DEBUG_NEW
#undef THIS_FILE
static char THIS_FILE[] = __FILE__;
#endif

const char* const COpenGLView::_ErrorStrings[]= {
            ("No Error"},                     // 0
            ("Unable to get a DC"},           // 1
            ("ChoosePixelFormat failed"},    // 2
            ("SelectPixelFormat failed"},    // 3
            ("wglCreateContext failed"},     // 4
            ("wglMakeCurrent failed"},       // 5
            ("wglDeleteContext failed"},     // 6
            ("SwapBuffers failed"},          // 7
            };

/////////////////////////////////////////////////////////////
// COpenGLView

IMPLEMENT_DYNCREATE(COpenGLView, CView)

BEGIN_MESSAGE_MAP(COpenGLView, CView)
    //{{AFX_MSG_MAP(COpenGLView)
    ON_WM_CREATE()
    ON_WM_DESTROY()
    ON_WM_ERASEBKGND()
    ON_WM_SIZE()
    //}}AFX_MSG_MAP
    END_MESSAGE_MAP()

/////////////////////////////////////////////////////////////
// COpenGLView construction/destruction

COpenGLView::COpenGLView() :
    m_hRC(0), m_pDC(0), m_ErrorString(_ErrorStrings[0])
```

Listing 6.3 The COpenGLView Source File (continued)

```
{
    // TODO: add construction code here
}

COpenGLView::~COpenGLView()
{
}

BOOL COpenGLView::PreCreateWindow(CREATESTRUCT& cs)
{
    // TODO: Add your specialized code here and/or
    // call the base class

    // An OpenGL window must be created with the
    // following flags and must not include
    // CS_PARENTDC for the class style.
    cs.style |= WS_CLIPSIBLINGS | WS_CLIPCHILDREN;

    return CView::PreCreateWindow(cs);
}

/////////////////////////////////////////////////////
// COpenGLView drawing

void COpenGLView::OnDraw(CDC* pDC)
{
    COpenGLViewClassDoc* pDoc = GetDocument();
    ASSERT_VALID(pDoc);

    // TODO: add draw code for native data here

    ::glClear( GL_COLOR_BUFFER_BIT | GL_DEPTH_BUFFER_BIT );

    PreRenderScene();

    ::glPushMatrix();
    RenderStockScene();
    ::glPopMatrix();
    ::glPushMatrix();
```

Listing 6.3   The COpenGLView Source File (continued)

```
        RenderScene();
        ::glPopMatrix();

        ::glFinish();

        if ( FALSE == ::SwapBuffers( m_pDC->GetSafeHdc() ) )
            {
            SetError(7);
            }
}


///////////////////////////////////////////////////////////////
// COpenGLView diagnostics

#ifdef _DEBUG
void COpenGLView::AssertValid() const
{
    CView::AssertValid();
}

void COpenGLView::Dump(CDumpContext& dc) const
{
    CView::Dump(dc);
}

COpenGLViewClassDoc* COpenGLView::GetDocument()
// non-debug version is inline
{
    ASSERT(m_pDocument->IsKindOf
        (RUNTIME_CLASS(COpenGLViewClassDoc)));
    return (COpenGLViewClassDoc*)m_pDocument;
}
#endif //_DEBUG


///////////////////////////////////////////////////////////////
// COpenGLView message handlers

int COpenGLView::OnCreate(LPCREATESTRUCT lpCreateStruct)
{
    if (CView::OnCreate(lpCreateStruct) == -1)
```

Listing 6.3 The `COpenGLView` **Source File (continued)**

```
        return -1;

    // TODO: Add your specialized creation code here
    InitializeOpenGL();
    return 0;
}


/////////////////////////////////////////////////////////
// GL helper functions

void COpenGLView::SetError( int e )
{
    // if there was no previous error,
    // then save this one
    if ( _ErrorStrings[0] == m_ErrorString )
        {
        m_ErrorString = _ErrorStrings[e];
        }
}


BOOL COpenGLView::InitializeOpenGL()
{
    // Can we put this in the constructor?
    m_pDC = new CClientDC(this);

    if ( NULL == m_pDC ) // failure to get DC
        {
        SetError(1);
        return FALSE;
        }

    if (!SetupPixelFormat())
        {
        return FALSE;
        }

    if ( 0 == (m_hRC =
        ::wglCreateContext( m_pDC->GetSafeHdc() ) ) )
        {
        SetError(4);
        return FALSE;
```

Listing 6.3   The COpenGLView Source File (continued)

```
            }

        if ( FALSE ==
            ::wglMakeCurrent( m_pDC->GetSafeHdc(), m_hRC ) )
            {
            SetError(5);
            return FALSE;
            }

        // specify black as clear color
        ::glClearColor(0.0f, 0.0f, 0.0f, 0.0f);
        // specify the back of the buffer as clear depth
        ::glClearDepth(1.0f);
        // enable depth testing
        ::glEnable(GL_DEPTH_TEST);

        return TRUE;
        }

BOOL COpenGLView::SetupPixelFormat()
    {
    static PIXELFORMATDESCRIPTOR pfd =
        {
        sizeof(PIXELFORMATDESCRIPTOR), // size of this pfd
        1,                              // version number
        PFD_DRAW_TO_WINDOW |            // support window
           PFD_SUPPORT_OPENGL |         // support OpenGL
           PFD_DOUBLEBUFFER,            // double buffered
        PFD_TYPE_RGBA,                  // RGBA type
        24,                             // 24-bit color
        0, 0, 0, 0, 0, 0,               // color bits ignored
        0,                              // no alpha buffer
        0,                              // shift bit ignored
        0,                              // no accum buffer
        0, 0, 0, 0,                     // accum bits ignored
        16,                             // 16-bit z-buffer
        0,                              // no stencil buffer
        0,                              // no auxiliary buffer
        PFD_MAIN_PLANE,                 // main layer
```

Listing 6.3   The COpenGLView Source File (continued)

```
            0,                              // reserved
            0, 0, 0                         // layer masks ignored
        };
        int pixelformat;

        if ( 0 == (pixelformat =
            ::ChoosePixelFormat(m_pDC->GetSafeHdc(), &pfd)) )
            {
            SetError(2);
            return FALSE;
            }

        if ( FALSE ==
            ::SetPixelFormat(m_pDC->GetSafeHdc(),pixelformat,&pfd))
            {
            SetError(3);
            return FALSE;
            }
        return TRUE;
    }


void COpenGLView::OnDestroy()
{
    CView::OnDestroy();

    // TODO: Add your message handler code here

    if ( FALSE == ::wglDeleteContext( m_hRC ) )
        {
        SetError(6);
        }

    if ( m_pDC )
        {
        delete m_pDC;
        }
}


BOOL COpenGLView::OnEraseBkgnd(CDC* pDC)
{
    // TODO: Add your message handler code here and/or
```

Listing 6.3   The COpenGLView Source File (continued)

```
        // call default

        // return CView::OnEraseBkgnd(pDC);
        return TRUE; // tell Windows not to erase the background
    }

    void COpenGLView::OnSize(UINT nType, int cx, int cy)
    {
        CView::OnSize(nType, cx, cy);

        // TODO: Add your message handler code here
        GLdouble aspect_ratio; // width/height ratio

        if ( 0 >= cx || 0 >= cy )
            {
            return;
            }

        SetupViewport( cx, cy );

        // select the projection matrix and clear it
        ::glMatrixMode(GL_PROJECTION);
        ::glLoadIdentity();

        // compute the aspect ratio
        // this will keep all dimension scales equal
        aspect_ratio = (GLdouble)cx/(GLdouble)cy;

        // select the viewing volume
        SetupViewingFrustum( aspect_ratio );

        // switch back to the Modelview matrix
        ::glMatrixMode(GL_MODELVIEW);
        ::glLoadIdentity();

        // now perform any viewing transformations
        SetupViewingTransform();
    }

    ////////////////////////////////////////////////////////////
    // COpenGLView helper functions
```

Listing 6.3   The COpenGLView Source File (continued)

```cpp
BOOL COpenGLView::SetupViewport( int cx, int cy )
{
    // select the full client area
    ::glViewport(0, 0, cx, cy);
    return TRUE;
}


BOOL COpenGLView::SetupViewingFrustum(GLdouble aspect_ratio)
{
    // select a default viewing volume
    ::gluPerspective(40.0f, aspect_ratio, 0.1f, 20.0f);
    return TRUE;
}


BOOL COpenGLView::SetupViewingTransform()
{
    // select a default viewing transformation
    // of a 20 degree rotation about the X axis
    // then a -5 unit transformation along Z
    ::glTranslatef( 0.0f, 0.0f, -5.0f );
    ::glRotatef( 20.0f, 1.0f, 0.0f, 0.0f );
    return TRUE;
}


BOOL COpenGLView::RenderScene()
{
    // draw a red wire sphere inside a
    // light blue cube

    // rotate the wire sphere so it's vertically
    // oriented
    ::glRotatef( 90.0f, 1.0f, 0.0f, 0.0f );
    ::glColor3f( 1.0f, 0.0f, 0.0f );
    ::auxWireSphere( 0.5 );
    ::glColor3f( 0.5f, 0.5f, 1.0f );
    ::auxWireCube( 1.0 );
    return TRUE;
}
// Draw a square surface that looks like a
// black and white checkerboard
void COpenGLView::RenderStockScene()
{
```

Listing 6.3   The `COpenGLView` Source File (continued)

```
// define all vertices   X      Y      Z
GLfloat v0[3], v1[3], v2[3], v3[3], delta;
int color = 0;

delta = 0.5f;

// define the two colors
GLfloat color1[3] = { 0.9f, 0.9f, 0.9f };
GLfloat color2[3] = { 0.05f, 0.05f, 0.05f };

v0[1] = v1[1] = v2[1] = v3[1] = 0.0f;

::glBegin( GL_QUADS );

for ( int x = -5 ; x <= 5 ; x++ )
    {
    for ( int z = -5 ; z <= 5 ; z++ )
        {
        ::glColor3fv( (color++)%2 ? color1 : color2 );

        v0[0] = 0.0f+delta*z;
        v0[2] = 0.0f+delta*x;

        v1[0] = v0[0]+delta;
        v1[2] = v0[2];

        v2[0] = v0[0]+delta;
        v2[2] = v0[2]+delta;

        v3[0] = v0[0];
        v3[2] = v0[2]+delta;

        ::glVertex3fv( v0 );
        ::glVertex3fv( v1 );
        ::glVertex3fv( v2 );
        ::glVertex3fv( v3 );
        }
    }
::glEnd();

}
```

Try This

Once you get used to using the `COpenGLView` class (or your own implementation of it), you'll find that creating an OpenGL view is as effortless as creating any other MFC view class. The next chapters will further modify the `COpenGLView` class to give it even greater capabilities. But before you read on, you might want to take the time to try some experiments of your own.

- Try creating your own `COpenGLView` class, using the text.

- Instead of having a wire cube and a sphere as the default scene, add in some lines that indicate the major axes, using green for the positive axes and red for the negative.

- Replace the default scene with the solid-teapot routine from the auxiliary library. Then you'll see why we had wire-frame objects in the default scene.

7
Display Lists and Fonts

It is a capital mistake to theorize before one has data.

—Sherlock Holmes

Caching OpenGL Commands

In chapter 6 we created a stock background for our default OpenGL view. Although we can easily generate a background for our model, it's time consuming to go through all those calculations every time we need to rerender the scene. After all, the stock scene doesn't change from frame to frame. Only the viewpoint or the model will change. If we have to rerender something that doesn't change, there should be a method of optimizing our program by caching those OpenGL commands. Well, there is, and it's called *display lists*, the subject of this chapter.

The limited commands that are acceptable between a `glBegin()`/`glEnd()` pair only describe an OpenGL primitive. Thus if you're going to repeatedly execute the same sequence of OpenGL commands, you can create and store a display list and then have this cached sequence of calls repeated with minimal overhead, since all of the vertices, lighting calculations, textures, and matrix operations stored in that list are calculated only when the list is created, not when it's replayed. Only the *results* of the calculations end up being stored in display lists; thus any complicated calculations can usually benefit from being placed in a display list and having them replayed at a different time. This speeds up your program and is called *display-list*, or *deferred* or *retained mode:* The commands are compiled, not executed. In contrast, *immediate mode* refers to putting OpenGL commands into the graphics pipeline when they are encountered.

Dynamic or Adaption Tessellation

A particularly useful feature of display lists is that they enable you to cache changes in models without having to compute them more than once. For example, suppose that you're trying to model a flight simulator above a busy airport. You could draw each type of airplane and hangar from a display list to save time, but if the plane or hangar is a kilometer or more away from the current viewpoint, that level of detail in the original model might be too much. Instead it's a simple matter to generate three or four display lists that gradually simplify a model as the distance from the viewpoint becomes large enough to overwhelm any visible differences. This greatly speeds up the rendering time required for the simulation, especially when there's more than one model to render.

Creating a Display List

Creating a display list is very simple. Let's suppose that we have some code that creates a static model. The important part of the code is within the `glBegin()`/`glEnd()` pair. The normal function for the stock scene does something like this:

```
// start rendering the stock scene
glBegin( GL_POLYGON );
    ..... details don't matter
glEnd();
// finished rendering the stock scene
```

A display list records the *results* of a `glBegin()`/`glEnd()` sequence and saves the resulting vertices, matrices, materials, lighting calculations, raster images, and textures. Thus when you record a display list, the current state of OpenGL is used to create the display list; when the list ends, the current state is whatever the original state was *plus* any changes made during the recording of the display list. Replaying the display list uses the current state, *not* the state that was in effect when the list was recorded. When the replay ends, the current state is the state when the replay started *plus* any changes to the state that were replayed as part of the display list.

This concept can be used to distinct advantage. Remember, when recording and playing back display lists, you have to be aware of the state that was in effect when the list was recorded, the states that are changed by executing the display list, and the state in which you'll be executing the list. You usually don't want to save all state information and pop it afterward; after all, we're doing this to speed up the program! However, you'll need to understand what the current states are and to push/pop or in some other way reset those states that need to remain unchanged after the display list executes. We'll go over this in an example in a later section. For now let's examine how you go about recording a display list.

Recording a Display List

When creating a display list, you use the `glNewList()` and `glEndList()` commands as separators. The first function—`glNewList()`—takes two arguments: The first is a unique integer argument used to identify the display list; the second is a flag indicating whether to simply compile the display list or to compile and immediately execute the display list. The second parameter is useful for the lazy evaluation of display lists. The `glEndList()` function takes no arguments and simply serves as a delineator.

Creating a display list is pretty simple:

```
// define a unique number for our display list
#define MYLIST    1
// start recording the display list
::glNewList( MYLIST, GL_COMPILE ); // just record for now
    // start rendering the display list
    ::glBegin( GL_POLYGON );
        ..... details don't matter
    ::glEnd();
    // finished rendering the display list
::glEndList();
// finshed creating the display list
```

The commands executed between a `glNewList()` and `glEndList()` pair use the parameter values in effect when the list was created, not values when the list is replayed. Thus if you generate a display list that's based on a vector pointer, only the values of the pointer are used, not the pointer itself. In other words, you can't set up the array of vertices, create the display list using that array, change the vertices in the array, and then execute the display list and expect the new array values to be in effect.

In addition to the restrictions on the commands that can be placed in `glBegin()` and `glEnd()` pairs, there are further restrictions on commands that can be used in display lists but not in the `glBegin()` and `glEnd()` pairs. These commands aren't compiled into the display list but are executed immediately, regardless of the display list mode. Most of these commands are listed below.

- `glIsList()`
- `glGenLists()`
- `glDeleteLists()`
- `glFeedbackBuffer()`
- `glSelectBuffer()`
- `glRenderMode()`
- `glReadPixels()`
- `glPixelStore()`
- `glFlush()`
- `glFinish()`
- `glIsEnabled()`
- `glGet*()`

These are commands that can be stored on the server and not on the client. For example, only the client knows its current state, so any commands that query the current state can't be placed in a display list, in keeping with OpenGL's client/server architecture. Remember, even though you might be running Windows95, OpenGL can run on many other platforms. So those functions that query the state, such as `glGet*()`, or routines that depend on clients' state, such as `glFinish()`, can't be compiled in display lists. You should also note that calling `glNewList()` while inside another `glNewList()` generates an error. You can, however, call a display list while creating a display list, as we'll see later.

Executing a Display List

Once you've created a display list, it's a simple matter to execute it. Executing a display list is done with one of two functions. One is a specialized form that is used for sequences of display lists, a topic we'll cover in a later section. The other function is the basic method of calling a single display list. The `glCallList()` command takes a single argument, the unique integer ID that you gave a previously defined display list. If the ID doesn't correspond to a valid display list, nothing happens. When a display list is executed, it's as if the display list commands were inserted into the place where you made the `glCallList()` command, except that any state variables that have changed between the display list creation and execution times are ignored. However, if any state variables are changed from within the display list, they remain changed after the display list completes execution. The OpenGL commands `glPushAttrib()` and `glPopAttrib()` were created for such cases. These commands save and restore state variables. If you also want to save and restore the current matrix, you'll need to use the `glPushMatrix()` and `glPopMatrix()` commands.

To call the display list we generated previously, we'd issue the following command:

```
::glCallList( MYLIST ); // execute my list
```

The state of OpenGL after a display list is executed depends on what's in the list. For example, suppose that our list was created as follows:

```
::glNewList( MYLIST, GL_COMPILE );
    // start rendering the stock scene
    ::glBegin( GL_QUAD );
    ::glVertex3f( 1.0f, 0.0f,-1.0f );
    ::glVertex3f( 1.0f, 0.0f, 1.0f );
    ::glVertex3f(-1.0f, 0.0f, 1.0f );
    ::glVertex3f(-1.0f, 0.0f,-1.0f );
    ::glEnd();
    ::glTranslatef( 1.0f, 0.0f, 1.0f );
::glEndList();
```

Note that there's a translation after the vertices have been defined. This causes the vertices following the execution of this display list to be translated. We could use this to draw the same square repeatedly, having it translated each time, and have the squares connected at the corners. In order to get five connected squares, we would use the following commands:

```
::glCallList( MYLIST );
::glCallList( MYLIST );
::glCallList( MYLIST );
::glCallList( MYLIST );
::glCallList( MYLIST );
```

This sequence would also leave the Modelview matrix translated five units in the +z and +x directions. You'd have to be careful about what commands you executed before and during display list creation to make sure that these are the ones really needed.

Generating a Unique Display List ID

Some complications can arise in getting a unique display list ID. You can hope that your programs will always be so simple that when someone adding a feature doesn't accidentally reuse a display list ID. But it's easy enough to guarantee that all your IDs are unique. Windows provides the function `RegisterWindowsMessage()` so that you can get a guaranteed unique message ID from the operating system, necessary when processes need to communicate. Display list IDs are unique to each RC that's running, so if you're just working on an application that's going to have a short lifetime and is pretty much self-contained, you're probably safe in assuming that you don't have to worry about nonunique IDs. However, if this is for your job, then you're probably aware that prototypes have a nasty habit of turning into product.

The `glIsList()` Function

Much as you can generate unique message IDs using the operating system, OpenGL provides two functions to guarantee the uniqueness of display list IDs. The `glIsList()` function takes an ID and returns `GL_TRUE` if the ID is already in use. Since there is nothing special about display list IDs, it's a pretty simple matter to construct a function to generate a unique ID. If we allocate the IDs in order and keep track of the last ID issued, we can easily construct a function to always return a unique ID. Listing 7.1 shows how you might implement such a function. Note two features: The `m_LastDisplayListID` variable should be considered a member of the `COpenGLView` class; second, the purpose of the variable is to retain the last ID dispensed. The range of valid IDs doesn't include 0, so it's reserved to indicate either that a display list needs to be generated (or else it would have an ID) or that the function failed to return an ID.

Listing 7.1   Generating a Unique Display List ID Using `glIsList()`

```
GLint COpenGLView::GetNewDisplayListID()
{
    GLint first, last;
    first = m_LastDisplayListID; // in class definition
    last = first+10001;
```

Listing 7.1   Generating a Unique Display List ID Using `glIsList()` (continued)

```
      ASSERT( last > first );
      while( ++first <= last )
         {
         if ( GL_TRUE == ::glIsList( first ) )
            continue;
         // we found a unique ID, return it
         return (m_LastDisplayListID = first);
         }
      // reserve 0 as failure
      return 0;
   }
```

This function is fine when you need to generate only a few IDs at a time. However, sometimes you need to generate a whole stream of unique, continuous IDs, as described next.

The `glGenLists()` Function

This function takes one argument, the *range*, and returns an ID such that the next *range* IDs are continuous. (In other words, if ID *n* is returned, the last valid ID would be *n + range –1*). The display list IDs that are generated are empty display lists. They are marked as reserved but are empty. If you fail to assign a display list to any of these IDs, they are wasted. If the display lists can't be generated for some reason, 0 is returned and no lists are generated.

Deleting and Reusing Display List IDs

Occasionally you might want to release or free up some display list IDs. The `glDeleteLists()` function deletes a contiguous group of display lists. The two parameters the function requires are the ID of the first list to delete and the range of lists to delete. After the function returns, the display lists *n* though *n + range –1* are now available. All storage locations allocated to the specified display lists are freed, and the names are available for reuse. Any IDs within the range that do not have an associated display list are ignored. If the range is 0, nothing happens.

If you want to immediately reuse one or more display list IDs, you can simply reuse the ID(s) immediately by using the `glNewList()` function with the IDs to be reused. When a display list ID is reused, it is replaced only when `glEndList()` is called.

Sequential Display Lists

The command for creating display list IDs is `glGenLists()`. The primary purpose of this command is convenience, as verifying a series of potential IDs for availability is tedious at best, so OpenGL has provided a mechanism for reserving a sequence of unique display list IDs. This is where the range parameter for the `glGenLists()` comes in.

This feature is particularly handy for rendering objects that exist (or are created) in some order, such as 3D character sets. An example in the *OpenGL Programming Guide* uses this technique to generate stroked fonts. Each character is assigned to a display list ID that corresponds to its ASCII value. For example, the letter *A* is ASCII value 65, so display list ID 65 is assigned the strokes for generating the character A. These steps are repeated for the rest of the letters needed, and then the display lists are executed by using the `glCallLists()` function. Unlike the `glCallList()` function seen earlier, `glCallLists()` function takes three arguments. The last argument is a void pointer to a vector that contains the order of the display list IDs you want executed. The middle parameter tells `glCallLists()` the size (in bytes) of each element of the vector, using one of a series of enum values provided by OpenGL.

What use is this for generating more than one set of sequential display lists? Well, there is one more OpenGL command that is provided to make sequential display lists easier to use (but *not* easier to create!). The `glListBase()` command takes an integer value that is used as an offset when calling subsequent `glCallLists()` commands. Note that it has no effect on either `glCallList()` (singular) or `glNewList()`. Thus when you use `glGenLists()`, the returned value is used as the base value when you make calls to `glCallLists()`. However, you have to manually add this base value when you define a display list.

Generating a Display List for a Character Set

For example, let's generate a list for the twenty-six uppercase characters in the ASCII character set. First, we'd reserve twenty-six consecutive display list IDs for the characters and reserve the returned value, as follows:

```
GLuint base = ::glGenLists(26);
```

We have no control over the returned value; we know only that there are now twenty-six reserved IDs, from **base** to **base+25**. A convenient way of calling display lists for characters is to use the value of the character. Thus we could allocate some extra space at the beginning of the reserved display list

IDs to account for the initial value of our first vector index (in this case it's 65, or 'A'). Or we could subtract the initial value from the generated base value, which is preferred if you're going to be generating lots of lists. The other alternative makes it simpler if you don't have that many. An added complication is that `glGenLists()` returns an unsigned int, and thus you'd have to be careful with the calculations to avoid wrapping the values around. For example, using the **base** value generated earlier and letting **RenderLetter** be some function that takes an index into an array of rendering commands for each letter, we have:

```
for ( GLint i = 0 ; i < 25 ; i++ )
    {
    ::glNewList( base+i, GL_COMPILE );
    RenderLetter(i);
    ::glEndList();
    }
```

Then, to have the text rendered, you'd create a sequence of display list indices that spelled out what you wanted. This is made easier because we've associated the value of each ASCII letter with the corresponding display list. Thus to render a text string, the code might look like this:

```
char *text = "THIS IS SOME OPENGL TEXT";
::glCallLists( strlen(text), GL_BYTE, text );
```

Note that a **GL_BYTE** is the same size as an ASCII char, but if you are using Unicode, you'll have to make the appropriate changes.

Finally, you may wonder just what the **RenderLetter()** routine does. It does whatever it has to—it's entirely up to you. Since serial display lists were made to accommodate a sequence of display lists, not just character rendering, you are entirely responsible for the definition of each display list. For character rendering you probably want to render each letter in the xy or xz plane, making them either flat or extruded, and probably performing a translation after you're done rendering, placing the updated origin just after the end of the character that you've just rendered. This allows sequential display lists to be strung together and to have the rendered characters positioned one after the other. This is the end of OpenGL's support of character lists. However, *wgl* provides some extra support for Windows character sets, and we'll explore these features later in this chapter.

Sharing Display Lists between RCs and Threads

When you create an OpenGL rendering context, it has its own display list space. Sometimes you don't want to go through the process of re-creating display lists, particularly if they are common to most of your OpenGL programs. The OpenGL function `wglShareLists()` was designed just for this purpose; it enables a rendering context to share the display list space of another RC. Any number of rendering contexts can share a single display list space. All the IDs and definitions of display lists in a shared display list space are shared. Once a rendering context shares a display list space, the rendering context always uses the shared space until the rendering context is deleted. When the last rendering context of a shared space is deleted, the shared space is deleted.

You can share display lists with rendering contexts only within the same process. However, not all rendering contexts in a process can share display lists. Rendering contexts can share display lists only if they use the same implementation of OpenGL functions. All client rendering contexts of a given pixel format can always share display lists.

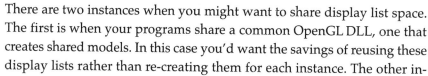

There are two instances when you might want to share display list space. The first is when your programs share a common OpenGL DLL, one that creates shared models. In this case you'd want the savings of reusing these display lists rather than re-creating them for each instance. The other instance is when you're performing multithreaded OpenGL rendering. Remember that a thread can have only one *current* rendering context at a time. A process can have multiple rendering contexts by means of multithreading. An application can perform multithreaded drawing by making different RCs current to different threads and supplying each thread with its own RC and DC. If you want to share display lists, you should note that it's available only with the updated OpenGL version 1.0 that came with Windows NT 3.51 or Windows 95.

Hierarchical Display Lists

When you call `glCallList()` inside the definition of a new display list, you are creating *nested*, or *hierarchical*, display lists. Nested display lists are useful when the object you're compiling into a display list is itself made up of repeated parts. When `glNewList()` encounters a call to `glCallList()`, the command that is inserted is a call to that display list, not the commands represented by that display list. For example, consider the following code:

```
// create three display lists
::glNewList( LIST_ONE, GL_COMPILE );
    ... some code
::glEndList();

::glNewList( LIST_TWO, GL_COMPILE );
    ... some code
::glEndList();

::glNewList( LIST_THREE, GL_COMPILE );
    ... some code
::glEndList();
```

This simply creates three unique display lists. To generate a hierarchical display list composed of these three lists, we'd write the following:

```
// create a hierarchical display list
::glNewList( NESTED_LIST, GL_COMPILE );
    ::glCallList( LIST_ONE );
    ::glCallList( LIST_TWO );
    ::glCallList( LIST_THREE );
::glEndList();
```

The following line will execute the nested display list and thus call the three display lists nested inside:

```
::glCallList( NESTED_LIST );
```

That's all pretty straightforward. But say that you now wanted to modify the **LIST_TWO** sequence, retain the other two, and execute this modified sequence. This is the advantage of hierarchical display lists; you can modify the commands associated with a display list ID and have the new commands executed in other display lists that use this ID.

```
// modify the second list
::glNewList( LIST_TWO, GL_COMPILE );
    ... some code that's different
::glEndList();

// now execute the modified hierarchical list
::glCallList( NESTED_LIST );
```

You can see the power associated with this feature. If you're writing an application that uses many static objects in nonstatic ways, such as an architectural program that creates buildings out of standard parts, the ability to cache objects and to replay them whenever you need, plus the ability to nest them, provides the basis for a very powerful modeling feature.

Using Display Lists in the `COpenGLView` Class

Now let's incorporate display lists into the `COpenGLView` class. A natural place to use them is the `RenderStockScene()` function. After all, we had only one stock scene, and users of the `COpenGLView` class would probably like to define some stock scenes for their own use. So let's add another stock scene.

We'll use the surface made up of triangles arranged about the origin that we created in chapter 6 and will call this routine `StockSceneTriangles()`, shown in Listing 7.2. All it does is render the triangles about the current origin in the *xz* plane.

Listing 7.2   A Triangled Surface on the *XZ* Plane

```
// Draw a square surface of red and blue triangles
// all touching the origin.
void COpenGLView::StockSceneTriangles( )
{
    // define all vertices     X       Y       Z
    GLfloat surface0[3] = {  0.0f,  0.0f,  0.0f };
    GLfloat surface1[3] = {+5.0f,  0.0f,  0.0f };
    GLfloat surface2[3] = {+5.0f,  0.0f, -5.0f };
    GLfloat surface3[3] = {  0.0f,  0.0f, -5.0f };
    GLfloat surface4[3] = {-5.0f,  0.0f, -5.0f };
    GLfloat surface5[3] = {-5.0f,  0.0f,  0.0f };
    GLfloat surface6[3] = {-5.0f,  0.0f, +5.0f };
    GLfloat surface7[3] = {  0.0f,  0.0f, +5.0f };
    GLfloat surface8[3] = {+5.0f,  0.0f, +5.0f };
    GLfloat surface9[3] = {+5.0f,  0.0f,  0.0f };

    // define the two colors
    GLfloat color1[3] = { 0.5f, 0.0f, 0.0f };
    GLfloat color2[3] = { 0.0f, 0.0f, 0.5f };

    ::glBegin( GL_TRIANGLES );
        ::glColor3fv( color1 );
```

Listing 7.2   A Triangled Surface on the XZ Plane (continued)

```
                    ::glVertex3fv( surface0 );
                    ::glVertex3fv( surface1 );
                    ::glVertex3fv( surface2 );
                    ::glColor3fv( color2 );
                    ::glVertex3fv( surface0 );
                    ::glVertex3fv( surface2 );
                    ::glVertex3fv( surface3 );
                    ::glColor3fv( color1 );
                    ::glVertex3fv( surface0 );
                    ::glVertex3fv( surface3 );
                    ::glVertex3fv( surface4 );
                    ::glColor3fv( color2 );
                    ::glVertex3fv( surface0 );
                    ::glVertex3fv( surface4 );
                    ::glVertex3fv( surface5 );
                    ::glColor3fv( color1 );
                    ::glVertex3fv( surface0 );
                    ::glVertex3fv( surface5 );
                    ::glVertex3fv( surface6 );
                    ::glColor3fv( color2 );
                    ::glVertex3fv( surface0 );
                    ::glVertex3fv( surface6 );
                    ::glVertex3fv( surface7 );
                    ::glColor3fv( color1 );
                    ::glVerte3fv( surface0 );
                    ::glVertex3fv( surface7 );
                    ::glVertex3fv( surface8 );
                    ::glColor3fv( color2 );
                    ::glVertex3fv( surface0 );
                    ::glVertex3fv( surface8 );
                    ::glVertex3fv( surface9 );
               ::glEnd();
          }
```

We'll also rename our original stock scene function to StockScene-Checkerboard(), and we'll add another, empty routine, called StockScene-User(), which is available for derived classes to override. To generate the stock scenes, we'll add a function that uses a user-set member variable to determine which stock scene to render. Listing 7.3 shows how this function looks.

Listing 7.3   Selecting a Stock Scene to Render

```
// Call the routines to render the stock scene
BOOL COpenGLView::GenerateStockScene( eStockSceneID id )
{
    // if the display list for the stock
    // scene hasn't been generated, then do so
    // we'll reuse this ID for all stock scenes
    if ( 0 == m_StockSceneListIndex )
        {
        // get a unique id
        m_StockSceneListIndex = GetNewDisplayListID( );

        if ( 0 == m_StockSceneListIndex ) // failed
            {
            return FALSE;
            }
        }

    // we have an ID, so set (or reset) it
    // and create the new stock scene

    ::glNewList( m_StockSceneListIndex, GL_COMPILE );
    GenerateThisStockScene( id );
    ::glEndList();

    return TRUE;
}

// This routine generates the stock scenes. The functions
// called are simply expected to render a scene
void COpenGLView::GenerateThisStockScene( eStockSceneID id )
{
    switch( id )
        {
        case eStockSceneSet:
        case eStockSceneNone:
            ; // an empty list
            break;

        case eStockSceneUserDefined:
            StockSceneUserDefined();
            break;
```

Listing 7.3　Selecting a Stock Scene to Render (continued)

```
        case eStockSceneTriangles:
            StockSceneTriangles();
            break;

        case eStockSceneCheckerboard:
            StockSceneCheckerboard();
            break;

        default:
            break;
        }
    }
```

Finally, we can rewrite the **RenderStockScene()** function to work on a member variable that can be set, **m_SelectedStockScene**. This member is selected directly or by calling the function **SelectStockScene()**. Since you typically want to set up all the parameters of a view when it's created, you'd normally do this in the constructor. However, it's impossible to generate an OpenGL display list without first initializing an OpenGL RC. We get around this problem by letting the stock scene display list be generated just before the display list is used. If **m_SelectedStockScene** is set, a new display list is to be generated. After the display list is generated and the display list ID for the stock scene is saved, **m_SelectedStockScene** is cleared. Listing 7.4 shows this updated function. Note that the stock scene can also be dynamically changed and that this will cause a new display list to be generated, but the *original* stock scene display list ID is reused.

Listing 7.4　`RenderStockScene()` Using a Display List

```
void COpenGLView::RenderStockScene()
{
    // if the display list for the stock
    // scene hasn't been generated, then do so
    // the selected variable is used only to change
    // the stock scene
    if ( m_SelectedStockScene )
        {
        GenerateStockScene( m_SelectedStockScene );
        m_SelectedStockScene = eStockSceneSet; // clear it
        }
```

Listing 7.4 `RenderStockScene()` **Using a Display List (continued)**

```
    if ( 0 != m_StockSceneListIndex )
        {
        ::glCallList( m_StockSceneListIndex );
        }
    }
```

Rendering Windows Fonts in OpenGL

Probably the most glaring deficiency in OpenGL's implementation is its lack of direct support of text objects. However, the reasoning is simple. Since text depends on there being a font in which to display the characters, there needs to be a description of these glyphs somewhere. OpenGL is a system-independent API, and there is really no reason to carry around the baggage of some font-rendering code when the host machine's operating system no doubt has its own font-rendering software. Indeed this is the approach found on all OpenGL implementations, Windows being no exception.

In fact, if you've used GDI fonts before, you're already familiar with the setup for using them in OpenGL. There are just a few twists to watch out for. If you're using a double-buffered window, you can't use GDI calls in your OpenGL window. You have to generate the glyphs for each character and then save them, which is where display lists come in handy. In fact, you'll see that most of the display list commands we have examined are designed to support text rendering.

The steps for generating a display list of a particular font under Windows are as follows:

1. Select the desired font characteristics.
2. Select and then generate that font, using the current DC.
3. Call one of the two *wgl* functions to automatically generate the glyphs and assign them to display list IDs sequentially.
4. Deselect that font from the DC. (We have the display lists we need.)

This is surprisingly easy, because two *wgl* functions have been added that take care of generating the display lists for the font glyphs for us. In fact, with the proper wrapping, it can be easier to use fonts under OpenGL than in GDI! Let's look at the two functions that save us a lot of work.

The `wglUseFontBitmaps()` **Function**

The `wglUseFontBitmaps()` function creates a set of bitmap display lists based on the glyphs in the currently selected font in the current DC for use in the current OpenGL RC. These bitmaps can then be used to draw characters in an OpenGL image. The `wglUseFontBitmaps()` function takes a DC argument and then values that indicate the starting character, the number of characters to create, and the value to use as the base offset for the generated display lists.

The documentation on the `wglUseFontBitmaps()` function tells us that each of the display lists consists of a single call to `glBitmap()`. Thus each display list consists of a rendering of a bitmap on the screen. In other words, the bitmap is rendered directly on the frame buffer. This indicates that `wglUseFontBitmaps()` is useful when your text doesn't need to change size and you need only a flat representation of text.

Also you'll have to specify where the bitmap is drawn in terms of a *raster position*, or window coordinates. Therefore these display lists are useful only when you want text that doesn't rotate or scale with the rest of your model. For example, if you want to label part of your model and need to make sure that the text is always readable no matter what the user's selected viewpoint or orientation, you'd use the function `wglUseFontBitmaps()`. A nice feature is that the current raster position is updated after *each* bitmap, which places the current raster position just after the last bitmap displayed. In this manner we can simply provide a starting position and then a string of bitmaps, and each bitmap will be correctly positioned so that the following bitmap is positioned correctly after it.

But how are you going to get your text labels to follow around the objects they are supposed to label when the model is spinning around? Never fear! The `glRasterPos*()` command is used for positioning bitmaps. This command introduces the concept of a current position. In this case it's the starting position for raster operations and thus is used to position the current raster position for such commands as `glBitmap()`, `glDrawPixels()`, and `glCopyPixels()`.

In the case we're interested in, you use `glRasterPos*()` just as you would a `glVertex*()` command; you set the coordinates (in 3D space) and expect the coordinates to get transformed to raster coordinates. The only difference is that the *position* is being transformed, not the object associated with the position. In this case we're simply transforming the starting location to render our display lists of bitmaps. Thus when you use `wglUseFontBitmaps()` to generate display lists and then call them, the resulting text is displayed, starting at the current raster position, and the bitmaps are copied to the raster buffer, giving the effect of always having the text positioned in the *xy* plane of the screen.

Thus you'd use `wglUseFontBitmaps()` when you need to make sure that the text is always visible to the user and that the size of the text relative to its distance from the viewpoint doesn't matter. The transformations are done only on the current raster position, not on the bitmap. When the current raster position is transformed to screen coordinates, *then* the bitmap is copied to the raster buffer. The bitmap will always be the same size, no matter how far away from the viewpoint it is positioned. It may not always be visible, however, since the raster position is checked for clipping before the bitmaps are displayed. Therefore if the initial raster position is outside the clipping area, no text will be displayed, even if that text flows into the viewing volume.

Finally, the utility library provides two commands that make it relatively easy to get from screen coordinates to object coordinates and back. These commands are `gluProject()` and `gluUnProject()`. You use these commands to position text so that it is always in the same location in the viewport window.

Adding Bitmapped Text to `COpenGLView`

We can use the `wglUseFontBitmaps()` function to create a set of bitmap display lists from a specified font name. In order to use this function, you must first select the desired font into the current DC. Since we have the current DC saved away, it's easy to simply pass in the font name, select that font as the current one, use `wglUseFontBitmaps()` to generate the display lists, and then deselect the font to return the DC to its previous state.

We'll create such a function in the `COpenGLView` class so that we can easily display flat text in our OpenGL window. Since we can't be sure of what fonts are available on the current machine, let's build in a default that selects the **SYSTEM_FONT** if a null name is passed in. This way we can always fall back to a font we know exists. We'll also make use of the `GetNewDisplayListIDs()` function to generate our display list IDs. Listing 7.5 shows the initial implementation. The return value is the display list ID that identifies the font bitmaps. This value is used as the base value before using the font.

Listing 7.5   Generating a Bitmapped Font

```
GLuint COpenGLView::GenerateBitmapListForFont(
        char* fontname )
{
    GLuint id;

    if ( 0 == m_pDC ||
```

Listing 7.5   Generating a Bitmapped Font (continued)

```
                        (GLuint)0 == (id = GetNewDisplayListIDs(256)) )
                        {
                        return 0;
                        }

                CFont newfont;
                CFont* oldfont;
                BOOL success;

                if ( NULL != fontname )
                    {
                    LOGFONT logfont;
                    // select 12 point font for now
                    logfont.lfHeight        = -12;
                    logfont.lfWidth         = 0;
                    logfont.lfEscapement    = 0;
                    logfont.lfOrientation   = logfont.lfEscapement;
                    logfont.lfWeight        = FW_NORMAL;
                    logfont.lfItalic        = FALSE;
                    logfont.lfUnderline     = FALSE;
                    logfont.lfStrikeOut     = FALSE;
                    logfont.lfCharSet       = ANSI_CHARSET;
                    logfont.lfOutPrecision  = OUT_DEFAULT_PRECIS;
                    logfont.lfClipPrecision = CLIP_DEFAULT_PRECIS;
                    logfont.lfQuality       = DEFAULT_QUALITY;
                    logfont.lfPitchAndFamily =
                            FF_DONTCARE|DEFAULT_PITCH;

                    lstrcpy ( logfont.lfFaceName, fontname );

                    // CreateFontIndirect returns 0 if it fails
                    success = newfont.CreateFontIndirect( &logfont );
                    oldfont = m_pDC->SelectObject( &newfont );
                    ASSERT( 0 != oldfont );
                    }
                else
                    {
                    // make the system font the device context's
                    // selected font
                    oldfont = (CFont*)m_pDC->SelectStockObject(
                            SYSTEM_FONT );

                    ASSERT( 0 != oldfont );
```

Listing 7.5   Generating a Bitmapped Font (continued)

```
        }
    // Create a set of display lists based on the glyphs
    // of the font. Notice that we really waste the first
    // 32 spaces....
    // if there's a problem delete the display lists
    if ( 0 == success ||
        FALSE == ::wglUseFontBitmaps( m_pDC->m_hDC,
                0, 256, id ) )
        {
        ::glDeleteLists( id, 256 );
        id = 0;
        }
    else
        {
        // replace old font
        m_pDC->SelectObject( oldfont );
        }
    return id;
    }
```

Thus to generate a bitmapped font and then use it, you'd simply supply the font name (or null, if you wanted the system font) and then use the returned ID as the base value for the font display list. A simple routine to take the font ID and a text string is shown in Listing 7.6.

Listing 7.6   The Display List GLTextOut Function

```
void COpenGLView::GLTextOut( GLuint id,
        const char * const textstring )
{
    if ( 0 == id || 0 == textstring )
        {
        return;
        }

    GLsizei size = strlen( textstring );

    ::glListBase( id );
    ::glCallLists( size, GL_UNSIGNED_BYTE,
        (const GLvoid*)textstring );
}
```

Windows 95 and Windows NT have some differences. Particularly when selecting a font using the Windows **LOGFONT** structure, there are differences in the behavior if you use some of the flags to attempt to customize the generated font. Also, some combinations give different behavior between Windows 95 and Windows NT, so unless you write operating system–aware code, you should avoid changing the **LOGFONT** structure unless you absolutely have to. The routines presented here will work on both operating systems.

The routines shown here are ANSI routines. If you must write for an international market and use Unicode, the text-processing routines presented here must be modified to use the macros provided in the compiler-supplied header files. These are simple wrappers that simplify writing code that must be compiled for both ANSI and Unicode.

The `wglUseFontOutlines()` Function

The `wglUseFontOutlines()` function creates a set of 3D polygon- or line-based primitive display lists, based on the glyphs in the currently selected *TrueType* font in the current DC for use in the current OpenGL RC. Stroke and raster fonts are *not* supported. These objects can then be used to draw 3D characters in an OpenGL image. The em-square size of the font is mapped to 1.0 in the *x* and *y* directions, and the characters are positioned in the *xy* plane in the display lists.

The `wglUseFontOutlines()` function takes a DC argument and then values that indicate the starting character, the number of characters to create, and the value to use as the base offset for the generated display lists. So far this looks like the `wglUseFontBitmaps()` function. However, additional arguments control the *extrusion* of the 3D characters in the +z direction (the depth of the generated characters), the *deviation* of the generated primitive vertices from the design outline of the font (how *blocky* you want the resulting characters to be), whether to generate filled polygons or a wire-frame primitive, and finally an array of structures to hold the metrics of each of the generated characters. This last function gives you tighter control over the positioning of the font by letting you do it yourself, if you want.

The `wglUseFontOutlines()` function approximates glyph outlines by subdividing the quadratic B-spline curves found in the TrueType outline into line segments until the distance between the outline and the interpolated midpoint is within the value specified by the *deviation* parameter you've supplied. This is the final format used when generated format is specified as line segments. When you specify polygons as the format, the outlines are further tessellated into separate triangles, triangle fans, triangle strips, or quadrilateral strips to create the surface of each glyph.

Each display list ends with a translation specified with the **gmfCellIncX** and **gmfCellIncY** fields of the corresponding **GLYPHMETRICSFLOAT** structure. This translation enables the drawing of successive characters in their natural direction with a single call to **glCallLists()**. A routine to generate true 3D characters is shown in Listing 7.7; we provide a routine that takes the name of a TrueType font and generates the display lists for each character. The return value is the ID for use as the base offset. These display lists are then used with the **GLTextOut()** routine discussed in Listing 7.6.

Listing 7.7   Generating a 3D Display List Font

```
GLuint COpenGLView::GenerateDisplayListForFont(
        char* fontname, double xt )
{
    GLuint id;

    if ( 0 == m_pDC ||
        (GLuint)0 == (id = GetNewDisplayListIDs(256)) )
        {
        return 0;
        }
    LOGFONT logfont;
    GLYPHMETRICSFLOAT gmf[256];

    // lfHeight can't be used to change the font size
    logfont.lfHeight        = -12;
    logfont.lfWidth         = 0;
    logfont.lfEscapement    = 0;
    logfont.lfOrientation   = logfont.lfEscapement;
    logfont.lfWeight        = FW_NORMAL;
    logfont.lfItalic        = FALSE;
    logfont.lfUnderline     = FALSE;
    logfont.lfStrikeOut     = FALSE;
    logfont.lfCharSet       = ANSI_CHARSET;
    logfont.lfOutPrecision  = OUT_DEFAULT_PRECIS;
    logfont.lfClipPrecision = CLIP_DEFAULT_PRECIS;
    logfont.lfQuality       = DEFAULT_QUALITY;
    logfont.lfPitchAndFamily =
            FF_DONTCARE|DEFAULT_PITCH;

    lstrcpy ( logfont.lfFaceName, fontname );
```

Listing 7.7   Generating a 3D Display List Font (continued)

```
CFont newfont;
// CreateFontIndirect returns 0 if it fails
BOOL success = newfont.CreateFontIndirect( &logfont );
CFont* oldfont = m_pDC->SelectObject( &newfont );
ASSERT( 0 != oldfont );

// Create a set of display lists based on the glyphs
// of the TrueType font
// notice that we really waste the first 32 spaces....
// if there's a problem delete the display lists
if ( 0 == success ||
    FALSE == ::wglUseFontOutlines( m_pDC->m_hDC,
            0,   256,
            id, 0.0f,
            (float)xt, WGL_FONT_POLYGONS, gmf) )
    {
    ::glDeleteLists( id, 256 );
    id = 0;
    }
else
    {
    m_pDC->SelectObject( oldfont );
    }
return id;
}
```

Both the flat font and the 3D font routines are included as part of the
COpenGLView class. A member function called **GenerateDefaultFonts()** provides a default flat font and a default 3D font as part of **COpenGLView** initialization. For an example of what these fonts provide, take a look at the following
code when it is placed inside a **RenderScene()** member function. You'll get
bitmap text that is always legible and outline text that'll rotate with the view.

```
::glColor3f( 0.0f, 0.0f, 1.0f );
::glRasterPos2f( 0.5f, 0.2f );
GLTextOut( m_DefaultFlatTextID, "OpenGL Bitmap Text" );

::glColor3f( 1.0f, 0.0f, 0.0f );
::glTranslatef( -2.5, 0.0, 0.0 );
```

```
::glScalef( .8f, .6f, 0.6f );
GLTextOut( m_DefaultTextID, "OpenGL 3D Text" );
```

As you can see, using the functionality provided by the `COpenGLView` class, you can easily add text to your OpenGL scene.

Summary

Using display lists enables you to speed up the rendering process by precalculating models or parts of models. The wrapped display list manipulation routines found in the `COpenGLView` class make it very easy to generate your own display lists and to later replay them. The added benefit is that you can also use these routines to assist in generating flat and 3D fonts that you can use in your model, with less effort than is normally required to select a GDI font. Since these fonts are stored in display lists, it's easy to be able to mix calls to different fonts, with nothing more than merely changing the display list ID that you want to render with.

 If you find yourself writing modeling code that resembles something you've written before, you should examine the code you're writing to see whether you can replace all similar code with a call to a display list. If only minor parts are different, consider writing a hierarchical display list that encapsulates the differences. It's easy to make a top-level display list call sublists and to dynamically modify those sublists merely by reassociating their IDs with different display lists. Even if you use a routine only once each time a scene is rendered, you still might get a big boost to your rendering speed by creating a display list, simply because of the way display lists are precomputed. With the `COpenGLView` class it's easy to experiment and see what works out best.

Try This

- Rewrite the `GetNewDisplayListID()` function described in this chapter to take an argument for the number of sequential display list IDs to generate. Make this new function use `glGenLists()`. Compare your code to the `GetNewDisplayListIDs()` function in the shared implementation of `COpenGLView`.

- Write your own stock scene and use it.

- Now make your stock scene a display list and use it.

8

OpenGL and Animation

The only reason for time is so that everything doesn't happen all at once.

—Buckaroo Banzai

Now we've reached the heart of the matter! Probably most people reading this book want to know how to not only program an OpenGL Windows program but also get as much rendering speed as possible out of their programs. You can use the following tips to make sure that you are getting the maximum performance from your program:

- Draw only what you need to.
- Use display lists and connected primitives whenever possible.
- Turn off depth testing when you don't need it; when rendering a background, for example.
- Use "illuminated" texture-maps instead of real lights, or simply modify the appropriate vertex colors instead of using lighting.
- Disable smooth shading, lighting, and dithering when you don't need them.
- Use double buffering to smooth out the animation.
- Use the vector forms of the OpenGL commands.
- Avoid pixel operations, as they're notoriously slow!
- Take advantage of any extensions that are available in the currently running version of OpenGL. (See chapter 12.)
- Minimize the OpenGL features your program requires. If possible, allow the user to select the richness of the animation by turning off specific graphics features, such as texture maps or lighting.

- Try to avoid changing the state.

- Perform your own rough object culling, based on the current viewpoint and view vector.

- Dynamically adjust your models, based on the current frame rate.

- Take advantage of distance from the viewpoint to simplify (or eliminate!) polygons, textures, materials, or entire objects.

- Use high-quality models when the user is stationary. Use simpler ones when the viewpoint-object distance and direction are changing.

- Try a smaller window.

- Do any bookkeeping calculations *after* you swap buffers.

Are you looking for raw speed, the more the better? Ahh. You're greedy. Perhaps your application has to display some sort of complex model and animate it in response to a user direction. Perhaps it is a model of a plane that allows the user to grab onto one end and spin it about its center; you're interested in getting as much raw speed as possible.

In this chapter we'll discuss how to hog the processor to varying degrees, as well as how to get to a maximum frame rate (but no more). Of course, all the acceleration techniques discussed so far need to be heeded. Sloppy code is no excuse for mediocre animation. You should hone your code, looking for ways to speed it up. Measuring execution times and experimenting with various forms of code will give you valuable experience with being able to write fast OpenGL code. When you've done all that, you're ready to hog the processor to achieve that last iota of speed you might need.

Animation Loops in Windows

You should be forewarned that the following code is considered "bad form" for the Windows message queue. Once you understand that, nearly all other operations on the machine—any automatic backups or disk defrags, background communications, or *anything* that's trying to run along with your program—are going to come to a near total halt. That said, let's look at various ways of being a processor hog.

The basic problem is that Windows is a multitasking messaging-based operating system; you're supposed to share the processor with other running applications, including the operating system. The traditional method of fast repainting is to use a `PeekMessage()` loop to take up all available idle time. You'd typically see something like the code in Listing 8.1 in animated Windows programs:

Listing 8.1   A Typical Windows Animation Loop

```
while ( 1 ) // forever
    {
    if ( ::PeekMessage( &msg, 0, 0, 0, PM_REMOVE ))
        {
        // we have a message in the msg struct,
        // so process it

        // ...local message processing goes here

        // if it's not processed here, pass it on
        ::TranslateMessage( &msg );
        ::DispatchMessage( &msg );
        }
    else // there is no message in the queue, so animate
        {
        // if the program is animated
        if (AnimationRunning() )
            RunAnimation(); // my function
        else // no message, no animation
            ::WaitMessage(); // waste some cycles
        }
    }
```

To a Windows programmer Listing 8.1 looks like rather unfriendly code. You're basically spinning in a loop while checking for messages after the animation runs. A typical application should use a **PeekMessage()** loop for as little time as possible. A Windows-based application should, as soon and as often as possible, inform Windows that it's idle. An application is idle when the **GetMessage()** or **WaitMessage()** function is called and no messages are waiting in the application's message queue. Using any messaging method of animation will eat up processor time and run down any battery-powered computer. But you probably don't care about battery-powered computers, just in fast rendering, so this is the avenue you're forced to travel. It's not the most cooperative way of achieving Windows animation, but it works.

At least it works if you're not programming in MFC. MFC's messaging structure dosen't adapt well to this methodology. In MFC each thread has its own message loop, and MFC has its own background processing requirements. Listing 8.2 shows some of the considerations you should be aware of when using MFC for animation or any other task that requires background processing.

Listing 8.2   An MFC-Style Animation Loop

```
while ( TRUE == bAnimate )
    {
    while( ::PeekMessage(&msg, 0, 0, 0, PM_REMOVE ))
        {
        // we have a mesage

        // if it's a Quit message
        if (msg.message == WM_QUIT)
            {
            bAnimate = FALSE; // turn off loop
            ::PostQuitMessage(nExitCode);
            break;
            }
        if ( !AfxGetApp()->PreTranslateMessage( &msg ) )
            {
            ::TranslateMessage( &msg );
            ::DispatchMessage( &msg );
            }
        }
        // Update UI
        AfxGetApp()->OnIdle(0);
        // Free any temp objects
        AfxGetApp()->OnIdle(1);

        // Perform your background processing here
        }
```

These examples show how to embed a message loop in one of your (non-CWinThread-derived) classes.

If you look at the main message loop found in the Run() member function in MFC's CWinThread class, you'll see how MFC processes its messages. Another, safer variation is to make the message loop perform many of the same functions that MFC needs to perform in its message loop, by modifying what MFC does in its own message loop. Listing 8.3 shows how you might write such a loop.

Listing 8.3   The Preferred MFC Animation Loop

```
while ( bAnimated )
{
    while ( ::PeekMessage( &msg, 0, 0, 0, PM_NOREMOVE ) )
    {
```

Listing 8.3   The Preferred MFC Animation Loop (continued)

```
if ( !PumpMessage( ) )
    {
        bAnimated = FALSE;
        ::PostQuitMessage( );
        break;
    }
}
LONG lIdle = 0;
while ( AfxGetApp()->OnIdle(lIdle++ ) )
    ; // let MFC have the first crack

// Perform animation here
RunAnimation();
}
```

You use this code by embedding it in a function that will get called after Windows is up (in response to a **WM_PAINT** message is a good place, as in the **On-Draw()** member function). The code will run as long as there is animation to do. The **PeekMessage()** function is repeatedly called, just as in the previous examples. If a message is found, the undocumented **CWinThread::PumpMessage()** function is called to perform the normal message translation and dispatching. (This is right out of the MFC source code. Look in the MFC file THRDCORE.CPP to see how it works.)

All of these examples have one thing in common: They assume that your animation code is not in its own **CWinThread**-derived class. If you're writing your own multithreaded application to perform animation, you can do your own animation in the **OnIdle()** function. Creating a multithreaded application with one thread responsible for OpenGL rendering is a unique avenue to fast rendering speed. If your target machine is a multiprocessor, this is definitely the way to go. However, multithreaded application programming is itself the subject of a small book and beyond the scope of this one. If you want to pursue this subject further, look at the GLTHREAD example program included with Visual C++ and read Jeffery Richter's *Advanced Windows*. (If you're serious about Windows 95 and Windows NT programming, you should already have this book in your library!)

If you're using a multithreaded app, you should be aware that **PeekMessage()** looks only at the message queue of the calling thread. A queue attached to another thread won't get messages even if they belong to the same process. However, you can *post* a message to another thread (so long as it's got a message queue and it's made at least one call to a USER32 or GDI function, using `PostThreadMessage()`. You can use this function to kickstart an animation thread.

A Slightly Less Extreme Animation Loop

Another alternative to programming your own loop is to use *Windows* as the looping mechanism. This is pretty simple in that the programming requirements are less, and the Windows user interface will still work at nearly the same speed when the program is running as when it isn't. You will see that background operations will be severely timesliced; for example, background repainting of windows not in focus will proceed in a blocky manner, background printing will slow to a crawl, and so on.

The code is very simple. At the end of the scene rendering, we simply invalidate the window and send a message to repaint it, thus forcing Windows to loop through its own message queue, assign priorities, do a little background processing, and then repaint the window, at which time another repaint message is sent. Listing 8.4 shows the code that you need to add to your `OnDraw()` function.

Listing 8.4   MFC Animation without a Direct Loop

```
if ( bAnimated )
    {
    InvalidateRect( 0, FALSE );
    GetParent()->PostMessage(WM_PAINT);
    }
```

The code is pretty simple and doesn't disrupt the Windows messaging system. The code tells Windows that the entire client rectangle is invalid and to not erase the background of the window. Then we *post* a message to paint the window not *send* a message. *Posting* a message merely places a message in a window's message queue and returns to the caller without waiting for the window (in this case, ourselves) to process the message. *Sending* a message by using `SendMessage()` would call the window's message loop directly and would wait until the message had been processed before control returned. An endless loop is not what we want, so we use the `PostMessage()` function instead.

If your application is either always maximized (taking up the full screen with no Minimize button) or its window can't be moved, you might be able to get away with a more extreme messaging system. If you can, you'll gain a great deal of speed by performing your own region updating. For example, if you're animating a set scene, such as a 3D bar graph, a CAD model, or another model that occupies a specific area of the screen at any given time, you can update the region yourself. The point is to avoid clearing the entire screen using `glClear()`. You'll need to set the region to be updated to the proper color (and depth) values, most easily done by drawing a rectangle of the background color. Another way is to select the region to be updated, using the stencil buffer. It's a bit more work, but it's also faster. On the other hand, if your program is a flight simulator, the entire scene can change from frame to frame, and you might have to redraw the entire scene at each frame. However, you still might need only part of the window for the outside scene, if, for example, you're also drawing the cockpit controls and some window frame supports. In this case you can use the stencil buffer to select where to update the window. (You also might examine the GL_WIN_swap_hint and GL_EXT_clip_volume_hint extensions.)

The point is to avoid redrawing the whole scene if you don't have to. The `COpenGLView` class generically erases the entire window simply because this takes care of all cases. If your program has a geometry such that you can predict beforehand which areas of the window will need to be updated, you can significantly affect your rendering speed by taking this into account in your redraws. Remember, the way to get fast drawing is to draw as little as possible! (In other words if you spend some brain cycles to figure out a way to use some CPU cycles to calculate what needs to be updated rather than just blindly updating everything, this will almost always yield faster results.)

Letting Windows Tell Us When to Redraw

The safest method of animation is to use a Windows *timer,* a Windows routine that periodically fires off a **WM_TIMER** message to your message queue. You'd use the following code to set up a timer event in your initialization code:

```
if ( bAnimated )
    // Turn on a timer
    SetTimer(1, 50, NULL);
else
    // Turn off the timer
    KillTimer(1);
```

You'll also need to provide a `KillTimer()` in your `OnDestroy()` member function. This code will send off a `WM_TIMER` message, which you can easily intercept in MFC by setting up an `OnTimer()` member function to handle the timer messages. This code is pretty simple, as shown in Listing 8.5.

Listing 8.5   Using Animation for a Timer Event

```
void CMyView::OnTimer( UINT nIDEvent )
{
    // You did save the DC and RC, right?
    RunAnimation();

    // call the CView's timer routine
    CView::OnTimer(nIDEvent);

    // Remove any extra timer messages
    MSG msg;
    while( ::PeekMessage(&msg, m_hWnd,
            WM_TIMER, WM_TIMER, PM_REMOVE));
}
```

This method is very simple but does have its drawbacks. Windows timers let you specify timers with millisecond accuracy. However, they respond at only about 55 milliseconds for Windows 95 (10 milliseconds for NT). This is the famous clock "tick" that triggers 18.2 times a second. It's a holdover from the old DOS days, when an 8086 chip was the latest in personal computing. Nonetheless, it's still pretty useful for triggering periodic events. However, for really smooth animation, you need *at least* 15 frames per second (which is still choppy to some people), and you'd really like 24 frames per second. That's right up there with how motion pictures are filmed. The nice thing about timers is that we can tell them when to notify us that it's time to redraw. The bad things are that the standard Windows timer doesn't have the resolution that we require and that the time you specify is actually a *minimum* time, not an absolute time.

Timer messages are on the bottom of the message pecking order and are serviced only when no other messages are in the queue. So you might specify 55 milliseconds, but in reality the messages might come in later—sometimes *much* later. If your rendering takes some time, you might get another timer message queued while the rendering is going on. That's why Listing 8.5 has some code to eat any extra timer messages. If the events going on swamp the queue, timer messages will get tossed out of the queue. In fact, the timer is not really meant for such precise timings as animation requires.

However, if you really want to use timers and really want better accuracy, the multimedia extensions have a timer routine that provides such resolution. But, it's a lot more work than the other methods outlined here; you have to create the routines in a DLL, for example. However, if you're really enamored with timers, investing the time to set them up might be worth it.

One routine that we can make immediate use of from the multimedia extensions is the `timeGetTime()` routine. We'll use it in the next section to get an accurate system time down to 1 millisecond.

Getting the Smoothest Animation Possible

This is where I expect most sane people to spend their time. After all, we're willing to be cutthroat only up to the point where faster rendering time does us no good, since the animation already looks smooth to the user. After a certain point our animation is fast enough so that any additional rendering does us no good and might in fact hurt us!

If all things were perfect, we could tweak our code to get the maximum speed out of it and be satisfied with the result. If we needed to add a little more detail to one item, we'd expect to pay a small-time penalty for that extra detail, say, dropping the frame rate from 25 frames per second to 20. Unfortunately there is a dividing line that the unwary can cross.

We generally use double buffering in animation because we don't want the user to see the scene being rendered; we just want the entire scene to appear, completed. Double buffering means that OpenGL draws to an off-screen block of memory (ideally on the video card) and that when we signal the graphics system that we are done and it's time to swap the buffers, the front and back buffers are swapped in the time it takes to refresh the screen, usually about 60 to 80 times a second. It depends only on the refresh rate, since the memory isn't physically copied; it's just that a pointer to one buffer is changed to point to the other buffer. The time depends on the rates of the video card and monitor that the scene is being displayed on.

ADVANCED If you've just added a little bit of code to your program, the screen-clearing time, message-processing time, and rendering time, which just barely fit into that 60-times-a-second window (or about 16 ms for the entire sequence), now just tops 16 ms. Thus we can't refresh the window as often as we could have before. If it now takes 17 ms to complete the rendering, you'll be updating the scene only every 32 ms—17 ms to render and 15 ms waiting for the screen to refresh. The processor can be doing other things in the meantime, but even if you *could* be rendering, you can get out a new scene only at every screen refresh, which is a limitation that you have no control over (other than getting a monitor with a 120 Hz or better refresh rate!).

This means that you're working on your project, adding features when suddenly the motion becomes much more jerky than it was before. You've just crossed over the boundary that forced you into alternate refreshes. That's the bad news. The good news is that we need a refresh rate of only about 25 frames per second, or about once every 40 ms or so. So we could drop our frame rate from once every 60 times (1/60, or 16 ms/frame) to 2/60 (33 ms/frame)—still quite acceptable—to 3/60 (67 ms/frame), or about 20 frames per second, which is slightly less than we'd like. Unfortunately if the user simply has a faster video refresh rate, say, 75 Hz, 3/75 equals 25 frames per second, an ideal target. Without some sophisticated timings, you won't be able to tell what the current machine's refresh rate is. So as mentioned earlier, it's a good idea to give the user some control over the complexity of the rendering.

This is where knowing how you're spending your time becomes important. The **WM_PAINT** message is just above the **WM_TIMER** message in the priority queue, but at least that's a step in the right direction. I prefer the method of posting a repaint message to oneself. If you examine the shared **COpenGLView** class sources, you'll see Listing 8.6, the function to turn on the animation flag.

Listing 8.6 OnAnimate Control Function

```
void COpenGLView::OnAnimate()
{
    // TODO: Add your command handler code here
    m_bAnimationRunning = !m_bAnimationRunning;

    if ( m_bAnimationRunning )
        {
        InvalidateRect( 0, FALSE );
        UpdateWindow();
        }
    else
        {
        // turn off animation message
        GetParentFrame()->
            SetWindowText( (const char*)m_WindowTitle );
        }
}
```

The part we're interested in is where the control toggles the animate flag. If the animation is turned on, we have to start by forcing a repaint of the scene. Turning the animation off resets the view's title. While the animation is running, timing mechanisms in the code allow the code to optimize itself. Some of the information is quite useful. While the scene is animated, the frame rate is updated in the window's title. You can change the window's size and watch the frame rate change. Not too surprisingly, you can watch it jump from one rate to another as the rate jumps through the quantum levels of video-refresh rates as the window size changes.

The frame rate is calculated on the basis of how quickly the last frame was rendered. Listing 8.7 shows how the frame rate is calculated.

Listing 8.7   Calculating Frame Rates

```
int COpenGLView::FramesPerSecond( void )
{
    int rate;

    if ( m_previousFrameRateTime == m_ElapsedTime )
        return 0;

    // elapsed time is the current rendering system time,
    // while previous is the previous rendering system
    // time (in ms) convert to frames/second and return.

    rate = (int)(1000/(m_ElapsedTime -
        m_previousFrameRateTime));
    m_previousFrameRateTime = m_ElapsedTime;
    return ( rate );
}
```

The two timing values are system time, fetched by means of the **timeGet-Time()** routine. The difference between the two values is the elapsed time to render one frame; thus we can convert it to the frame rate. Watching the rate halve as you make a small change in the window size is quite instructive.

But more important is the fact that we can use timing to avoid doing spurious renderings. Any rendering rate faster than 24 frames per second is probably wasting CPU cycles, so at the top of the **OnDraw()** member function, you'll see a snippet of code that looks like this:

```
if ( m_bAnimationRunning &&
    ElapsedTimeinMSSinceLastRender( currTime ) < 30 )
```

```
{
InvalidateRect( 0, FALSE );
GetParent()->PostMessage(WM_PAINT);
return;
}
```

This is a check to see whether the animation is running faster than we require. The function `ElapsedTimeinMSSinceLastRender()` does just that: returns the elapsed time since the last render. If this value is less than 30 ms, we simply post another repaint message and return without rendering. This way we won't hog the processor any more than we need to.

Finally, we need a way to limit the animation rates—the rate at which we are animating our scene. For example, if we are rotating the viewpoint about the center of a terrain map, we'd probably like the rotational rate to be constant and not to depend on the window size. If the user makes the window very small, the terrain shouldn't whiz around like an angry hornet. The idea is to make the animation independent of other factors that could eat CPU cycles. If the user makes the scene full screen and there's a fair number of polygons, the refresh rate probably isn't going to be 24 frames per second. However, we can easily make the rotational rate the same no matter what size (or amount of CPU time) we have by getting the current system time (accurate to a millisecond) just before each render. This way we can specify rotational or transitional rates in real, natural, terms (i.e., 5 degrees per second) and have the animation run at the same speed, no matter what the frame rate.

This has the advantage of always allowing the user to know beforehand what a transformation command, such as a command to rotate about the origin, will do, no matter what the machine, screen size, or current load on the CPU. It also makes things simpler for the programmer, since you get to specify things naturally and can then expect them to behave in a predictable manner. Examine the code in some of the examples in the next chapters, and you'll see how to use these timing values to specify time-based animations.

Try This

- Try creating your own animations using the functionality provided by the `COpenGLView` class. Create a scene and dynamically change the Modelview matrix so that your viewpoint spins around the origin, always oriented toward it.

9

Colors, Materials, and Lights

Some people are always grumbling because roses have thorns; I am
thankful that thorns have roses.

—Alphonse Karr

One of the basic tenets of creating a good scene is that you have to make it
look interesting. There's no better way to achieve this than to make good
use of lighting and textures. This chapter will cover the basics of creating and using color, materials, textures, and lighting in your OpenGL programs.

Color

OpenGL supports two color models. The first is RGBA mode, where you select
the value for each of the red, blue, green, and alpha (or opacity) parameters. The
second is color-index mode, whereby you fill a palette with the colors that you'll
need in your program. Palette programming is one of the banes of Windows programmers, since until a few years ago you could still expect to find sixteen-color
platforms. Today most people are running on SVGA cards and have at least 16-bit
color in some mode of the video card. This book will focus on RGBA mode, since
most of the interesting things you can do involve lighting and textures, which are
difficult or impossible to do using a color palette.

Color and Lighting

There's an important differentiation you need to understand. When you are using lighting or texture-mapping effects (lighting is turned on), the color of a vertex is the cumulative effect of the material color *and* the light that's shining on that

vertex. When lighting is turned off, the color of a vertex is the effect of the color setting—and that color is different from the material color. Thus you can toggle the color of a vertex by toggling the lighting state. This section will cover un-lighted, non-texture-mapped color. The color you specify is the color you get, un-affected by lighting or texturing (but perhaps affected by the palette if you've specified color-index mode).

Color and Shading

Color in RGBA mode is set by specifying the red, green, blue, and alpha intensi-ties. The `glColor*()` function comes in a variety of formats. Windows program-mers will be familiar with the **COLORREF** struct, which defines an RGB triplet as 3-byte values in the range 0–255. This followed the natural evolution of the PC's video card from a 16-color device to one of 16 million colors. OpenGL has simi-larly tailored versions that take everything from single-byte arguments to quad-byte ones, including the normal floating-point versions. Throughout this book you'll see the floating-point versions simply because it's easy to remember that the values have to be in the range [0,1].

OpenGL's state machine applies the currently selected color to the current ver-tex. Thus you need to set the color of a vertex before specifying the vertex. If you wanted to specify a bright red triangle, you would use the following commands:

```
glColor3f( 1.0f, 0.0f, 0.0f ); // no alpha value form
glBegin( GL_TRIANGLES );
    glVertex3f( -1.0f, 0.0f, 0.0f );
    glVertex3f( 1.0f, 0.0f, 0.0f );
    glVertex3f( 0.0f, 1.0f, 0.0f );
glEnd();
```

Note that the `glColor*()` function can be placed inside a `glBegin()`/`glEnd()` pair. Therefore you can specify individual colors for each individual vertex if you desire.

You might be wondering what the color is between two vertices of different colors. For example, what's the color of the center of the triangle in the following code?

```
glBegin( GL_TRIANGLES );
    glColor3f( 1.0f, 0.0f, 0.0f );// red
    glVertex3f( -1.0f, 0.0f, 0.0f );
    glColor3f( 0.0f, 1.0f, 0.0f );// green
```

```
    ::glVertex3f( 1.0f, 0.0f, 0.0f );
    ::glColor3f( 0.0f, 0.0f, 1.0f );// blue
    ::glVertex3f( 0.0f, 1.0f, 0.0f );
::glEnd();
```

The answer is it depends on the shading model you've specified. If *smooth* shading (the default) is specified, the color values are interpolated between vertices. In this case the color at the center would be gray (the mixture of pure red, pure blue, and pure green). If *flat* shading is specified, the one vertex is selected as being representative of all of the vertices; thus the entire primitive is displayed using one single color. Which vertex is used depends on which primitive type you are drawing. Chapter 4 discusses this in greater detail.

If you examine the program sources in the "Chapter 9/Color" subdirectory, you'll find the unlighted color-shading example, which uses the color cube to show the effects of the various shading models. I've left the top off the cube and placed a small black sphere inside the cube so that you can see the effects of smooth shading. Listing 9.1 shows the model for the program.

Listing 9.1   The Color Cube (Minus Top)

```
// Render the color cube, but leave the top off....
// so we can see the sphere inside
BOOL CColorView::RenderScene( void )
{
    ::glColor3f( 0.0f, 0.0f, 0.0f );
    ::auxSolidSphere( .3f );

    // define the colors
    GLfloat color1[3] = { 1.0f, 0.0f, 0.0f }; // red
    GLfloat color2[3] = { 0.0f, 1.0f, 0.0f }; // green
    GLfloat color3[3] = { 0.0f, 0.0f, 1.0f }; // blue
    GLfloat color4[3] = { 1.0f, 1.0f, 1.0f }; // white
    GLfloat color5[3] = { 0.0f, 0.0f, 0.0f }; // black
    GLfloat color6[3] = { 1.0f, 0.0f, 1.0f }; // magenta
    GLfloat color7[3] = { 0.0f, 1.0f, 1.0f }; // cyan
    GLfloat color8[3] = { 1.0f, 1.0f, 0.0f }; // yellow

    // Connect the four sides
    ::glBegin(GL_QUAD_STRIP);
        ::glColor3fv( color6 );
        ::glVertex3f(-1.0f, 1.0f, 1.0f);
```

Listing 9.1   The Color Cube (Minus Top) (continued)

```
    ::glColor3fv( color1 );
    ::glVertex3f(-1.0f, -1.0f, 1.0f);

    ::glColor3fv( color4 );
    ::glVertex3f(1.0f, 1.0f, 1.0f);

    ::glColor3fv( color8 );
    ::glVertex3f(1.0f, -1.0f, 1.0f);

    ::glColor3fv( color7 );
    ::glVertex3f(1.0f, 1.0f, -1.0f);

    ::glColor3fv( color2 );
    ::glVertex3f(1.0f, -1.0f, -1.0f);

    ::glColor3fv( color3 );
    ::glVertex3f(-1.0f, 1.0f, -1.0f);

    ::glColor3fv( color5 );
    ::glVertex3f(-1.0f, -1.0f, -1.0f);

    ::glColor3fv( color6 );
    ::glVertex3f(-1.0f, 1.0f, 1.0f);

    ::glColor3fv( color1 );
    ::glVertex3f(-1.0f, -1.0f, 1.0f);

::glEnd();

// The Bottom
::glBegin(GL_QUADS);

    ::glColor3fv( color1 );
    ::glVertex3f(-1.0f, -1.0f, 1.0f);

    ::glColor3fv( color8 );
    ::glVertex3f(1.0f, -1.0f, 1.0f);

    ::glColor3fv( color2 );
    ::glVertex3f(1.0f, -1.0f, -1.0f);
```

Listing 9.1 The Color Cube (Minus Top) (continued)

```
        ::glColor3fv( color5 );
        ::glVertex3f(-1.0f, -1.0f, -1.0f);
    ::glEnd();

    return TRUE;
}
```

This model draws the color cube—red, green, and blue as one triplet; cyan, magenta, and yellow as another triplet; with a diagonal axis representing the white-black axis. Plate 9.1 shows the effect of smooth shading. You can see how just by specifying the colors of the vertices, smooth shading interpolates to provide nearly every color representable. You should also note how difficult it is to see the edges where the faces of the cube meet. With no lighting effects, it's nearly impossible to distinguish between the faces of the polygons that make up an object. You can use this effect to your advantage. Plate 9.2 shows the same scene with flat shading. The color of each face is entirely the result of the order in which the vertices were specified. A different order would yield a totally different color for a flat-shaded model.

 Lighting effects let you make a model that instantly has a realism to it by the effects of the shading provided by the lighting calculations. However, adding lighting calculations increases the complexity of the calculations that OpenGL must go through to render the scene. If your model requires lighting effects, there's no way around it. However, you can selectively turn lighting effects on and off for certain parts of your model. If you need to let the user differentiate between the polygons of a model, you might consider subtly changing the color of the polygons that make up the model or applying a texture map. This might let you get away with little or no requirement for calculated lighting in your model. Also remember that infinite lights are much simpler to compute than local lights.

Another optimization (or simplification) to your model is deciding when you need smooth shading versus flat shading. You can toggle the shading method used for various parts of your model just as you can toggle the lighting effects. This lets you selectively increase or decrease the complexity of the calculations required to render your model. If you need lighting calculations, you might be able to design your model such that you don't need smooth shading. If an area of the model looks too faceted, you can always increase the polygon count in that area. Be aware, however, that there's a point of diminishing returns if you take tessellation too far.

Materials

OpenGL's materials are descriptions of what things are made of—or at least what they *appear* to be made of—by describing how they reflect light. If you were shown a picture of a room with a black marble floor, you'd probably be able to distinguish it from a picture of a room with a black carpeted floor. Although both floors may be black, the differences between the way that marble and carpet reflect light make them easily distinguishable. Although you can't specify marble or carpet as materials, OpenGL makes it fairly easy to describe the reflective properties of each material to achieve the same visual result.

Types of Material Properties

OpenGL has five properties that describe how a surface dissipates light. These properties are typically described by RGBA values that stipulate the color of the dissipated light. For example, a blue sphere under a white light looks blue because the reflected light is blue. If the light were to change to red, the sphere would appear black, because there would be no blue component for the sphere to reflect back. Thus the color of a surface of an object is a complicated summation of the color(s) of any light(s) that are shining, the angle(s) that those lights are in relationship to the surface, and the color and reflective and emissive properties of that surface.

Diffuse and Ambient Properties

The *diffuse* and *ambient* reflective material properties are a type of reflective effect that is independent of the viewpoint. *Diffuse* lighting describes how an object reflects a light that is shining on the object. In other words, it's how the surface diffuses a direct light source. *Ambient* lighting describes how a surface reflects the ambient light available. The ambient light is the indirect lighting that's in a scene: the amount of light that's coming from all directions so that all surfaces are equally illuminated by it. A surface that has no direct light sources shining on it appears the color of its ambient material—assuming that there's ambient light available.

Specular and Shininess Properties

The *specular* and the *shininess* properties of the surface describe the reflective effects that *are* affected by the position of the viewpoint. *Specular* light is reflected light from a surface that produces the reflective highlights in a surface. The *shini-*

ness is a value that describes how focused the reflective properties are. A ceramic teapot will return less specular light than a plastic one, whereas a metal teapot will have a higher shininess value than both.

Emissive Property

Emissive light is the light that an object gives off by itself. A light source is typically the only object that you might give an emissive value. Lamps, fires, and lightning are all objects that give off their own light. Note that specifying an emissive value is not the same as specifying a light source (something that's going to illuminate other objects). If you wanted to render a scene with a lamp in it, you render the lamp with an emissive value (so that the lamp appears to be glowing) and place a light source in the lamp (so that the lamp appears to be illuminating the objects around it).

Specifying a Material Property

Specifying a material property is about the same as specifying a color. You provide an RGBA value. If you're using color-index mode, you should look at the articles from the *Microsoft Systems Journal* listed in the bibliography section of "OpenGL Sources." The following discussion deals only with RGBA mode.

Let's specify a gray material for both the ambient and diffuse properties. The code to specify a dark gray ambient material and a light gray diffuse material might look like this:

```
GLfloat materialDiffuse[] = { 0.2f, 0.2f, 0.2f, 1.0f };
GLfloat materialAmbient[] = { 0.5f, 0.5f, 0.5f, 1.0f };
::glMaterialfv( GL_FRONT, GL_DIFFUSE, materialDiffuse);
::glMaterialfv( GL_FRONT, GL_AMBIENT, materialAmbient);
```

Note that we specify an RGBA quartet, since we're specifying the color that's perceived under certain lighting conditions. The OpenGL function `glMaterial*()` is a new one, and its various forms are used to specify the materials properties that make up the resultant color of a surface. The first parameter indicates which face of a polygon the property should be applied to. You can specify the front, back, or both faces. Typically you want only the front face to be illuminated, but under certain conditions you might want the back face illuminated. This also means that you can specify *different* parameters for the front and back faces. The *OpenGL Programming Guide* contains a nice example of a teapot illuminated on the outside with one set of parameters and on the inside with a different set of parameters. A clipping plane neatly slices off some of the teapot so that we can see inside.

Selecting an Object's Material Properties

Choosing the material properties of an object determines how it will look. The steps are as follows:

1. Decide on the diffuse and ambient colors. The ambient color defines the color that results from ambient light falling on the object and will be the dominant color when no direct illumination is on that part of the surface. The diffuse reflecting color comes into play when the surface is illuminated. For most physically based materials, or real-world materials, these are the same values. OpenGL conveniently has a parameter for `glMaterial*()` to specify this fact: `GL_AMBIENT_AND_DIFFUSE`.

2. If the object has a hidden interior, you'll probably want only the front faces to be included in the calculations, so you'd use the `GL_FRONT` parameter.

3. Decide on the shininess of the object. Pewter, silver, and chrome differ in the perceived shininess of their surfaces. The two controls for this reflective property are the specular and the shininess parameters. It may seem odd that you can specify the color characteristics of the highlights. Generally you'll want this color to be white, but you might want to color the highlight the same color as the ambient and diffuse values. If you're modeling some colored crystal, the highlights of a white light shining on the crystal are generally colored the same as the crystal, whereas a chrome surface reflects the color of the light shining on it. The shininess parameter controls the focus of the highlight. A low value spreads the reflectance over the surface (according to the mathematics of the lighting calculations), whereas a high value concentrates the highlight, making it smaller and brighter.

4. Finally, decide whether the object is giving off light. If it is, assign it the emissive properties you need.

How do you get these values? Trial and error, although after a while you get a collection of values for the materials that you use. One particularly useful thing to do is to write a program to run the gamut of properties and just watch how they vary. This is exactly what the LIGHTING 1 project in the "Chapter 9 / Lighting 1" subdirectory does.

The program creates a 4 × 4 × 4 matrix of blue spheres that varies the ambient and diffuse properties along the *y*-axis, the specular property along the *x*-axis, and the shininess along the *z*-axis. The material properties matrices that are used are as follows:

```
// The Specular values
GLfloat materialSpecular[4][4] = {
    { 0.1f, 0.1f, 0.1f, 1.0f },
    { 0.33f, 0.33f, 0.33f, 1.0f },
    { 0.67f, 0.67f, 0.67f, 1.0f },
    { 0.9f, 0.9f, 0.9f, 1.0f },
    };

// The Ambient and Diffuse values
GLfloat materialAmbDiff[4][4] ={
    { 0.0f, 0.0f, 0.12f, 1.0f },
    { 0.0f, 0.0f, 0.25f, 1.0f },
    { 0.0f, 0.0f, 0.50f, 1.0f },
    { 0.0f, 0.0f, 1.00f, 1.0f },
    };

// The Shininess values
GLfloat materialShininess[4][1] = {
    { 0.0f },
    { 35.0f },
    { 70.0f },
    { 128.0f }
    };
```

These values were chosen because they give a relatively even increase in each property as the values change. Plate 9.3 illustrates the changes that these properties bring when combined. The colors of the spheres are defined by the ambient and diffuse values, and you can see from both the array and the illustration that the colors start off as a very dark blue and rise to a bright pure blue.

The shininess effect can be seen as the highlight goes from being spread across the entire illuminated hemisphere to a point of light on the surface. If you rotate the matrix about the *y*-axis, you'll see that the highlight disappears when the angles of reflection no longer hit the viewpoint. The other interesting thing to note is that lighting is turned off for the text by using `glDisable( GL_LIGHTING )` and setting the color to yellow. The text is generated by using the default 3D text created by the `COpenGLView` class. See chapter 7 for more information on creating and using text in OpenGL.

Creating Your Own Material Properties

Let's create a material that we can use in the next section. We're going to use some 3D text made out of something like chrome. The next section is about lighting, and a chrome surface will give nice highlights. The first step is to decide on the color. Chrome is a neutral color; most of its visual effect stems from its highly reflective properties. We choose a medium gray for the ambient color. The diffuse color is a bit brighter, because we want to emphasize the diffuse reflective properties of the surface. The values used in the program are

```
GLfloat materialAmbient[4] = { 0.25f, 0.25f, 0.25f, 1.0f };
GLfloat materialDiffuse[4] = { 0.4f, 0.4f, 0.4f, 1.0f };
```

The reflective effects are next, and we select highly reflective and shiny values for these properties:

```
GLfloat materialSpecular[4] = { 1.0f, 1.0f, 1.0f, 1.0f };
GLfloat materialShininess[1] = { 128.0f };
```

Finally, these values are placed in the program, using the following calls:

```
::glMaterialfv( GL_FRONT, GL_DIFFUSE, materialDiffuse );
::glMaterialfv( GL_FRONT, GL_AMBIENT, materialAmbient );
::glMaterialfv( GL_FRONT, GL_SPECULAR, materialSpecular );
::glMaterialfv( GL_FRONT, GL_SHININESS, materialShininess );
```

Note that we set them for only the front faces, since the text back faces are hidden. In order to get the visual effect of the material, we need to add some lights to the scene, and that's what we do in the next section.

Lighting

OpenGL has two types of lighting: global lighting, or the ambient light and its associated parameters, and individual light sources, which have position and direction. The calculations involved in determining how much light is reflected off a surface are quite complex. They are an intricate combination of all of the lights that are turned on; the ambient light; the position of the lights; the position of the objects and the viewpoint; the angles among all the lights, the object, and the viewpoint; and, finally, all of the parameters that are set for each material and each light. The *OpenGL Programming Guide* has an entire section devoted to explaining the mathematics involved in lighting calculations.

Enabling Lighting

You must do a few steps before you'll get lighting effects in your program. Since lighting calculations are expensive, you'll first need to turn these calculations on. This is done, as are many things in OpenGL, by turning on a state variable. In this case the `glEnable()` function is called with `GL_LIGHTING`. This will turn on lighting calculations, and the default values for the global ambient light will let you see any objects in your scene.

In addition to the global ambient light, you can turn on at least eight individual lights. The actual number depends on the OpenGL implementation that's running. You enable each individual light by using a `GL_LIGHT*` argument to `glEnable()`, where * is a number from 0 to 7 (or more). Default values for `GL_LIGHT0` let its effects be visible; the other lights have default values set so that they are disabled and don't enter into the lighting calculations. Some hardware implementations are optimized for a single light.

Global Lighting

The `glLightModel*()` function is used for setting global lighting parameters. You can select the RGBA value for the global ambient light that's present in your scene. You'll probably want a small value of light, such as the default, so that all the objects in your scene will be visible even if no individual light is shining on them.

Next, you can set calculations for specular highlights. Highlights are calculated either from an infinite viewpoint (the default) or by taking into account the position of the viewpoint. In *local-viewpoint* mode, the highlights are calculated by taking into account the angle between the viewpoint and the vertex reflecting the light. This will yield a more realistic scene but at the expense of more complicated lighting calculations. The default is to assume that the angles should be calculated using a viewpoint at infinite distance. Although this greatly simplifies the lighting calculations, some authenticity is lost. The program LIGHTING 2 in the "Chapter 9/Lighting 2" subdirectory uses the local-viewpoint mode to increase the "realness" of the reflections. Plate 9.4 shows a scene from the program.

Finally, by default OpenGL calculates ambient reflections only for front faces. If you wanted the back or inside of an object to be visible, you'd need to turn on the mode for two-sided global lighting calculations, using the `GL_LIGHT_MODEL_TWO_SIDE` argument. By default this value is turned off.

If you need to turn on either two-sided lighting or the local-viewpoint mode, you should be judicious and turn it on only for the part of the model that requires it. Globally turning on complicated lighting calculations when you don't need them is a good way to slow down rendering time.

Individual Light Sources

Once you've got the global lighting set, you'll probably notice that although you can see individual sides of objects, there's no difference in the light among them. An individual light source will bring into sharp detail the differences between differently illuminated sides. After enabling an individual light source, you'll probably want to set the ambient and diffuse RGBA values for the light. The ambient part of the light's setting contribute to the overall global ambient light. By default there is no ambient light component. The command used to set an individual light's values is the `glLight*()` function. The parameters passed in are the particular light's enum value, the enum of the parameter you want to change, and the value of the parameter.

Setting the Illuminating Parameters

The diffuse RGBA value is the color that the light contributes to the reflectance off an object and is what you can consider the "color" of the light. Shining a light with red diffuse RGBA settings on a white sphere would give a red coloring to that part of the sphere that the light illuminates.

The specular component is the color of the highlights that reflect off a shiny surface. Typically you'd set the specular value to be the same as the diffuse value, since the reflected highlight is usually the same color as the light. Plate 9.4 is a scene from the LIGHTING 2 program in the "Chapter 9/Lighting 2" subdirectory. There are three white, mildly reflective spheres. The sphere in the middle has a light with white diffuse and specular light shining on it. The sphere on the left has a green diffuse and white specular light shining on it. The sphere on the right has a white diffuse and a green specular light shining on it. You can easily see the green specular component shining through the white diffuse glow on the sphere on the left. If you animate the scene, you can see the highlight moving around on the sphere while the diffuse component is stationary.

Setting the Position

You can position individual lights by passing in a four-element position into `gl-Light*()`. You can select two types of light positions. The first is called a *direc-*

tional light position. The *x, y, z* values specify a point that, when connected to the origin, defines the line to which all of the light rays are parallel. A directional light is considered to be at an infinite distance from the origin, and hence all of the light coming from the light source is parallel to the line specified between the origin and the point given. Remember that the Modelview matrix transformations work for light positions, as well as for vertex positions!

The second type is called a *positional* light source. In this case the position vector that is passed in is the position of the light. It's the origin of the light, and all the light rays originate from this position. By default this light radiates in all directions and is equally bright no matter the distance of a surface from the light.

The method for selecting positional versus directional light sources lies in the *w* component of the position vector that you pass in. If the *w* value is 0, the light is taken to be a directional one. If the *w* value is not 0, it's used like it normally would be, although usually *w* is set to 1 in this case.

Setting Attenuation

Attenuation is the reduction in the intensity of the light as the distance increases. OpenGL has three modifiable parameters for calculating the attenuation factor. GL_CONSTANT_ATTENUATION is the constant, and by default its value is 1.0. The other parameters—GL_LINEAR_ATTENUATION and GL_QUA-DRATIC_ATTENUATION—are used in the calculations to reduce the light as a function of distance. See the *OpenGL Programming Guide* for more information on the formula used for calculating attenuation. You can set the attenuation only for a positional light. It doesn't make sense to attempt to do it for a light that's located at infinity.

Creating a Spotlight

The last setting that affects a light turns an omnidirectional light source into a spotlight. The position of the light is set, the same as for a positional light (it makes sense only for a positional light to be turned into a spotlight). You constrict the range of light dispersion with the GL_SPOT_CUTOFF parameter, which specifies the angle from the centerline of the spotlight's direction. See Figure 9.1. Thus a value of 15 degrees, for example, defines a cone 30 degrees wide. By default this value is 180 degrees, yielding a full 360 degrees. The acceptable range is [0,90], except for the special value of 180.

To set the direction of the spotlight, use the GL_SPOT_DIRECTION parameter. This vector is in object coordinates, and it's affected by whatever matrix transformations are in effect. By default it's pointing down the negative *z*-axis.

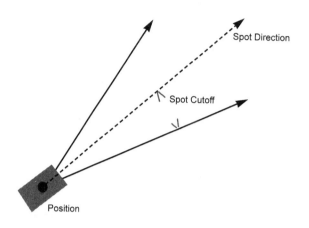

Figure 9.1 Components of a Spotlight

The final setting for spotlights controls how intense the light is at its center. The `GL_SPOT_EXPONENT` controls how to concentrate the light's intensity. By default the light is equally bright across the diameter of the spotlight. The exponent value is the power of the exponent on a cosine of the angle from the center of the spot. The higher the value, the more concentrated the light will be at the center.

IMPORTANT
If you want to illuminate a large surface, you should remember that the interior of a surface is colored by interpolating the color at the vertices. If you have a light source close to the middle of one large polygon, the center will be dark, because the middle color is interpolated from vertices that are far away from the light source. The solution is to break up the large polygon into smaller polygons so that there are more vertices from which to interpolate.

Creating a Scene with Multiple Light Sources

Let's create a scene with some dramatic lighting effects. We'll use multiple lights to create a scene that shows OpenGL's lighting model capabilities. Earlier we discussed how to create a set of material properties to get a highly reflective surface. We'll now use that set of properties in combination with what we've learned about lighting to create a spectacularly illuminated scene. The source code for this section can be found in the "Chapter 9/Lighting 3" subdirectory. Plate 9.5 shows a rendering of the scene.

The best scenes are simple, so this scene will consist of nothing more than the text "OpenGL & Windows," albeit dramatically lighted. I've chosen a font that contains a lot of extra serifs and details to better provide reflective surfaces. In the code that accompanies this section, I've commented out that line of code and re-placed it with a selection of Arial instead. To display the text is simply a matter of generating the font's display list and then using the `GLTextOut( )` member function of the `COpenGLView` class. Since we've already discussed how the materials were set, all that's required is to generate the display list and to render the text with these two lines of code:

```
GLuint myFont =
    GenerateDisplayListForFont( "Arial", 0.2f );
GLTextOut( myFont, "OpenGL & Windows" );
```

The scene has four lights. Two directional white lights generally illuminate the scene and are placed above the text, one in front and one behind. The one in front provides some general illumination of the letters; the one in back provides white highlights. Being directional, unattenuated lights, they provide a general, global illumination of the entire scene.

The next two lights are positional lights, both of which are placed under and behind the text string to provide localized highlights across the text. One light is red and the other blue, and they are placed about a third of the way from each end of the string. The rest of this text is easier to visualize if you examine Plate 9.5. The letters closer to the lights show the effects of that light (although, being un-attenuated, distance from the light usually has no meaning). I've placed a red and blue sphere at the same position as the light of that color. This makes it easier to see how the lights reflect off the text as it rotates. In particular note the red and blue highlights reflecting from the text. The purple highlights on the "O" are the result of illumination from both the red and blue lights.

The global ambient light has been turned off (set to 0,0,0,1), so illumination is strictly the result of calculations involving the four lights placed in the scene. Note that even though there are letters in the way, the "O" seems fully illuminated by the red light. This demonstrates one simplification of OpenGL's lighting model that becomes evident when you're trying to create realistic scenes. This limitation is discussed briefly in the next section.

Ray Tracing

You may have noticed the absence of shadows in the scene. It's particularly obvious when you rotate the text. OpenGL has no provisions for letting objects obscure one another from lighting. The lighting model that does do this is called *ray tracing,* and it refers to the method of tracing each ray of light on its way to illuminating each pixel in the scene. If it sounds computationally expensive, it is. However, many people write their own illumination models, including ray tracing ones to use with OpenGL. If you want to find out more about ray tracing, consult one of the general graphics texts listed in the bibliography.

The Module for the Scene

A nonoptimized version of the source code for the module is shown in Listing 9.2. (You wouldn't place all these light and material commands in the redraw loop.) The important things to note are the positioning of the lights, the selection of the materials, and the fact that the global ambient light has been set to 0.

Listing 9.2   The RenderScene( ) Member Function for Plate 9.5

```
BOOL CLightingView::RenderScene( void )
{
    // select the font
    static GLuint myFont =
        GenerateDisplayListForFont("Arial",0.2f);
    GLfloat materialSpecular[4] = {1.0f, 1.0f, 1.0f, 1.0f};
    GLfloat materialShininess[1] = { 128.0f };
    GLfloat materialAmbient[4] = {0.25f,0.25f,0.25f,1.0f};
    GLfloat materialDiffuse[4] = {0.4f, 0.4f, 0.4f, 1.0f};
    GLfloat local_ambient[] = { 0.0f, 0.0f, 0.0f, 1.0f };

    ::glEnable(GL_DEPTH_TEST);
    ::glDepthFunc(GL_LESS);
```

Listing 9.2   The `RenderScene( )` Member Function for Plate 9.4 (continued)

```
::glLightModelfv(GL_LIGHT_MODEL_AMBIENT,local_ambient);

    // The red light
    GLfloat ambient0[] = { 0.0f, 0.0f, 0.0f, 1.0f };
    GLfloat diffuse0[] = { 1.0f, 0.0f, 0.0f, 1.0f };
    GLfloat specular0[] = { 1.0f, 0.0f, 0.0f, 1.0f };
    // note positional setting
    GLfloat position0[] = { 2.0f, -1.5f, -1.5f, 1.0f };

    // the back white light
    GLfloat ambient1[] = { 0.0f, 0.0f, 0.0f, 1.0f };
    GLfloat diffuse1[] = { 1.0f, 1.0f, 1.0f, 1.0f };
    GLfloat specular1[] = { 0.5f, 0.5f, 0.5f, 1.0f };
    // note directional setting
    GLfloat position1[] = { 2.0f, 1.0f, -1.0f, 0.0f };

    // The blue light
    GLfloat ambient2[] = { 0.0f, 0.0f, 0.0f, 1.0f };
    GLfloat diffuse2[] = { 0.0f, 0.0f, 1.0f, 1.0f };
    GLfloat specular2[] = { 0.0f, 0.0f, 1.0f, 1.0f };
    GLfloat position2[] = { -0.5, -0.5, -1.0f, 1.0f };

    // the other white light (in front)
    GLfloat ambient3[] = { 0.0f, 0.0f, 0.0f, 1.0f };
    GLfloat diffuse3[] = { 1.0f, 1.0f, 1.0f, 1.0f };
    GLfloat specular3[] = { 0.0f, 0.0f, 0.0f, 1.0f };
    GLfloat position3[] = { 2.0f, 0.5f, 0.5f, 0.0f };

    // Now set up the individual lights
    ::glEnable(GL_LIGHT0);
    ::glLightfv(GL_LIGHT0, GL_AMBIENT, ambient0);
    ::glLightfv(GL_LIGHT0, GL_POSITION, position0);
    ::glLightfv(GL_LIGHT0, GL_DIFFUSE, diffuse0);
    ::glLightfv(GL_LIGHT0, GL_SPECULAR, specular0);

    ::glEnable(GL_LIGHT1);
    ::glLightfv(GL_LIGHT1, GL_AMBIENT, ambient1);
    ::glLightfv(GL_LIGHT1, GL_POSITION, position1);
    ::glLightfv(GL_LIGHT1, GL_DIFFUSE, diffuse1);
    ::glLightfv(GL_LIGHT1, GL_SPECULAR, specular1);
```

Listing 9.2   The RenderScene( ) Member Function for Plate 9.4 (continued)

```
::glEnable(GL_LIGHT2);
::glLightfv(GL_LIGHT2, GL_AMBIENT, ambient2);
::glLightfv(GL_LIGHT2, GL_POSITION, position2);
::glLightfv(GL_LIGHT2, GL_DIFFUSE, diffuse2);
::glLightfv(GL_LIGHT2, GL_SPECULAR, specular2);

::glEnable(GL_LIGHT3);
::glLightfv(GL_LIGHT3, GL_AMBIENT, ambient3);
::glLightfv(GL_LIGHT3, GL_POSITION, position3);
::glLightfv(GL_LIGHT3, GL_DIFFUSE, diffuse3);
::glLightfv(GL_LIGHT3, GL_SPECULAR, specular3);

// Set up the material properties
::glMaterialfv( GL_FRONT, GL_SPECULAR,
   materialSpecular );
::glMaterialfv( GL_FRONT,GL_SHININESS,
   materialShininess);
::glMaterialfv( GL_FRONT, GL_DIFFUSE,
   materialDiffuse);
::glMaterialfv( GL_FRONT, GL_AMBIENT,
   materialAmbient);

// Now that the setup is all done (it has to be
// done only once) perform the actual rendering

// turn off lighting to draw regular old wire
// spheres to show where the lights are
::glDisable( GL_LIGHTING );

::glPushMatrix();
::glColor3fv( diffuse0 );
::glTranslatef( position0[0],
   position0[1], position0[2] );
::auxWireSphere(0.15f);
::glPopMatrix();

::glPushMatrix();
::glColor3fv( diffuse2 );
::glTranslatef( position2[0],
   position2[1], position2[2] );
::auxWireSphere(0.15f);
::glPopMatrix();
```

Listing 9.2   The RenderScene( ) Member Function for Plate 9.4 (continued)

```
        // Turn lighting back on
        ::glEnable( GL_LIGHTING );

        // Now, draw the text
        ::glPushMatrix();
        ::glTranslatef( -3.0f, 0.0f, 0.0f );
        GLTextOut( myFont, "OpenGL & Windows" );
        ::glPopMatrix();
        return TRUE;
}
```

As you can see, most of the routine is setup and would be better placed in an initialization routine. The difficult part is understanding how the lights interact with one another and with the materials. As you rotate the scene, note that you can see the red or blue highlights only when you're looking directly at the text, because the lights have to reflect off a surface such that they can reflect into the viewpoint. Think of each surface as a mirror; if the light or your viewpoint drops below the plane of a mirror, no light will be reflected from that mirror.

Optimizing the Rendering of Dynamically Changing Material Properties

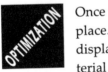
Once you've set the materials for your scene, you generally leave them in place. If you have more than one set of materials, encapsulate them in a display list. Occasionally you might want to dynamically change the material properties on the fly. If the changes are fairly simple, such as changing the diffuse color of an object, you can use OpenGL's optimized call for such an occasion.

The glColorMaterial() function allows you to change the source of a material property's values to the RGBA values set by the glColor*() function. Recall that when lighting is enabled, the glColor*() function has no effect. If you enable the glColorMaterial() function with a call to glEnable() with the argument GL_COLOR_MATERIAL, you can selectively change a material property's source RGBA values to those stored by means of the glColor*() function.

It works like this: You enable the function, then use the glColorMaterial() function to select the face(s) you want to affect and the material property you want to switch over to, using the `glColor*()` functions values. To change that material's RGBA values, you make a call to `glColor*()`.

For example, suppose you wanted to draw a shiny red, green, and blue triangle. You could use the `glColorMaterial()` function to do it, as in the following code segment:

```
// Set up ambient, shininess, and specular materials values
// using glMaterial*() calls
// turn on glColorMaterial()
::glEnable( GL_COLOR_MATERIAL );
// select the property we want to change
::glColorMaterial( GL_FRONT, GL_AMBIENT_AND_DIFFUSE );
// glColor()'s values are now hooked to the ambient and
// diffuse color
// Now let's do some rendering
::glBegin( GL_TRANGLES );
    for ( int i = 0 ; i < 10000 ; i++ )
        {
        // position and draw red vertex
        ::glColor3f( 1.0f, 0.0f, 0.0f );; // select red
        ::glVertex3f( 0.0f, 0.0f, 0.0f );
        // position and draw green vertex
        ::glColor3f( 0.0f, 1.0f, 0.0f );; // select green
        ::glVertex3f( 1.0f, 0.0f, 0.0f );
        // position and draw blue vertex
        ::glColor3f( 0.0f, 0.0f, 1.0f );; // select blue
        ::glVertex3f( 0.5f, 1.0f, 0.0f );
        // now do some rotating or translating to the
        // next triangle position...
        .... move to next position
        }
::glEnd(); // all done rendering
// turn off glColorMaterial()
::glDisable( GL_COLOR_MATERIAL );
```

It's a good idea to always turn off the `glColorMaterial()` rerouting when you're done with it. Nothing is more frustrating than to wonder why you can set specular and highlight for something, but the ambient and diffuse color is always white! This is a powerful command, but it obfuscates the way that colors normally work, so be careful when using it.

Try This

- Rewrite the LIGHTING 1 example to add a light source. Then vary such things as the specular reflection. If the animation is too slow, try making the spheres cubes.

- Try using a flat shading model in LIGHTING 2. Compare the visual effects and the rendering speed for both shading models. How about turning the lighting effects off?

- Play with the LIGHTING 3 (chrome text) example. Try rewriting it so that the red and blue lights are spotlights.

- Try making the red and blue lights attenuated. (Try setting the quadratic term to 2.0.) How does this affect the color reflecting off the "O"?

- Make the light in front a spotlight with a narrow beam. However, make the light positioned at and aligned with the viewpoint. (See the *OpenGL Programming Guide* if you need help on how to do it. *Hint:* Set the light position *before* the viewing transformation. Did you remember the default viewpoint location?)

10

Textures _____

If I had two loaves of bread, I would sell one and buy hyacinths, for
they would feed my soul.

—The Koran

Textures are to 3D graphics what scenery is to the theater, that is, a way of
making something *appear* rich and complex even though it's not. This is a
good thing. Anything that gives us depth at little cost is to be strived for in 3D
graphics. Texture mapping is a result of attempts to make 3D objects more interesting and realistic, and its popularity easily demonstrates how successful
it's been.

This chapter covers applying a texture to a surface—from converting a Windows bitmap to OpenGL's format to automatically creating multiple levels of detailed images to speed up rendering. By the way, if you're using color-index
mode in your program, this section will be strictly academic for you. Texture
mapping works only in RGBA mode.

Windows Bitmap Files

Images in Windows are typically stored in bitmap or BMP files. These BMP files
are also referred to as DIB files, or device-independent bitmaps. You'll typically
see such files with BMP or DIB extensions. These files—essentially a header
with an array of color values attached—can be compressed, although this is un-
usual. By themselves the files are pretty useless for OpenGL, since OpenGL
uses a different format for storing images. This may not matter if you are running OpenGL 1.1. Microsoft has added an extension to 1.1 to handle Windows
bitmaps.

A Quick Look at Windows DIB Format

As mentioned, the bitmap format consists of a header and an array of color values. The header of a bitmap file is in fact two headers. The first is the **BITMAP-FILEHEADER**, which contains, among other things, the "signature" of a bitmap file (the letters *BM*), the file size, and the offset to the bitmap. The second header contains such things as the depth of the color array and the compression method used in the file. Windows DIBs may have color formats of 1, 4, 8, 16, 24, and 32 bits per pixel and a variety of compression types.

So far, so good. We just have to read in the DIB file and convert it to OpenGL's format. But in addition to converting, say, an 8-bit color format to a 24-bit format, we need to put the colors into the correct order. For some reason DIB-file RGB triples are in blue-green-red order, whereas OpenGL's pixels formats require red-green-blue ordering. Rather than torture you with descriptions of converting 8-bit, then 16-bit, then 32-bit formats, and so on, I'll give you the benefit of someone else's groundwork on converting DIB files to OpenGL format.

A Special Microsoft Extension

If you're writing your own code and you know you'll be running on OpenGL 1.1 on a Windows platform, there are the EXT_bgra extensions that Microsoft provides to avoid the nastiness of the transformation code. This makes it convenient to share DIBs between OpenGL and Windows. See chapter 12 to find out how to access OpenGL extensions.

Since you're reading this book, I can assume that you've seen the OpenGL screen savers. Most of them allow you to specify a bitmap for the images they render, so someone at Microsoft has already figured out how to generically read a DIB and use it in OpenGL. Better yet, that source code is included in Visual C++ (at least, the *pipes* sources are included). And it's from spelunking this code that we discover that buried deep in the auxiliary library sources is a routine for reading in a Windows bitmap file and massaging it into OpenGL's format. The basic algorithm is to use GDI to translate the DIB from its original format to a 32-bit format. Using 32-bit instead of 24-bit means that you don't have to worry about boundary padding. The code then rearranges the bytes from 32-bit blue-green-red ordering to an OpenGL-usable 24-bit red-green-blue ordering.

The transformation can be done in a variety of ways, and if you're interested in learning more about how to do it, examine Dale Rogerson's articles in the Microsoft Development Network. He explains a few ways to go about the transformation, including the method used in the auxiliary library. A good resource for learning more about bitmap files and the DIB format is Marv Luse's *Bitmapped Graphics Programming in C++*. Look in the bibliography under "OpenGL Resources" for more information on these resources.

 If you do end up writing your own method of converting a DIB into an OpenGL-readable format, you should be aware that Windows 95 and Windows NT handle DIBs differently. The method described here is compatible with both Windows NT and Windows 95. Make sure that whatever method you use will work on both platforms.

Reading a Windows Bitmap into an OpenGL Image

OpenGL images can be stored in a variety of formats. If you're interested in writing portable code, this is something that you'd be interested in. However, if you're interested in reading in DIB files, you're probably running Windows, so we'll set the storage mode of native Windows and then not worry about it anymore. The **glPixelStore*()** function sets the storage mode that OpenGL uses. If you're interested in any pixel operations, such as texture maps, polygon stippling, or reading or writing pixels, you should be aware of this function and what it does.

In this case we're simply going to set it up for Windows usage and then forget it. The *OpenGL Programming Guide* has an entire chapter on how to perform pixel operations. The functions **glReadPixels*()**, **glDrawPixels*()**, **glBitmap()**, **glPolygonStipple()**, **glTexImage()**, **glTexImage1D()**, and **glTexImage2D()** are all affected by the pixel storage mode. In the parlance of *The OpenGL Reference Manual*, "pack" refers to putting images into memory, and "unpack" to reading them from memory. If you're writing portable code that reads an image read on a different machine, you can control things like the byte ordering and the alignment of the bytes.

We'll use the following command to tell OpenGL that images are aligned on single-byte boundaries:

```
glPixelStorei( GL_UNPACK_ALIGNMENT, 1 );
```

Then OpenGL knows how to interpret the memory images that we pass in. Finally, we have to tell OpenGL exactly *what* we are passing into it. For images we're going to be dealing strictly with RGB and RGBA values stored as unsigned bytes, since these structures are compatible with Windows.

Once you have a texture map read into memory, the individual elements are called *texels*, just like an image's individual elements are called *pixels*. Since we're going to bypass the whole Windows-to-OpenGL format issue, we won't be dealing with texels as such, but you should know what they are.

Rather than write and test our own code, however, it's much simpler to ask someone else to do it. The following line takes a path to the BMP file and reads in the bitmap, massages it, and then returns a pointer to the OpenGL-compatible format:

```
m_pRGBImage = auxDIBImageLoadA( (const char*)bmpfile );
```

The trick here is to remember that this function uses `malloc()` to allocate memory for the image, and the responsibility to clean up falls on you.

IMPORTANT Once the image is in memory, it's *not quite* ready to use. OpenGL images that you're going to use as a texture *must* have dimensions of a power of 2. Thus 8 × 32, 64 × 64, 128 × 128, and 256 × 512 are all valid image sizes to use as texture maps. If you're going to write your own texture mapping routines, you'll have to resize the image to acceptable dimensions. (Alternatively, if your texture *has* to be some particular aspect ratio, you can simply leave that extra portion of your image blank and not use that part of the texture map at all.)

Changing an Image's Size

You could use GDI routines to scale the image, and if the image is in a DIB, you probably should use `StretchBlt()`. If you're not using a DIB format, then OpenGL provides a routine that does exactly what we need. The `gluScaleImage()` function takes an image of one size and returns an image of the specified size. It's pretty simple to use and does the job with a minimum of effort on our part.

Specifying a Texture

OpenGL has two types of textures: 1D textures are similar to stipple patterns for lines, except that you can specify RGB values for the pixels and set the length; 2D image textures are what we're really interested in. The `glTexImage2D()` function specifies the data to use as a texture map. In addition to passing in the expected data pointer, format, storage type, and image dimensions, you pass in the *level* parameter.

You can specify multiple copies of the same bitmap but rendered at different levels of detail. This is useful so that OpenGL can decide which image is of sufficient detail to use. This speeds up the code by allowing OpenGL to use smaller and smaller images as the object getting textured gets smaller and smaller. The first resolution starts with number 0. If there's only one image, it's also given level 0. The way this works is that there is only one bitmap available at any one time. A call to the `glTexImage2D()` function changes the currently selected image, except when the level value is changed.

Multiple Images and Large Images

If you require multiple images, you must make repeated calls to the `glTexImage2D()` function. If your image is larger than the largest image size (the generic implementation has a limit of 1024 × 1024), you'll have to load the image in parts and render each part before loading the next part of the image. An alternative would be to scale the image to a smaller size.

 If you require multiple images, you can avoid repeated image swapping (which is expensive) by creating a metaimage that contains all of the images you'll need (keeping in mind the maximum image size). You can then select the appropriate portion of the metaimage to use, thus keeping all of the images in memory at one time.

Generating Images of Multiple Levels of Detail

Once you start using texture maps, especially in animated scenes, you'll quickly discover that scaling the image can generate some visual artifacts that detract from the texturing. One way of avoiding these artifacts is to generate texture maps of varying sizes from a large original, called *mipmapping,* and letting OpenGL automatically switch among these various sizes. You can use the `gluScaleImage()` function to generate these images, or *mipmaps* and, with a little work, automate the process. Fortunately a function in the utility library performs this function for us. The `gluBuild2DMipMaps()` function constructs a series of mipmaps for you by using the `gluScaleImage()` and `glTexImage2D()` functions. Therefore it also *selects* the image for you; since it takes a while to do all this scaling and image generation, generate them sparingly!

Introducing the COpenGLImage Class

A lot of complicated things go on with using texture maps in OpenGL. Such details are best encapsulated in a class. Just as the complexities of using OpenGL in an MFC program were hidden in the COpenGLView class, we can do the same with the problems of converting Windows bitmaps into an OpenGL image and managing those images. I've collected the techniques we've touched on in the previous sections into the COpenGLImage class, a class designed expressly to be used as an interface between Windows bitmaps and OpenGL textures. There's not much to the COpenGLImage class other than wrapping up the complexities of bitmap and image management; however, you do have a few choices that give you control over how the image is going to be used.

Deciding between Decal and Modulation Mode

When you apply a texture map to a polygon, you can decide whether the texture is to be applied like a decal, that is, the texture is considered opaque, and the underlying color is obscured. The other choice is to modulate the colors. This means that the underlying color of the polygon pixel is multiplied by the decal's color at that pixel location.

For example, if you're designing a tank simulation, you can create a texture map of a gray camouflage pattern and then color one team's tanks green and the other's brown. Applying the same texture to each in modulation mode would result in each team's having camouflaged green tanks and the other camouflaged brown tanks.

The modulation mode is specified by the glTextEnv*() function. The default for the COpenGLImage class is DECAL mode, but you can change it when you specify the bitmap file to initialize the image with. The following calls show how to read in a bitmap and change the mixing mode:

```
// just read in a bitmap, DECAL is default style
myImage1.InitFromDIB( "\windows\system\marble.bmp" );
// read in another and use it as a decal
myImage2.InitFromDIB("another.bmp", GL_DECAL );
// read in another and modulate it with the surface
myImage3.InitFromDIB(" additional.bmp", GL_MODULATE );
```

After this code is executed, three images are in memory, but none of them has been given to OpenGL yet. Listing 10.1 shows you the basic COpenGLImage routine that reads in a bitmap file and converts it to OpenGL format. When it's done, an OpenGL image is in memory, ready to be selected by OpenGL.

Listing 10.1   Reading in a DIB for Use as a Texture Map

```
BOOL COpenGLImage::InitFromDIB( const CString dibfile,
      GLint texFunc )
{
    // free any previous images
    if ( 0 != m_pRGBImage)
        {
        //use same routine that allocated it
        LocalFree( m_pRGBImage );
        }

    // Load the bmp file using the library routine.
    // This routine resides in the AUX lib sources,
    // so you'll need to have it loaded (or create
    // your own version.
    // It uses only GDI calls, no OpenGL.
    // If it fails, it returns NULL
    // (Takes an ANSI string, use auxDIBImageLoadW()
    // for others)
    m_pRGBImage = auxDIBImageLoadA( (const char*)dibfile );

    if( 0 == m_pRGBImage )
        return FALSE;

    // save the file name (cast away const'ness)
    // Kids, don't try this at home!
    CString* pNameTemp = (CString*)&m_DIBFileName;
    *pNameTemp = dibfile;

    // select the texture mixing function. Since we're using
    // RGB format, then we're restricted to either DECAL
    // mode (the default) or MODULATE
    m_TextureFunction = texFunc;

    return TRUE;
}
```

Note that you can reinitialize a **COpenGLImage** if you need to, that the auxiliary function does almost all of the work for us, and that you're limited to either **GL_DECAL** or **GL_MODULATE** (it's more a limitation of using an RGB format, but the code enforces this). That's it. All of the nasty details of handling bitmaps are taken care of. If you're thinking of using this in a product, I'd probably rewrite **auxDIBImageLoad()** to be a little more friendly, as it will attempt to post an error message if it runs into problems (or call **tkErrorPopups(FALSE)**!).

Using COpenGLImage to Select the Image

Once you've read in an image—be warned, an image may take a while to read in if it's big—you'll most probably want to show it. That's done by using the **selectImage()** member function, as the following lines illustrate:

```
COpenGLImage myImage;
// Now read in the bitmap file
myImage.InitFromDIB( "myDecal.bmp" );
// now tell OpenGL to use the image
myImage.SelectImage();
```

The code for **selectImage()** is show in Listing 10.2.

Listing 10.2   Selecting an Image for OpenGL to Use

```
BOOL COpenGLImage::SelectImage( void )
{
    if ( 0 == m_pRGBImage )
        {
        return FALSE;
        }

    ::glEnable( GL_TEXTURE_2D );
    ::glPixelStorei( GL_UNPACK_ALIGNMENT, 1 );
    ::glTexParameteri( GL_TEXTURE_2D,
        GL_TEXTURE_WRAP_S, GL_REPEAT );
    ::glTexParameteri( GL_TEXTURE_2D,
        GL_TEXTURE_WRAP_T, GL_REPEAT );
    ::glTexParameteri( GL_TEXTURE_2D,
        GL_TEXTURE_MAG_FILTER,GL_LINEAR );
    ::glTexParameteri( GL_TEXTURE_2D,
        GL_TEXTURE_MIN_FILTER,GL_LINEAR_MIPMAP_NEAREST );
    ::glTexEnvi( GL_TEXTURE_ENV,
```

Listing 10.2   Selecting an Image for OpenGL to Use (continued)

```
        GL_TEXTURE_ENV_MODE, m_TextureFunction );

    // Generate a series of texture maps of decreasing size
    gluBuild2DMipmaps( GL_TEXTURE_2D, 3,
        m_pRGBImage->sizeX, m_pRGBImage->sizeY,
        GL_RGB, GL_UNSIGNED_BYTE,
        m_pRGBImage->data );

    return TRUE;
}
```

After this function returns, the image is selected. This function sets up the parameters for the texture and then generates the mipmaps. Note that there is no checking of the dimensions of the image before we call `gluBuild2DMipmaps()`, because it's done for us. The *OpenGL Programming Guide, Release 1*, incorrectly states that you need to size the image before calling `gluBuild*DMipmaps()`. In reality `gluBuild*DMipmaps()` checks the size for us and rescales the image if necessary. However, it *is* true that `glTexImage*()` requires the image to be correctly scaled. Always check the online documentation, especially if you are using OpenGL 1.0 references and running on an OpenGL 1.1 implementation.

Controlling Image Quality

A number of parameters are set in the default implementation of the `SelectImage()` member function so that you generate a high-quality image suitable for animation. However, these defaults take more time to load. If you're interested in simpler image generation or you want to limit the image size, a number of parameters are available for you to set. Check the header file for the `COpenGLImage` class to find out how to use them.

That's pretty much it for using `COpenGLImage`. The things to watch out for are errors in reading in the file and memory errors in trying to read in too many images. Both `InitFromDIB()` and `SelectImage()` return `BOOL` values that indicate whether they were successful in their execution.

Applying a Texture to a Surface

Just as we specified the normals and the colors for the vertices in an object, we also can specify the *texture coordinates*. And just as colors are interpolated between vertices, so are textures. But using textures has one twist. The Modelview matrix transformations are *not* applied to texture coordinates. (There *is* a texture matrix, so you can select the texture matrix and perform transformations, if you like.) This makes sense. If you're applying textures to a square and you move the square away from the viewpoint, the square appears to get smaller. However, the textures are applied to the vertices that are transformed, so you get the expected results.

In order to keep this dichotomy apparent, we use *texture coordinates* to refer to parts of a texture. What's more strange is that instead of the usual x,y,z,w coordinates, we refer to s, t, r, q, when we're talking about texture space, and these values are limited to the range 0 to 1. That is, since our texture image is a rectangular shape, the s gamut of the texture (the horizontal value) runs from 0 to the left edge to 1 on the right. Similarly, the vertical component (the t component) also runs from 0 at the bottom to 1 at the top. This is texture space. When you specify a value from 0 to 1, you're specifying some point across a dimension of the texture. Since the object space and the texture space are independent, you can have the texture span across a large object or get scrunched up in a small area. You can literally think of it as pinning the texture (composed of a *very* stretchy fabric) to the corners of a polygon in object space.

The command for specifying texture coordinates is the `glTexCoord*()` function. As you'd expect, it takes s, t, r, and q as arguments and "attaches" them to make them current when the next vertex is instantiated. For example, in the "Chapter 10/Texture 1" project the following code enables the texture to be mapped to the rotating face:

```
// texture already selected
::glBegin( GL_QUADS );
        // define texture origin
        ::glTexCoord2f( 0.0f, 0.0f );
        // define polygon origin
        ::glVertex3f( -2.0f, -2.0f, 0.0f );
        // upper-left corner of texture
        ::glTexCoord2f( 0.0f, 1.0f );
        // upper left of polygon
        ::glVertex3f( -2.0f, 2.0f, 0.0f );
        //upper right of texture
        ::glTexCoord2f( 1.0f, 1.0f );
```

```
                    // upper right of polygon
                    ::glVertex3f( 2.0f, 2.0f, 0.0f );
                    //lower-right corner of texture
                    ::glTexCoord2f( 1.0f, 0.0f );
                    // lower right of polygon
                    ::glVertex3f( 2.0f, -2.0f, 0.0f );
            ::glEnd();
```

This code takes the current texture and maps it directly to the polygon in a 1:1 relationship.

Frequently you want to define just a small texture and use it repeatedly. For example, the **brick.bmp** used in the program is designed so that the edges will match when multiple images are tiled. You can achieve tiling in OpenGL simply by extending the texture coordinates beyond the [0,1] range. In the Texture 1 program the other side of the polygon is drawn with the following code:

```
    ::glBegin(GL_QUADS);
        // the side with the multiple images
        ::glTexCoord2f( 0.0f, 0.0f );
        ::glVertex3f( -2.0f, -2.0f, 0.0f );
        ::glTexCoord2f( 0.0f, 8.0f );
        ::glVertex3f( -2.0f, 2.0f, 0.0f );
        ::glTexCoord2f( 8.0f, 8.0f );
        ::glVertex3f( 2.0f, 2.0f, 0.0f );
        ::glTexCoord2f( 8.0f, 0.0f );
        ::glVertex3f( 2.0f, -2.0f, 0.0f );
    ::glEnd();
```

If you compare this code with the previous code, you'll see that there's no difference between the polygon coordinates, but the texture coordinates now extend from 0 to 8. This tells OpenGL to repeat the texture eight times across the face of the polygon, achieving the effect of tiling the brick texture across the face of the polygon, giving us the impression of a brick wall. You can do other things, such as rotate the texture or even reverse it across the face of the polygon by applying the appropriate texture coordinates.

Repeating Textures and the `glTexParameter*()` Function

The tiling effect happens in our example because the **COpenGLImage** class is designed this way. The following section is what does it:

```
::glTexParameteri( GL_TEXTURE_2D,
    GL_TEXTURE_WRAP_S, GL_REPEAT );
::glTexParameteri( GL_TEXTURE_2D,
    GL_TEXTURE_WRAP_T, GL_REPEAT );
```

The **glTexParameter*()** function controls how textures are applied to a surface. We've already seen how modulation is set up. The **GL_TEXTURE_WRAP_S** and **GL_TEXTURE_WRAP_T** parameters select the *s* and *t* axes. Then we set the wrap for these axes to **GL_REPEAT**, which tells OpenGL to repeat the image across each unit of the texture coordinate. The other setting is **GL_CLAMP**, which tells OpenGL to stop repeating the texture after it's been used. I've set the **COpenGLImage** class to use tiling as the default, since in most cases you want to either apply the texture once or repeat it across the face of a polygon. The default settings let you do either one.

Texture Quality and Filtering

If you want to restrict the interpolation of textures across the face of a polygon, you can set other parameters with the **glTexParameter*()** function. The **COpenGLImage** class uses the following lines:

```
::glTexParameteri( GL_TEXTURE_2D,
    GL_TEXTURE_MAG_FILTER,GL_LINEAR );
::glTexParameteri( GL_TEXTURE_2D,
    GL_TEXTURE_MIN_FILTER,GL_LINEAR_MIPMAP_NEAREST );
```

These lines of code select how OpenGL handles magnification and minification of the texture. If you need faster texture rendering at the cost of introducing some visual artifacts, you can change these parameters to select simpler algorithms. The defaults used by the **COpenGLImage** class are selected for their smooth results.

Texture Objects in OpenGL 1.1

Under OpenGL 1.1 there is additional functionality called *texture objects*. Texture objects allow you to load multiple images in memory and save the images as named textures, as you would with named display lists. The image loading is performed exactly the same way as in OpenGL 1.0. In fact, OpenGL 1.1 has a reserved image ID, (the value zero), that can be thought of as the default images that **glTexImage1D()** and **glTexImage2D()** normally operate on. The difference is that you generate a new ID, select that ID as the current image, and then perform all the texture operations that you need to. When you change IDs all the state information associated with the old image is saved and those states for the new image are made current. This feature alone makes OpenGL 1.1 much more friendly to those who need to perform texture mapping. Combined with the *vertex array* functionality (discussed in chapter 12), this feature shows that the priorities of the ARB—making OpenGL one of the fastest and most capable 3D graphics API available—are in the right place. See chapter 12 for a full discussion of texture objects.

Other Texture-Mapping Features

The art of texture mapping is quite involved, and I've provided only the barest minimum to allow you to do some real applications. The OpenGL texture-mapping capabilities are quite advanced, and you might want to peruse the *OpenGL Programming Guide* for more information. For example, if you need to stitch some texture maps together, you can specify a texture map with a border and match the borders to the adjacent texture maps. If you need to generate a contour on a surface or to simulate a reflective surface, you can use texture mapping. Texture mapping is an extremely powerful technique, and the effects you can achieve with it are limited only by your ingenuity.

Try This

- Try creating your own bitmap for tiling. You'll have to make sure that all the edges match correctly.

- Create a rotating cube and texture map it.

- Make the surface of the cube highly reflective and place a white light and a colored light on the left and right sides of the rotating cube, respectively. Make only the cube rotate, not the lights, and see the effects of switching on texture-mapping in different modes.

- Use a highly detailed bitmap, especially one generated from a photograph on the cube, and see how that looks.

- Finally, try using different filtering effects to see what happens.

11

Picking Objects in 3-Space

You don't resign from these jobs, you escape from them.

—Dawn Steel

Manipulating OpenGL Objects

It's possible to let the user select an object in an OpenGL view. It's not terribly difficult once you've done it; it's just a matter of understanding the steps you have to go through. Using the mechanisms provided in OpenGL, you've got some viewport coordinate, typically the location of the cursor when the user clicks a mouse button, but it could also be input from a joystick to a SpaceBall. The point is you've got some coordinates from the user. You then change the rendering mode of OpenGL, define the area of interest, let OpenGL see whether anything was drawn in that area, and then fetch the list of objects that were in that area. OpenGL's selection mechanism, although an important feature of the language, isn't really well designed for interactive 3D manipulation. However, if you don't need a high degree of interactivity or if your models are fairly simple, OpenGL's picking mechanism might be just the thing.

Using Selection Mode

In order to see what the user has selected, you have to change the rendering mode by using the `glRenderMode()` function. This function changes the mode from the default, which is to rasterize primitives into the frame buffer, to either selection mode (which we are interested in here) or feedback mode. Selection mode does no rendering and makes no changes to the frame buffer. Rather, it's used to make a record of the names of objects that *would* have been drawn. These names are returned in what's called the *selection buffer*. Feedback mode is similar to selection mode but returns the coordinates and attributes of vertices that would have been rendered. In order to use selection mode, you first have to initialize the name stack.

Creating Names and a Name Stack

Objects—either primitives or complex objects—can be given a name. If the current object or part of the object is picked, this is the name returned. Since the current name may be a combination of multiple objects (just as an object may have subassemblies), the picked object may return a collection of picked objects. For example, if you draw a row of bicycles, each bike and each wheel on each bike could have its own name. Thus you can determine when the user has selected Bike 1, Front Wheel. The name and the object, Front Wheel, is shared by all the bikes, and its name is pushed onto the name stack when the wheel is rendered.

To use a name, you'll use three OpenGL routines: `glInitNames()`, `glPush-Name()`, and `glLoadName()`. The first routine initializes the name stack so that there's nothing in it. The second command pushes a name onto the stack. The third command replaces the current name on the top of the name stack. It's a minor annoyance (but a performance optimization) that the name stack takes unsigned integers. Therefore the "names" that you push onto the stack are really just integers—the values that OpenGL returns to you. Thus in order to make picking an object easy to perform in your program, you should structure your rendering such that just before you render an object that you want to name, you're able to either push the name onto the name stack by using `gl-PushName()` or replace the current name at the top of the stack using `glLoad-Name()`.

Note that you can't use `glLoadName()` if there's nothing on the stack, so typically you push an empty name on the stack. I use 0, and the *OpenGL Programming Guide* uses –1, which I have trouble seeing as an unsigned int. You can't use these calls between a `glBegin()`/`glEnd()` pair. Finally, you should use these calls only if the current mode is `GL_SELECT`.

Structure your rendering code such that you can call it either when you need it to be rendered or when you need to see what objects have been hit. The difference between the behaviors is that when you're in selection mode, you'll need to push the names onto the name stack before you render the objects.

Determining Which Objects Are Picked

When the user clicks the mouse button and you want to determine what objects are under the cursor, you need to change the rendering mode to select, create a selection buffer, initialize the name stack, define the viewing volume, rerender the objects (pushing the names onto the name stack), and then query the selection buffer. You can examine the examples in the *OpenGL Programming Guide* for some examples.

What's not clear is that you need to, in essence, rerender your scene so that OpenGL can look and see what's near the cursor. OpenGL doesn't know anything about the cursor, of course, so you limit OpenGL's area of interest by defining a viewing volume that's arranged around the cursor. OpenGL will return all the things that are rendered in this viewing volume, so you want to make it pretty small. In other words, if a primitive intersects the clipping volume defined by the viewing frustum, that primitive generates a hit. If a polygon is culled, no hit is generated.

Equally confusing is that since more than one object can be "under" the cursor, the buffer specified to return the "hit list" is an array consisting of the number of

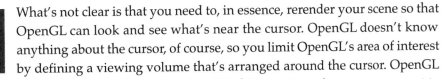

Top of selection buffer

1st Hit	5 (# in name stack for this hit)
	minimum Z value
	maximum Z value
	12, 5, 4, 10, 6 (name stack)
2nd Hit	1
	minimum Z value
	maximum Z value
	1
3rd Hit	7
	minimum Z value
	maximum Z value
	2, 7, 5, 4, 6, 1, 3
Last Hit	1
	minimum Z value
	maximum Z value
	3

Figure 11.1 Format of the Selection Buffer

objects hit, depth values, which are normally in the range 0.0–1.0, are mapped to unsigned ints in the range 0–MAX, where MAX is the largest unsigned int value on the current platform. Its FFFF FFFFh on 32-bit Windows platforms. The smaller the value, the closer to the viewer. And finally a number of object names. To set the selection buffer, you use the `glSelectBuffer()` function. You select the buffer before you call `glInitNames()`.

After you've done the selection mode rendering, you see whether anything is in the selection buffer by returning the mode to GL_RENDER. The number of hits in the buffer is returned by the `glRenderMode()` function if the previous mode was `GL_SELECT`.

Figure 11.1 shows what's in the selection buffer if there's a hit. The hit record consists of the number of names in the name stack at the time of hit, followed by the minimum and maximum depth values of *all* vertices that were hit since the previous event (that is, the range of all vertices), followed by the name stack contents, starting with the bottommost element.

Summary

Allowing the user to select objects in 3-space is nonintuitive, especially using a 2D device, and as you can see from the previous discourse, it's not terribly easy, either. If you need to have the capability of selecting an object, you might consider writing your own code that uses a 3D object that the user can manipulate. For example, there's a 3D construct called a "dipstick" that's simply a rendering of a stick that the user can control. A user who wants to measure some property in some object, such as a level of pollution in an ocean simulation, simply "dips" the stick into the model of the ocean at the point of interest. Since you control the stick, you know its location, and it's a simple matter of looking up the value of pollution at that particular point of the ocean that's located at the dipstick position. Always try to make it easy for the user to select an object or a position in an intuitive manner. Just because OpenGL can generate a hit list from a viewport position doesn't mean that it's the only way to do it. You might also examine some of the toolkits built on OpenGL, such as GLUT or Open Inventor. These toolkits have much more sophisticated selection capabilities.

12

Advanced OpenGL Features

> A man should keep his little brain attic stocked with all the furniture that he is likely to use, and the rest he can put away in the lumber room of his library, where he can get it if he wants it.
>
> —Sherlock Holmes

Once you've got the basics of OpenGL down, it's time to hone your abilities. The previous chapters have covered the generic parts of OpenGL. No matter what your implementation—hardware accelerated or generic, the first Windows NT 3.5 release or the OpenGL 1.1 that ships with Windows NT 4.0 and Windows 95—all the previous information will work, with exceptions as noted in the text.

However, no one ever received accolades for making a program—especially graphics programs—merely adequate! There's something about squeezing the last scrap of speed out of a program with some finely honed code that makes a graphics programmer ecstatic. That's what this chapter is about. Although the techniques discussed in this chapter aren't related, they are all geared toward making your program faster, one way or another.

Overview of OpenGL Extensions

OpenGL is a dynamic standard. The ARB is driven by companies that want OpenGL to be a success and that receive user feedback on how to make the code better, faster, and more useful. Also, OpenGL is continually evolving; in a few years your OpenGL code will still be robust, and there will be state-of-the-art extensions to the language.

OK. So what is an extension? An extension is a value-added add-on to the language provided by either the software interface provider or the hardware provider. OpenGL 1.0 came with some extensions, the update (with NT 3.51) added more, and OpenGL 1.1 added more while promoting some of the previous extensions into full-fledged OpenGL functionality. If you're using a hardware accelerator, you've probably got even more extensions available.

In Pursuit of Extensions

Determining what extensions are available is a run-time operation, so it's possible to make a run-time evaluation only if a particular extension is available. Design your code so that you take advantage of available extensions, but don't require them if they aren't available. If you examine the **COpenGLView** class's **FetchExtendedInformation()** member function, you'll see that it gets information about the current OpenGL implementation. This information is supplied by whoever wrote the current OpenGL driver, probably either the generic Microsoft implementation or that of a hardware vendor. Listing 12.1 shows the **FetchExtendedInformation()** member function in the **COpenGLView** class and shows how to get these values.

Listing 12.1   Getting Run-time OpenGL Information

```
void COpenGLView::FetchExtendedInformation()
{
    char *e,*extensions;

    // GL_VENDOR
    // Returns the company responsible for this OpenGL
    // implementation.
    // This name does not change from release to release.
    m_pVendor = GetString( GL_VENDOR );

    // GL_RENDERER
    // Returns the name of the renderer. This name is
    // typically specific to a particular configuration of
    // a hardware platform.
    // It does not change from release to release.
    m_pRenderer = GetString( GL_RENDERER );

    // GL_VENDOR and GL_RENDERER together uniquely specify
```

Listing 12.1   Getting Run-time OpenGL Information (continued)

```
//   a platform and will not change from release to
     release.
//   They should be used to identify the platform.

//   GL_VERSION
//   Returns a version or release number.
     m_pVersion = GetString( GL_VERSION );

//   GL_EXTENSIONS
//   Returns a space-separated list of supported
//   extensions to OpenGL. Because OpenGL does not
//   include queries for the performance characteristics
//   of an implementation, it is expected that some
//   applications will be written to recognize
//   known platforms and will modify their OpenGL
//   usage based on known performance characteristics of
//   these platforms.

//   The format and contents of the string that
//   glGetString() returns depend on the implementation,
//   except that extension names will not include space
//   characters and will be separated by space characters
//   in the GL_EXTENSIONS string, and that all strings
//   are null-terminated.

//   member function extensions = GetString( GL_EXTENSIONS );
//   while (e = GetExtension String (extensions)
         {
         m_ExtensionArray.Add( e );
         }
}
```

The **glGetString()** function is used to get specific information from the driver. One of these bits of information is the current extensions included in the dri-

ver. If you call the `glGetString()` function with the `GL_EXTENSIONS` argument, you'll get a list of supported extensions. Note that these extensions are entirely dependent on the currently running implementation.

Once you've identified an extension (you have to know what a particular extension means in order to support it), you can get pointers to the function(s) that are implemented by the driver. For example, if one of the returned strings in the list is `GL_EXT_vertex_array`, an entire family of additional functions is supported by this extension. Thus you'll have to hard code in support for this extension. This is true for any extension. However, you'll find that generally extensions are supported by all recent implementations. For example, the `GL_EXT_vertex_array` is supported by both the OpenGL 1.0 generic driver and most of the hardware vendors that wrote their own OpenGL drivers. You'll also find extensions that are supported by only a specific hardware vendor, but this is more the exception than the rule.

You can identify general extensions from vendor-specific extensions by the names. A `GL_EXT` prefix indicates that multiple vendors have supported a particular extension. If you see an extension with a different prefix, it will typically be the initials of the vendor or operating system, such as `SGI` or `WIN`.

Getting an Extension's Address

Once you've identified a specific extension, you'll need code to get the address of the function(s) that make up that extension. Thus you have to know the names of the functions that an extension supports. For example, the name `GL_EXT_vertex_array` indicates support for a number of extensions. One of these extended functions is `glDrawArraysEXT()`. Note that extended functions have a particular suffix. In order to get the address of the `glDrawArraysEXT()` function, you'll need to call a *wgl* function, `wglGetProcAddress()`. The argument is a text string of the name of the function you want. The following code gets the address of the function:

```
PROC fcn;
fcn = ::wglGetProcAddress("glDrawArraysEXT");
```

(`PROC` is a typedef for `int (__stdcall *) (void)`.) Once you've found the extensions you want to support, fetched the function pointer, and enabled the extension, you're ready to use them.

The Vertex Array Extensions Found in OpenGL 1.0

Vertex array extensions are among the most important extensions in the OpenGL 1.0 generic implementation for Windows. Note: This is part of the OpenGL 1.1 implementation, and 1.0 no longer supports this functionality as an extension. You might have noticed that considerable vertex information is involved in setting up a surface of an object. You need to specify not only the vertex locations but also colors, normals, edges, and so on. Using the vector form of calls is always faster than using any other form. For example, `glColor3fv()` is faster than `gl-Color3f()`. Unfortunately you get to specify only *one* vertex's information with these calls. The vertex array extension takes this step further by allowing you to specify an *array* of values.

Enabling the vertex array extension lets you specify (optionally) arrays of vertices, colors (or color indices) edge flags, textures, and normals. You set up the arrays that you want, enable that particular array support (normals or colors or vertices, and so on), call the appropriate function to give OpenGL the array, and then call the `glDrawArraysEXT()` extension to specify which primitive, which array index, and how many array elements to use. This means that you'll have to set up the arrays so that a particular vertex's information corresponds to a particular array index. With some clever arranging you can reuse parts of the array. The `glArrayElementEXT()` function allows you to override the indexing through the array for a single primitive. You'd use this function if you wanted a single array element for the color or normal, for example, for a particular primitive.

Advanced Vertex Construction:
Vertex Arrays in OpenGL 1.1

In chapter 4 we discussed the varieties of vertex commands that OpenGL supports. One of the problems of OpenGL is that describing a reasonably complex object requires the use of many different commands that describe a vertex. For example, you might need to describe the texture, color, normal and edge flag of a particular vertex before the vertex command. When you describe the next vertex, you might have to respecify all the attributes before you issue the vertex command. This leads to programs that repeatedly issue huge strings of similar commands. When the ARB set about deciding what commands should be added for the OpenGL 1.1 release, a more efficient method of dealing with these types of situations was devised.

Instead of issuing a series of vertex commands, vertex arrays allow you to create a series of arrays of data that contain vertex coordinates, edge flags, texture coordinates, colors, color indexes, and normal vectors. These arrays can then be used to specify multiple vertex attributes through a single OpenGL call, greatly simplifying the overhead. To paraphrase Microsoft, these extensions allow "significantly greater performance over the OpenGL 1.0 API." So if you're writing a program that has a complex object or you just want the fastest implementation possible, you should consider taking advantage of the speed increase that comes with OpenGL 1.1, particularly the vertex arrays and the texture objects—which are described later in this chapter.

Using Vertex Array Pointers

The declaration for the OpenGL 1.1 command for specifying a vertex array is

```
void glVertexPointer( GLint size, GLenum type,
    GLsizei stride, const GLvoid* ptr );
```

The **size** parameter indicates the number of values per vertex that are stored in the array. The **type** parameter tells the function the data type of the array elements. The **stride** parameter is used when the elements aren't packed sequentially. If **stride** is zero, the elements are stored sequentially. This is the normal mode of storage and the one that you'll probably use. If **stride** is nonzero, it is the distance (in unsigned bytes for Windows implementations) between the ith and the $(i + 1)^{st}$ element of the array. The **ptr** parameter points to the memory location of the first element of the array, with the rest of the array located at higher addresses. The acceptable values for the **size** and **type** parameters for the **glVertexPointer()** function are as follows:

- Array sizes: 2 (for x,y), 3 (for x,y,z), and 4 (for x,y,z,w)
- Data types: GL_SHORT, GL_INT, GL_FLOAT, GL_DOUBLE

The way that you'd use this function is straightforward. If you remember, the very first polygon we created was a parallelogram. The code looked like this:

```
::glBegin( GL_POLYGON );
    ::glVertex2f( 0.0f, 0.0f );
    ::glVertex2f( 1.0f, 1.0f );
    ::glVertex2f( 0.0f, 1.0f );
    ::glVertex2f( -1.0f, 0.0f );
::glEnd();
```

Now, to use the `glVertexPointer()` function instead, we'd issue the following commands:

```
GLfloat myShape[4][2]; // a parallelogram

    // fill up the array with data
    myShape[0][0] = 0.0f; myShape[0][1] = 0.0f;
    myShape[1][0] = 1.0f; myShape[1][1] = 1.0f;
    myShape[2][0] = 0.0f; myShape[2][1] = 1.0f;
    myShape[3][0] = -1.0f; myShape[3][1] = 0.0f;
    // turn on the use of vertex arrays (discussed later)
    ::glEnableClientState( GL_VERTEX_ARRAY );
    // place the vertex array pointer into OpenGL
    ::glVertexPointer( 2,GL_FLOAT,0,(const void*)&myShape );
    // Now draw the parallelogram (discussed later)
    ::glDrawArrays( GL_POLYGON, 0, 4 );
```

Note that just as with the `glRect*()` function, we don't need to wrapper our drawing primitives with a `glBegin()`/`glEnd()` pair. Some commands were used that we haven't seen yet, and we'll come to them later. The important features to notice with this example are that we've replaced the four calls of the `glVertex*()` function with one call to `glVertexPointer()` to set up the vertex pointer and one call to `glDrawArrays()` to draw the parallelogram. If, instead of a four-vertex parallelogram, we had a 10,000-vertex surface, we'd still make only one call to `glVertexPointer()` and one to `glDrawArrays()`. This is where the power of the vertex array's addition to OpenGL becomes evident. The last item you might notice is that there is only one `glVertexPointer()` function, compared to the 24 varieties of the `glVertex*()` function. This is because the data type is passed to the function rather than there being a separate function for each data type.

Using Color Array Pointers

The declaration for the OpenGL 1.1 command for specifying a vertex color array is

```
void glColorPointer( GLint size, GLenum type,
    GLsizei stride, const GLvoid* ptr );
```

The arguments are essentially the same as we saw for the `glVertexPointer()` function. The **size** parameter indicates the number of color values per vertex that are stored in the array—either for RGB or for RGBA. The `type` parameter tells the function the data type of the array elements. The `stride` parameter is used when the elements aren't stored sequentially. The `ptr` parameter points to the memory location of the first element of the array. The acceptable values for the `size` and `type` parameters for the `glColorPointer()` function are as follows:

- Array sizes: 3 (for RGB) and 4 (for RGBA)
- Data types: `GL_BYTE`, `GL_UNSIGNED_BYTE`, `GL_SHORT`, `GL_UNSIGNED_SHORT`, `GL_INT`, `GL_UNSIGNED_INT`, `GL_FLOAT`, `GL_DOUBLE`

If we modify the parallelogram example to add color to each vertex, it would look like this:

```
::glBegin( GL_POLYGON );
    // vertex 0
    ::glColor3f( 1.0f, 0.0f, 0.0f );
    ::glVertex2f( 0.0f, 0.0f );
    // vertex 1
    ::glColor3f( 0.0f, 1.0f, 0.0f );
    ::glVertex2f( 1.0f, 1.0f );
    // vertex 2
    ::glColor3f( 0.0f, 0.0f, 1.0f );
    ::glVertex2f( 0.0f, 1.0f );
    // vertex 3
    ::glColor3f( 1.0f, 1.0f, 1.0f );
    ::glVertex2f( -1.0f, 0.0f );
::glEnd();
```

Now, to use the `glColorPointer()` function instead, we'd issue the following commands:

```
GLfloat myShape[4][2] = { // the parallelogram
    { 0.0f, 0.0f }, { 1.0f, 1.0f },
    { 0.0f, 1.0f }, { -1.0f, 0.0f} };
GLfloat myColor[4][3] = { // vertex RGB colors
    myColor[0][0] = 1.0f; // red
    myColor[0][1] = myColor[0][2] = 0.0f;
    myColor[1][1] = 1.0f; // green
    myColor[1][0] = myColor[1][2] = 0.0f;
    myColor[2][2] = 1.0f; // blue
    myColor[2][0] = myColor[2][1] = 0.0f;
    myColor[3][0] = // white
```

```
          myColor[3][1] = myColor[3][2] = 1.0f;

     // turn on the use of vertex & color arrays
     ::glEnableClientState( GL_VERTEX_ARRAY );
     ::glEnableClientState( GL_COLOR_ARRAY );
     // place the vertex array pointer into OpenGL
     ::glVertexPointer( 2,GL_FLOAT,0,(const void*)&myShape );
     // now place the vertex color array pointer into
     OpenGL
     ::glColorPointer( 3,GL_FLOAT,0,(const void*)&myColor );
     // Now draw the parallelogram (discussed later)
     ::glDrawArrays( GL_POLYGON, 0, 4 );
```

Note that the order of setting the arrays is unimportant. You can set them up in any order before you call OpenGL to render the vertices.

Using Color-Index Array Pointers

The declaration for the OpenGL 1.1 command for specifying a vertex color-index array is

```
void glIndexPointer( GLenum type, GLsizei stride,
    const GLvoid* ptr );
```

The arguments are essentially the same as in the previous examples, except that there is no **size** parameter, since the color index has only a single value. The **type** parameter tells the function the data type of the array elements. The **stride** parameter is used when the elements aren't packed sequentially. The **ptr** parameter points to the memory location of the first element of the array. The acceptable values for the **type** parameter for the **glIndexPointer()** function are as follows:

- Data types: **GL_UNSIGNED_BYTE, GL_SHORT, GL_INT, GL_FLOAT, GL_DOUBLE**

If you're using color-index mode, you should be able to convert the previous example to use color indices instead. Don't forget to enable **GL_INDEX_ARRAY** instead of **GL_COLOR_ARRAY**.

Using Normal Vector Array Pointers

The declaration for the OpenGL 1.1 command for specifying a vertex normal vector array is

```
void glNormalPointer( GLenum type,
    GLsizei stride, const GLvoid* ptr );
```

The arguments are essentially the same as before, except that there is no **size** parameter, since normals are always specified by three values. The **type** parameter tells the function the data type of the array elements. The **stride** parameter is used when the elements aren't packed sequentially. The **ptr** parameter points to the memory location of the first element of the array. The acceptable values for the **type** parameter for the **glNormalPointer()** function are as follows:

- Data types: **GL_BYTE**, **GL_SHORT**, **GL_INT**, **GL_FLOAT**, **GL_DOUBLE**

If we further modify the parallelogram example to add normals to each vertex, it would look like this:

```
::glBegin( GL_POLYGON );
    // vertex 0
    ::glNormal3f( 0.0f, 0.0f, 1.0f );
    ::glColor3f( 1.0f, 0.0f, 0.0f );
    ::glVertex2f( 0.0f, 0.0f );
    // vertex 1
    ::glNormal3f( 0.0f, 0.0f, 1.0f );
    ::glColor3f( 0.0f, 1.0f, 0.0f );
    ::glVertex2f( 1.0f, 1.0f );
    // vertex 2
    ::glNormal3f( 0.0f, 0.0f, 1.0f );
    ::glColor3f( 0.0f, 0.0f, 1.0f );
    ::glVertex2f( 0.0f, 1.0f );
    // vertex 3
    ::glNormal3f( 0.0f, 0.0f, 1.0f );
    ::glColor3f( 1.0f, 1.0f, 1.0f );
    ::glVertex2f( -1.0f, 0.0f );
::glEnd();
```

The normals for this example are all identical vectors pointing straight down the positive z-axis. To use the **glNormalPointer()** function instead, we'd issue the following commands:

```
GLfloat myShape[4][2] = { // the parallelogram
    { 0.0f, 0.0f }, { 1.0f, 1.0f },
    { 0.0f, 1.0f }, { -1.0f, 0.0f} };
GLfloat myColor[4][3] = { // vertex RGB colors
    myColor[0][0] = 1.0f; // red
    myColor[0][1] = myColor[0][2] = 0.0f;
    myColor[1][1] = 1.0f; // green
    myColor[1][0] = myColor[1][2] = 0.0f;
    myColor[2][2] = 1.0f; // blue
    myColor[2][0] = myColor[2][1] = 0.0f;
    myColor[3][0] = // white
    myColor[3][1] = myColor[3][2] = 1.0f;
GLfloat myNormal[4][3] = { // vertex normals
    myNormal[0][0] = myNormal[0][1] = 0.0f;
    myNormal[0][2] = 1.0f;
    myNormal[1][0] = myNormal[1][1] = 0.0f;
    myNormal[1][2] = 1.0f;
    myNormal[2][0] = myNormal[2][1] = 0.0f;
    myNormal[2][2] = 1.0f;

    // turn on the use of vertex, color, and normal
    // arrays
    ::glEnableClientState( GL_VERTEX_ARRAY );
    ::glEnableClientState( GL_COLOR_ARRAY );
    ::glEnableClientState( GL_NORMAL_ARRAY );

    // place the vertex array pointer into OpenGL
    ::glVertexPointer( 2,GL_FLOAT,0,(const void*)&myShape );
    // now place the vertex color array pointer into OpenGL
    ::glColorPointer( 3,GL_FLOAT,0,(const void*)&myColor );
    // now place the vertex color array pointer into OpenGL
    ::glNormalPointer( GL_FLOAT,0,(const void*)&myNormal );
    // Now draw the parallelogram
    ::glDrawArrays( GL_POLYGON, 0, 4 );
```

Note that the order of setting the arrays is unimportant. You can set them up in any order before you call OpenGL to render the vertices.

Using Edge-Flag Array Pointers

The declaration for the OpenGL 1.1 command for specifying a vertex edge-flag array is

```
void glEdgeFlagPointer( GLsizei stride, const GLvoid* ptr );
```

The arguments are essentially the same as in the previous examples, except that there is no **size** parameter and no **type** parameter, since edge flags are always of type **GLboolean**. The **stride** parameter is used when the elements aren't packed sequentially, and the **ptr** parameter points to the memory location of the first element of the array. To use edge-flag array pointers, you simply construct your array of edge flags set for the corresponding vertex array elements and use the following commands to enable edge-flag arrays:

```
// enable the feature
::glEnableClientState( GL_EDGE_FLAG_ARRAY );
// place the vertex edge-flag array pointer into OpenGL
::glEdgeFlagPointer( 0, (const void*)&myEdgeFlags );
```

Using Texture-Coordinate Array Pointers

The declaration for the OpenGL 1.1 command for specifying a texture-coordinate array is

```
void glTexCoordPointer( GLint size, GLenum type,
    GLsizei stride, const GLvoid* ptr );
```

The **size** parameter indicates the number of values per texture coordinate that are stored in the array. The **type** parameter tells the function the data type of the array elements. The **stride** parameter is used when the elements aren't packed sequentially. The **ptr** parameter points to the memory location of the first element of the array. The acceptable values for the **size** and **type** parameters for the **glTexCoordPointer()** function are as follows:

- Array sizes: 1 (for s), 2 (for s,t), 3 (for s,t,r), and 4 (for s,t,r,q)
- Data types: **GL_SHORT**, **GL_INT**, **GL_FLOAT**, **GL_DOUBLE**

Modifying the original parallelogram program once more, we get some code that looks like this:

```
::glBegin( GL_POLYGON );
    ::glTexCoord2f( 0.5f, 0.0f );
    ::glVertex2f( 0.0f, 0.0f );

    ::glTexCoord2f( 1.0f, 0.5f );
    ::glVertex2f( 1.0f, 1.0f );

    ::glTexCoord2f( 0.5f, 1.0f );
    ::glVertex2f( 0.0f, 1.0f );

    ::glTexCoord2f( 0.0f, 0.5f );
    ::glVertex2f( -1.0f, 0.0f );
::glEnd();
```

To use the **glTexCoordPointer()** function instead, we'd issue the following commands:

```
GLfloat myShape[4][2] = { // the parallelogram
    { 0.0f, 0.0f }, { 1.0f, 1.0f },
    { 0.0f, 1.0f }, { -1.0f, 0.0f} };
GLfloat myTexture[4][2] = { // the texture coords
    { 0.5f, 0.0f }, { 1.0f, 0.5f },
    { 0.0f, 1.0f }, { 0.0f, 0.5f } };

    // turn on the use of vertex arrays
    ::glEnableClientState( GL_VERTEX_ARRAY );
    // place the vertex array pointer into OpenGL
    ::glVertexPointer( 2,GL_FLOAT,0,(const void*)&myShape );

    // turn on the use of texture-coordinate arrays
    ::glEnableClientState( GL_TEXTURE_COORD_ARRAY );
    // place the tex-coord array pointer into OpenGL
    ::glTexCoordPointer( 2, GL_FLOAT, 0,
        (const void*)&myTexture );

    // Now draw the parallelogram
    ::glDrawArrays( GL_POLYGON, 0, 4 );
```

You can see that once the arrays are correctly set up, using texture arrays (or any of the arrays, for that matter) streamlines the rendering process. Since the data is already in memory, rendering by using the vertex array features of OpenGL 1.1 greatly speeds up the entire rendering pipeline. If you're considering using the texture-coordinate array feature, you might also consider looking at the *texture-objects* feature of OpenGL 1.1 that's discussed later in this chapter.

Enabling Vertex Array Functionality

In order to make use of vertex array function in OpenGL 1.1, you have to know about two commands that change the OpenGL state machine. These commands are similar to the **glEnable()** and **glDisable()** functions that we've seen before, but these new functions are for toggling various vertex array functionality. The declaration of these new functions is

```
void glEnableClientState( GLenum array );
void glDisableClientState( GLenum array );
```

The **array** parameter is one of the following: GL_EDGE_FLAG_ARRAY, GL_TEXTURE_COORD_ARRAY, GL_COLOR_ARRAY, GL_INDEX_ARRAY, GL_NORMAL_ARRAY, GL_VERTEX_ARRAY. These are used for enabling or disabling the respective array. If you plan to use vertex arrays, you should try to enable these state variables once in your OpenGL initialization code rather than each time you use the vertex array features. Remember, you should alter the OpenGL state as little as possible if you want your programs to be fast.

Rendering an Element of the Array

If you want to be able to select individual elements from the enabled arrays and make a primitive out of them, use the OpenGL 1.1 command:

```
void glArrayElement( GLint index );
```

The **index** parameter specifies the array element to pass to OpenGL. The **glArrayElement()** function can be used if you have a situation like the following code sequence:

```
::glBegin( mode );
    for ( int i = 0 ; i < count ; i++ )
        {
```

```
            // for some set of vertex array information:
            // select the texture coordinates, colors,
            // indices, normals, edge flags, and vertices for
            // vertex i using the appropriate gl*() functions,
            // this could be some sequence like the following:
            ::glColor3fv( myColor[i] );
            ::glEdgeFlagv( myEdgeFlag[i] );
            ::glIndexiv( myIndex[i] );
            ::glNormal3fv( myNormal[i] );
            ::glTexCoord2fv( myTextureCoords[i] );
            ::glVertex3fv( myVertex[i] );
            }
::glEnd();
```

That sequence can be replaced by the following when you are using the **glArrayElement()** function:

```
::glBegin( mode );
    for ( int i = 0 ; i < count ; i++ )
        {
        // render the enabled array elements
        ::glArrayElement( i );
        }
::glEnd();
```

Thus you can see that the **glArrayElement()** function can replace a sequence of the **glVertex*()**, **glIndex*()**, **glColor*()**, **glNormal*()**, **glTexCoord*()**, and **glEdgeFlag*()** functions, greatly accelerating placing data into the graphics pipeline.

Rendering All or Part of the Array

If you want to render all or part of the vertex arrays, OpenGL 1.1 has a single command, the **glDrawArrays()** function, that constructs geometric primitives from the enabled arrays. The declaration of the command is

```
void glDrawArrays( GLenum mode, GLint first, GLsizei count);
```

This command constructs the primitive specified by **mode**, where **mode** is one of the same ten primitive types that the **glBegin()** function accepts. The **first** and **count** parameters specify the elements of the array(s) to use. The elements **first** through **first+count-1** of each enabled array are used to construct the primitive specified by **mode**.

Just as **glArrayElement()** wraps up a series of calls to individual OpenGL functions, **glDrawArrays()** takes this encapsulation up a level. For example, suppose that you have the following code sequence:

```
::glBegin( mode );
    for ( int i = 0 ; i < count ; i++ )
        {
        // render the enabled array elements
        ::glArrayElement( i );
        }
::glEnd();
```

That sequence can be replaced with the following **glDrawArrays()** call:

```
::glDrawArrays( mode, first, count );
```

Note that you don't have to use the **glBegin()**/**glEnd()** commands, since these are encapsulated as part of the **glDrawArrays()** operation. You can see that the new functionality that OpenGL 1.1 brings greatly accelerates the specification and creation of geometric primitives.

Indirectly Rendering All or Part of the Array

You might notice that if you use the **glDrawArrays()** function, you are forced to reference the array(s) elements directly, by array index. In many instances you might want to share vertex information among models. For instance, if you have a complex object to render, such as a plane or a building, many of the vertices are shared among polygons. You could create a database of related vertices and then call **glDrawArrays()**, based on the indices that you need. Fortunately OpenGL 1.1 provides an alternative to **glDrawArrays()**, one that does this indirection for you. The **glDrawElements()** function allows you to provide an array of indices that are used in the construction of geometric primitives. This function is declared as follows:

```
void glDrawElements( GLenum mode, GLsizei count,
    GLenum type, const GLvoid* indices );
```

The **mode** parameter is one of the ten primitive types. The **count** parameter is the number of array elements to process. The **type** is the size of the index array elements and can be one of the following: GL_UNSIGNED_BYTE, GL_UNSIGNED_SHORT, GL_UNSIGNED_INT. These values indicate that the **indices** pointer points to an array of at least **count** elements made up of type GLubyte, GLushort, or GLuint. A call to the **glDrawElements()** function is equivalent to the following sequence of commands:

```
// assume that myIndices is the index pointer
::glBegin( mode );
    for ( int i = 0 ; i < count ; i++ )
        {
        // render the enabled array elements
        ::glArrayElement( myIndices[i] );
        }
::glEnd();
```

Compare this to **glDrawArrays()**, in which the arrays are referenced directly.

Manipulating Arrays of Vertex Arrays

The vertex array functionality is pretty straightforward: You pick the particular vertex feature you're interested in and set up the corresponding array. OpenGL 1.1 provides yet another function, **glInterleavedArrays()**, declared as follows:

```
void glInterleavedArrays( GLenum format, GLsizei stride,
    const GLvoid* ptr );
```

You'd use this function if you need to have just one vertex array that interleaved all of the setting for the individual vertex attributes. The **format** parameter is one of fourteen constants, each of which describes a particular combination of pointers, flags, and types that specify how the array pointer is formatted. The particular format descriptions are too complicated to enumerate here, but note that the **glInterleavedArrays()** function is useful for those instances when you have a collection of geometric objects stored in vertex arrays and you need to render them quickly.

The effect of a call to **glInterleavedArrays()** is the same as a series of calls to **glDisableClientState()**, **glEnableClientState()**, **glTexCoordPointer()**, **glColorPointer()**, **glNormalPointer()**, and **glVertexPointer()**. Note that the **glInterleavedArrays()** command doesn't support edge flags or color indices. This command is the apex of the new vertex array features found in OpenGL 1.1 and is one of the more complicated ones to use. However, if your modeling requirements are high, you'll greatly benefit from the speed that the `glInterleavedArrays()` command brings to your program.

When to Modify Vertex Array Data

Typically you'd set up the vertex array data and then perform your rendering. However, it's possible that you could make changes to the data stored in the array inbetween the calls to `glBegin()` and `glEnd()`. This is not a good idea, since the behavior of OpenGL in this situation is undefined. A change in the data may not immediately be reflected. In fact, it's possible that a changed value may be reflected in one call to `glArrayElement()` but not in a subsequent call. So don't do it.

IMPORTANT The state of current edge flags, texture coordinates, color, color index, and normal coordinates is indeterminate for any of the enabled arrays after the execution of one of the vertex array functions. Disabled arrays are not modified. This means that you should keep track of which arrays are enabled, so that you don't unnecessarily go about changing state variables if you don't have to.

OpenGL 1.1's Texture Objects

If you're running under OpenGL 1.1 and you need more than one texture, you can take advantage of a new feature, called *texture objects*. Texture objects allow OpenGL to have more than one texture (1D or 2D) in memory at one time. In fact, an entire OpenGL-image state array is constructed for each new image that you create. This allows you to load and manipulate an image, as outlined in the latter sections of chapter 10, and then load a new image and manipulate it while having all of the old image's information stored. This means that you can load images, create mipmaps, and assign them to texture coordinates, all without having to reload any images.

In order for this functionality to coexist with OpenGL 1.0, compatibility had to be maintained. This was achieved by adding commands that create a *texture namespace* and by having a default name already selected. Thus your OpenGL 1.0 program can run under OpenGL 1.1 and never know that it's manipulating the *default* texture—texture zero—of OpenGL 1.1 instead of the *only* texture of OpenGL 1.0.

Before you can create a new texture object, you have to generate a new texture ID:

```
void glGenTextures( GLsizei count, GLuint ptrTexNames );
```

This command takes parameter `count` as the number of IDs to generate and parameter `ptrTexNames` as the location of the array of size `count` to place the (perhaps noncontiguous) IDs. Once you have generated a texture ID, you are free to bind it to a texture state.

Binding a texture is the OpenGL phrase for creating (if the ID is a new one) and then selecting that texture object as the current texture object.

```
void glBindTexture( GLenum type, GLuint textureID );
```

In this function `type` is either `GL_TEXTURE_1D` or `GL_TEXTURE_2D`, signifying that you want to create either a 1D or a 2D texture object. When this command is executed, a new texture specified by `textureID` is created (assuming that `textureID` is a previously unused texture ID). For a new ID a new state vector is created for this texture and is set to the default initial values. You are then free to perform all of the normal texture operations—loading a texture with `glTexImage*()`, generating mipmaps, selecting the texture filtering, and so on.

When you want to select another texture object as the current object, you again use the `glBindTexture()` function. This will cause the currently selected state associated with the current texture to be saved, and the new texture will either be created (for a new texture ID) or reloaded (for an existing texture ID). Note that the reserved value of 0 will select the original, default 1D or 2D texture objects. Also note that you must bind only the correct type of texture (either 1D or 2D).

OpenGL 1.1 Extensions

In chapter 10 I mentioned the `EXT_bgra` extension to allow you to read in DIB formats as native OpenGL formats. Another extension that you'll find useful is the `EXT_paletted_texture` extension. This is essentially a more efficient storage mechanism for textures. It requires more work to set up and use, but if you find yourself running out of texture-map storage space, you might want to examine this extension.

The `WIN_swap_hint` and the `EXT_clip_volume_hint` extensions enable you to optimize redrawing. The `EXT_clip_volume_hint` in particular can speed up rendering by letting you indicate that you don't need clipping to particular primitives, and it allows the implementation to maximize rendering performance

The Silicon Graphics OpenGL Drivers—Cosmo OpenGL

If you've been active in OpenGL since it first appeared with Windows NT 3.5, you may have noticed that Microsoft's initial support seemed to wane for a bit, especially as there seemed to be some speculation that DirectDraw and Direct3D might be more important than OpenGL. I'm happy to say that Microsoft has realized that it needs to give full support to OpenGL and not just tout it as only for high-end applications. However, one fallout from Microsoft's lapse was to anger SGI. Remember all those 3D applications that SGI wants to sell for the Windows platform? SGI decided that Microsoft's software implementation failed to deliver on the speed capable of a software driver, and so it set about to write its own. I haven't tried Cosmo OpenGL yet, as it wasn't yet in production before I finished this book. However, I have talked to the engineers on the project, and they have told me the following information about the driver.

It's a replacement software driver for the Microsoft binaries. It's basically an optimized implementation that makes it easy to get faster performance overall. In particular, SGI has optimized the driver for circumstances that once typically finds (or will find) in many OpenGL programs. These circumstances include

- Geometry defined in vertex arrays
- No multiple or local lights, no two-sided lighting
- Minimal state changes (reduces pipeline revalidation)
- No use of feedback, selection, or accumulation buffers

These guidelines are pretty generic. Follow these, and your OpenGL implementation will be pretty fat anyway. What SGI has done is to identify these paths through the driver and optimize the code for them.

In addition to the reworked code, SGI is planning to add extensions. These include

- Compiled/cached vertex arrays. These allow OpenGL to reuse vertex information between adjacent primitives, such as polygon strips.
- Object-space vertex culling. If all the vertices in a polygon are not facing (for either front- or back-facing mode) the viewpoint, the polygon is culled. Culling is usually done after the transformation to screen space.

- Additive texture environment. This allows you to use texture mapping with a color index or ramp lighting.

- Compressed textures. Also called prefilter texture color table, this is essentially the same as the `EXT_paletted_texture` extension discussed previously.

- Texture mapping for color-index mode.

- Additional formats for interleaved vertex arrays.

You can see that SGI is pretty serious about boosting OpenGL performance. Cosmo OpenGL is going into production as I write this. It's probably a good idea to see if your applications can benefit from it. Check the online resources, and you'll probably find lots of places where they are available.

OpenGL and Windows 95

Sometimes I feel that Windows 95 is the charismatic, good-looking, but slightly slow younger brother to Windows NT. I really like the Windows 95 interface, plug and play, DirectX. But I miss the security, the stability, and the direct OpenGL support found in Windows NT. Now it's getting better, but occasionally you'll come across some difference between the two. I've noted in previous chapters differences between the versions as we come across them, and Microsoft is slowly merging the differences.

OpenGL has always come with Windows NT (since the release of version 3.5) but not with Windows 95. However, if you're distributing a Windows 95 product that uses OpenGL *and* you're a Microsoft Developer Network Level 2 or better member (which means that you get the OpenGL DLLs from Microsoft), you can distribute them royalty free. If you're not an MSDN member, then technically you can't. What you can do to get the DLLs is to go to or direct people to Microsoft's network sites, as follows:

- CompuServe: GO MSL

- Microsoft Download Service (MSDL): dial 206-936-6735

- Internet (anonymous FTP): ftp ftp.microsoft.com

- Internet: http:://www.microsoft.com/

Microsoft has made the DLLs available there. You might also look for SGI's binaries. In any case don't take what I say here as accurate. It's accurate *now,* but it'll probably change within a year.

Recently Microsoft decided to start bundling OpenGL with Windows 95, so the differences between Windows 95 and Windows NT are slowly fading. With the release of Windows NT 4.0 the most compelling differences between Windows 95 and NT—the user interface, plug-n-play, OpenGL, and DirectX—will go away. I've always had good luck with NT. It's been my development environment almost exclusively for the past several years, and on average I crash it about once or twice a year. Compare this to the nearly daily crashes that you can get using Windows 3.1 or even Windows 95, and you'll see why NT is rapidly becoming a favorite environment for software developers. So should you be concerned about the differences? Probably not. Windows 95 has a bunch of nice features; Windows NT is secure and stable. I'm sure that in the near future the features of Windows 95 will migrate over to NT and that 95 will slowly fade away.

If you're running Windows 95 and you don't have OpenGL 1.1 on your system, then you can get the binaries, libraries, and header files from the CD that accompanies this book. OpenGL 1.1 comes with Windows NT 4.0.

Measuring Code Speed

Once you've tried other methods of speeding up your code—choosing the best architecture, selecting fast algorithms, migrating code to data, *reducing you code size by some serious culling,* making use of display lists and extensions—then, and only then, is it time to start hand tuning the code. To do so you *must* implement some soft of instrumentation on your code. The frame-rate counter in the `COpenGLView` class is a good rough estimate as to overall program speed. In order to *really* find out where time is being spent, you must place your program in some sort of harness. You can implement timing code in your debug version, but it's much simpler and more informative to use the tools that Microsoft has delivered.

I'm about to impart a great pearl of wisdom, one that I've never seen mentioned anywhere in any publication. And I find this strange, since a really excellent tool is readily available, and yet no one has ever mentioned it. The tool is called CAP, or the Windows NT (32-bit) Call/Attributive Profiler (CAP) for x86, Mips, Alpha, and PowerPC platforms. CAP has been available on the Win32 SDK since NT 3.5. You can find it in the win32sdk/mstools/bin/winnt subdirectory, along with lots of other goodies, of your Microsoft Developer Network CD, Level 2 SDK CD-ROM. (If you're programming an OpenGL Windows program, you should *really* have a copy.) It's basically a profiler but with a great GUI interface that lets you "drill" down through function calls to find out where your program is taking most of its time. CAP is a general-purpose profiling tool that can be used to measure the function call performance of .EXEs and .DLLs in a variety of ways:

- from within an .EXE
- from within a .DLL
- from an .EXE to all of its DLLs
- from one .DLL to all of its DLLS
- to specified .DLLs, from any .EXE or .DLL

Online information about using CAP is plentiful, so I'll direct you there for more information. What you'll get when you CAP-enable your program is a database of your program's execution time. You use the CAP viewer, called CAPVIEW, to view this file. I have a few problems with the display, but it's orders-of-magnitude better than anything else out there (which is why I find it so amazing that I've never seen it mentioned).

CAP creates a call tree of all the functions called in the selected modules being profiled. CAPVIEW then lets you display the information. What makes it stand out is that there's a tree view. Examine Plate 12.1 for a look at the tree display. You can see the names of the functions (in this case the infamous Windows Solitaire game). The colors indicate relative time. Red boxes indicate a call tree that accounts for 20 percent or more of the total program running time. By clicking on the boxes, you can further break down the call tree to lower and lower levels until you find out where most of the time is being spent.

Once you enable profiling, you can and should run periodic measurement runs to compare previous versions of your program with the latest version. This can even be automated. If you combine the profiling with a standard functionality test, you can catch speed problems right when they occur rather than weeks later suddenly noticing that the program has slowed down when certain things happen. Just being aware of how your program is spending its time yields valuable insight into its operation, information that could lead you to seriously consider some architectural changes early in the product cycle rather than at the end. In addition to CAP, lots of other goodies are in the SDK. Check it out!

Shadows

Plate 12.2 shows the SGI logo with a spotlight shining on it, with a shadow being cast on a textured but *flat* surface. OpenGL doesn't directly support shadows, which would imply a more comprehensive lighting model. If you need to cast a shadow on a flat surface, one simple approach is to rerender the object in the shadow color, on the surface where the shadow is to be seen, with a transformation matrix such that the *y*-axis is squished to 0. If your implementation supports an alpha (translucency) plane, you can mix the shadow color with the color of the surface underneath.

If you need to project the shadow onto a nonflat surface, you can perform the operation onto each flat surface with the appropriate clipping planes. Another approach might be to perform your own lighting calculations. The *OpenGL Programming Guide* explains how to create a shadow matrix if you're interesting in generating shadows.

Fog

Images can be made to appear more natural by adding *fog,* which is used to make images seem to fade with distance. Fog is also useful to limit the depth that you have to render making things past a certain distance fade away. Fog is very easy to use in OpenGL. You enable it with a call to `glEnable()` and then set up the parameters of the fog equations.

As an object's distance increases from the viewpoint, the object's color is gradually mixed with the specified fog color. Since fog is applied to objects after lighting, texturing, and transformations, adding fog can actually *speed up* your calculations, since there's no point in drawing objects that are obscured by fog.

Fog settings are controlled by the function

```
void glFog*( GLenum pname, const GLtype* params );
```

In this function **pname** is the parameter you are setting with the current call. It's one of the following: GL_FOG_MODE, GL_FOG_DENSITY, GL_FOG_START, GL_FOG_END, GL_FOG_COLOR, or GL_FOG_INDEX. The settings tell OpenGL where things start to become foggy, where they disappear totally into the fog, the color of the fog (fog can be used most easily in RGBA mode, but you can get it to work in color-index mode as well), and the parameters of the fog equation (how fast it goes from no fog to total fog). See the online documentation or the *OpenGL Reference Manual* for an exact description of these parameters.

Hardware Accelerators

The final step in achieving speedy OpenGL programs is to throw hardware at it. (Hey, it worked for SGI!) If you're in a position to support hardware accelerator boards or if you have a hardware accelerator, you'll notice a significant speed increase. The various flavors of hardware cards are based on the video chip on which the card is assembled. Hardware chips that support OpenGL are the GLINT chip from 3Dlabs, the Real3D from Lockheed Martin, the SPC1500 from S-MOS Systems, and the 3GA from ARTIST Graphics. This list is by no means comprehensive, and there is a running list of 3D accelerators (both chips and end user cards) on the Internet. Look in "OpenGL Resources."

But why would you want to know about a hardware accelerator? It's not just high-end cards that support OpenGL anymore. The current crop of OpenGL accelerated cards indicates that there's a big interest in getting onto the Windows 95 bandwagon. Since Microsoft has plainly targeted Windows 95 as "the" games platform, it's no surprise that video card vendors are clearly hoping that this will create a rush for faster and better graphics support. So far there is every indication that this is happening.

If you're writing an application that requires faster rendering, you might require the user to have one of the OpenGL accelerated cards. The differences in the cards reflect a wide variety of philosophies about what functionality to provide. The next section illustrates three tiers of OpenGL accelerators. Things to look for are the features they provide versus the cost. Each tier provides a significant increase in features over the previous one. One caveat: You can pretty much ignore any claims about polygon rendering times. There is no standard test yet, so the best thing to do is test the cards on your own applications.

Creative Labs' 3D Blaster

The 3D Blaster, based on a custom variation of the GLINT 300SX chip from 3Dlabs, has been optimized for the 3D gaming market. It's got 2 MB of on-board memory (upgradable to 4 MB), a 16-bit z-buffer, and on-board texture memory. This is a good card for starting out with OpenGL, but the memory limitation means that you'll get small color depth at high resolutions. I tend to prefer getting at least 1024 by 768 3D resolution in 16-bit colors. However, if you're interested in the games market, this card might be the target hardware. The street price is about $350.

Omnicomp Corp.'s 3DEMON

The 3DEMON card comes in three flavors, a 4 MB frame buffer, a 4 MB local buffer card, and an 8 MB card for both buffers. This card is the next step up and can be considered in the realm of *professional* cards. It has a nice set of features and will pep up your OpenGL programs. At a street price starting at $1600, it's well beyond the impulse purchase, but if you're an OpenGL developer or user, this card delivers. If you need VGA support, you'll need to provide a separate VGA card. I've personally dealt with Omnicorp, and the people there are *very* helpful.

Dynamic Pictures' V192

The V192 3D Graphics Accelerator card is the first product in a new generation of workstation-performance cards for the Windows desktop market. The company compares its card's performance to an SGI Indigo/Extreme. It's got 16 MB of memory, 24-bit color, and a z-buffer at 1280 by 1024 resolution, as well as an 8-bit alpha buffer, a 4-bit stencil buffer, and stereo support but *no* support for Windows 3.x. The cost is about $4500. Dynamic Pictures is interested in assisting users and programmers to get the best possible performance, and they are most helpful.

Accelerator Summary

If you decide to go with a hardware accelerator and you want to find out how best to take advantage of the card, most manufacturers will provide you with a free SDK and lots of technical support. It's going to get vicious out there as everyone tries to get market share, which puts software developers in an excellent position.

Try This

- Find out what extensions are available in your system. Try implementing them. Do they change with the pixel format?
- Profile the program you just created with CAP. Compare the execution times for the nonextended and extended versions.
- Change the pixel format, say, reducing the color depth. Does CAP report any differences?

OpenGL Resources

Newsgroups

The newsgroup of the OpenGL community is comp.graphics.api.opengl. You can ask questions at any level here and probably get an answer within twenty-four hours.

The newsgroup about Windows graphics programming in general is comp.os.-ms-windows.programmer.graphics. Occasionally you'll see OpenGL or DirectX questions here as well.

SGI's OpenGL Web site, www.sgi.com/Technology/openGL, is where you can find out about the latest OpenGL information. Unfortunately there's not much about Windows OpenGL programming yet.

Microsoft's Developer Network News, www.microsoft.com/devnews, is where you'll find the latest information about all of Microsoft's development tools.

Blair MacIntyre's 3D Accelerator Site, www.cs.columbia.edu/~bm/3dcards/3d-cards1.html contains a wealth of information about the various OpenGL accelerator cards that are out there.

Bibliography

Foley, James, and Andries van Dam *et al. Computer Graphics.* Reading Mass.: Addison-Wesley, 1990. (Known as "Foley and van Dam," this is *the* text on 3D graphics. It's pretty dense; there's a lot of math and essentially no code. It is complete, though.)

Fosner, Ron. "Programming with OpenGL." *Dr. Dobb's Journal* (July 1995). (You can look for it on the Web at www.ddj.com.)

————. "Programming with OpenGL Primitives." *Dr. Dobb's Sourcebook,* #257 (May/June 1996).

Kilgard, Mark. "Texture Mapping." *The X Journal* (March/April 1995). (Mark runs a regular series on various OpenGL topics, and he also makes them available on SGI's Web site.)

Luse, Marv. *Bitmapped Graphics Programming in C++*. Reading, Mass.: Addison-Wesley, 1993. (A good book on how to manipulate bitmaps.)

Neider, Jackie, Tom Davis, and Mason Woo. *OpenGL Programming Guide: The Official Guide to Learning OpenGL*, Release 1. Reading, Mass.: Addison-Wesley, 1993. (This book is also known as the "Red Book." This book is a must.)

OpenGL Architecture Review Board. *OpenGL Reference Manual: The Official Reference Document for OpenGL*, Release 1. Reading, Mass.: Addison-Wesley, 1992. (This book is also known as the "Blue Book" and is also a must, but you *might* get by with the online doc.)

Prosise, Jeff. "Advanced 3-D Graphics for Windows NT 3.5: Introducing the OpenGL Interface, Part I." *Microsoft Systems Journal* (October 1994).

———. "Advanced 3-D Graphics for Windows NT 3.5: The OpenGL Interface, Part II." *Microsoft Systems Journal* (November 1994).

———. *Programming Windows 95 with MFC*. Redmond, Wash.: Microsoft Press, 1996. (If you don't know MFC and need to, this is the book I wish I had had when I started MFC programming.)

———. "Understanding Modelview Transformations in OpenGL for Windows NT." *Microsoft Systems Journal* (February 1995).

Richter, Jeffery. *Advanced Windows*. Redmond, Wash.: Microsoft Press, 1995. (Nothing on OpenGL, but a great book on advanced Win32 programming.)

Watt, Alan. *3D Computer Graphics*. Reading Mass.: Addison-Wesley, 1993. (A good general text on 3D graphics.)

Other Software Development Resources

Crain, Dennis. "Windows NT OpenGL: Getting Started." (April 1994) Microsoft Developer Network CD. (This was the first article on Windows OpenGL.)

Microsoft Developer Network (MSDN). (Get level 2 if you can. It costs about $500/year, and you get goodies on CDs every quarter, as well as betas of operating systems and DLLs. It includes most of the *Microsoft Systems Journal* articles, source code, and the Win32SDK.)

Microsoft Win32 Software Development Kit (SDK) for Windows. (Tools and source code you can use. A must have. See the MSDN entry.)

Rogerson, Dale. "Open GL I: Quick Start." (December 1994) Microsoft Developer Network CD.

———. "Open GL II: Windows Palettes in RGBA Mode." (December 1994) Microsoft Developer Network CD.

———. "Open GL IV: Color Index Mode." (January 1995) Microsoft Developer Network CD.

————. "Open GL V: Translating Windows DIBs." (February 1995) Microsoft Developer Network CD.

————. "Open GL VI: Rendering on DIBs with PFD_DRAW_TO_BITMAP." (April 1995) Microsoft Developer Network CD.

————. "Open GL VII: Scratching the Surface of Texture Mapping." (May 1995) Microsoft Developer Network CD.

————. "Open GL VIII: wglUseFontOutlines." (July 1995) Microsoft Developer Network CD.

Index